To War With the Walkers

To War With the Walkers

*One Family's Extraordinary Story
of Survival in the Second World War*

Annabel Venning

HODDER &
STOUGHTON

First published in Great Britain in 2019 by Hodder & Stoughton
An Hachette UK company

1

A CIP catalogue record for this title is available from the British Library

Hardback ISBN 978 1 473 67930 6
Trade Paperback ISBN 978 1 473 67931 3
eBook ISBN 978 1 473 67933 7

Typeset in Bembo MT Pro by Palimpsest Book Production Ltd, Falkirk, Stirlingshire

Printed and bound in Great Britain by Clays Ltd, Elcograf S.p.A.

Hodder & Stoughton policy is to use papers that are natural, renewable
and recyclable products and made from wood grown in sustainable forests.
The logging and manufacturing processes are expected to conform to
the environmental regulations of the country of origin.

Hodder & Stoughton Ltd
Carmelite House
50 Victoria Embankment
London EC4Y 0DZ

www.hodder.co.uk

For my parents, Richard and Venetia –
and in loving memory of Ruth

Contents

PART FOUR:
TRIUMPH AND LOSS

PART FIVE:
AFTER THE WAR

Prologue

——◆——

RUTH

LYING ON A straw mattress in the basement of the nurses' home at St Thomas's Hospital, Ruth Walker, my great aunt, tried desperately to sleep.

Only twenty-four hours earlier, the long-awaited Blitz had begun. To the east of the hospital, the Thames had turned orange with the reflected glow of the many fires that blazed, as the Luftwaffe pounded London's docks and nearby streets with bombs. It would be some time before the final death toll of that first night was confirmed, but everyone knew that it would be high. And they knew that St Thomas's, across the Thames from the Houses of Parliament, was vulnerable.

So, like many of those who had previously spurned the safety of the basement in favour of their own beds, Ruth headed down that evening when she came off duty. She was the youngest of six, with four older brothers, so she had learned early on to be resilient. Even so, it was hard not to feel anxious as the sirens wailed and the bombers began to drone overhead.

She was still awake when, at 2.30 a.m., the world exploded around her. Dim light gave way to dense darkness and the air became thick with choking dust. The roar and rumble of crashing masonry seemed to go on and on. The nurses' home had been hit and the upper storeys were in ruins. The basement was filled with rubble, twisted metal, bricks and glass.

Ruth was unhurt. A steel girder had bent over her, protecting her from falling masonry, but she did not dare move for fear of dislodging something that might crush her. She could not hear or see anything through the darkness.

And then she smelt it, the unmistakable stench of burning. With a

ix

calm fatalism that many Blitz victims would display she lay still and tried to resign herself to dying, aged only twenty-one. She had hoped that death, if it came, would be instantaneous. Burning was another matter. Perhaps rescue would reach her before the flames. She began to pray.

HAROLD

S IX NIGHTS LATER, Ruth's brother Harold, a medical student, was also in the basement at St Thomas's.

The youngest of the four brothers, Harold was one of life's enthusiasts. At school he had sung in the choir and been a champion boxer, while at St Thomas's he played top-level rugby and cricket. He was outgoing, sunny and optimistic, yet now he could not shake the feeling that something would happen to him, a premonition that he would become an air-raid casualty. Would it be tonight? He did not let that deter him as he scrubbed his hands in preparation for an operation.

An operating theatre had been set up in the basement of the main hospital building and, as surgical dresser, Harold was to assist the two surgeons, one of whom was a close friend named Peter Spilsbury.

The operation went well and just before 8.30 p.m. Harold and Spilsbury emerged from the theatre, chatting as they walked through the basement towards the hospital's College House.

At that exact moment a huge bomb crashed through the main corridor at St Thomas's, penetrating the basement and cutting the main building in two. Spilsbury's head was severed by a flying piece of metal. Harold's was struck by debris, fracturing his skull.

The gas mains had been hit and began blazing fiercely, flames whipping through the basement. The glass bottles in the dispensary shattered in the heat, pipes burst and masonry crumbled. A rescue party bravely ventured in, crawling through the wreckage of twisted bedsteads and a grand piano, calling for survivors. But Harold could not hear them: he was unconscious. At last the rescue party found him, bleeding but alive. If they could get him out, through the fire and debris, he might just live.

BEE

I T WAS A dry July day. In Downing Street the prime minister, Winston Churchill, was preparing to face down his enemies in the House of Commons: they had proposed a motion of 'no confidence' in the government, following a series of defeats. Most shocking of all had been the loss of Singapore, that supposedly inviolable fortress, several months earlier. Churchill had made the crucial decisions. Now he would have to answer for them.

Not far away from where Churchill was marshalling his famous oratorical powers, other preparations were taking place at the King's Chapel of the Savoy, just around the corner from the Savoy Hotel.

The bridegroom waiting at the altar wore RAF uniform although he was an American citizen. His name was Gaddis Plum and he had been a pilot in the Great War. In 1940 he had crossed the Atlantic again to join the RAF and 'help complete the job we evidently failed to finish before', as he put it.

The bride was Ruth and Harold's older sister, Beatrice Walker, a former Norman Hartnell model. Her pre-war prettiness chiselled by wartime rationing and age into a more angular beauty, Bee made a stunning bride. Her looks had attracted plenty of suitors, but her romances had not run smoothly and she had more than one broken engagement behind her.

Now, with Gaddis, she had her happy ending. As with many wartime weddings there were notable absentees. Of Bee's four brothers, only one was there. Two were in India and the third, Peter, had not been heard of since the fall of Singapore. His parents, Dorothea and Arthur, were desperate for news, but five months on they had still heard nothing. Had he been killed in battle, or taken prisoner? And if the latter, would he survive his captivity?

PETER

P ETER WAS THE Walkers' happy-go-lucky fourth child, the joker of the family, charming and jovial. He had been a tea-planter in India before the war with a large force of workers under his command. Now the tables were turned. He was no longer the boss but a labourer, and his life hung by the slenderest of threads, at the mercy of Japanese and Korean guards.

Some months into his captivity, his frame shrunken by malnutrition, his uniform hanging in rags, he was out with a working party of his fellow prisoners of war in Thailand when one of the guards turned upon a prisoner and began beating him mercilessly. As an officer Peter felt it his duty to intervene on behalf of the man and began remonstrating with the guard. Immediately, the guard turned upon Peter and set about him. Vicious blows fell until he crumpled to the ground.

Already many men had died from injuries inflicted during such beatings. Peter had scars from previous occasions. But this time the beating went on and on, the blows landing with shattering force on his battered body. At last the beating ceased. But his punishment was not over. There were other plans for him, a more ingenious, prolonged torment. He was dragged into the centre of the camp and tied to a stake. The beating had been bad, but something much worse was to come.

WALTER

O N A SMALL hill in the middle of the burning Burmese plain Walter was listening to the sounds of battle in the village below.

Walter was the commanding officer of the 4th Battalion of 8th Gurkha Rifles - 4/8th Gurkhas - and the battle in the valley below was one of the first that the battalion had fought under his command. Less than an hour before, he had gone out on patrol and selected the position that the company of Gurkhas was now defending.

It was a good position, but Walter's Japanese opponent thought so too, and was determined to dislodge the Gurkhas. Pinned down, pounded by mortars and shells, the Gurkhas fought magnificently as the Japanese rushed towards them in attack after attack, screaming their war-cry, '*Banzai!*'

The Gurkhas had now all but run out of mortars and grenades. Wounded men lay bleeding on the sandy soil. As the Japanese began to close in, trying to encircle them, the Gurkhas drew their kukris and prepared for a hand-to-hand fight.

All of Walter's life had been a rehearsal for this moment. Even as a schoolboy he had had a military mindset, sorting out bullies with his fists. As an army officer, he had fought in several battles, and for the last seven months, as commanding officer, he had trained his battalion relentlessly. Now he had committed them to battle. But how were they faring? He did not know. They were out of wireless contact.

A runner arrived from the battlefield to tell Walter of the situation. He received the message with outward calm. A decision had to be made and made fast if he were to rescue the situation. If his men could not continue to hold off the Japanese, their position would be overrun. The best hope of saving them was to meet fire with fire, to bring down an artillery strike on the Japanese attackers and stop them in their tracks.

But without wireless contact he could not know his men's exact positions in relation to the Japanese. With only yards between them, there was a chance that the shells might fall upon the Gurkhas in the forward positions.

Should he risk raining death upon his own men? Or hope that they could hold out while he sent up further ammunition and reinforcements? The Gurkhas would fight to the death, but so, too, would the Japanese. It would be a bloodbath. He did not want to lose the battle, with many fine men.

He had repeatedly told his men in training that the only bad decision in battle is to take no decision.

The decision was now his to take – his alone.

EDWARD

FOR THE LAST eight months Edward, the eldest of the Walker siblings, had been fighting in Italy. As the commanding officer of 1st Jaipur Infantry he had shivered with his men in the snowy Apennine mountains during a long, hard winter, and fought with them as they advanced that spring across the plain. He was a popular commanding officer, considerate towards his men and impressing his superiors with his dynamism and vigour.

Some German units were now surrendering as the Allies pushed forward but others fought on grimly, even though it was now clear that Italy was slipping from their grasp.

That morning the Jaipurs, under Edward's command, had liberated the town of Lugo. The mayor came out to greet them with a white flag in one hand and a bottle of wine in the other.

The Germans had sown landmines in the countryside all around Lugo, so every step into newly taken territory was fraught with risk. At 6.15 p.m. that evening Edward went forward to consult with the commanding officer of another regiment taking part in the attack, and the commander of the tank squadron who would be supporting them.

Then came news that the attack would have to be postponed, so Edward began walking back to his headquarters. He trod carefully but it was dark and impossible to see where soil might have been disturbed and a mine might lurk beneath the surface. One wrong step would bring his war and perhaps his life to an abrupt end. Would he be lucky? He pressed forward and then, with no warning, the world around him exploded.

Introduction

THERE IS A sepia photograph among my family's old albums. A group is arranged, a little stiffly, in front of a substantial Regency villa. Mother and father are seated on either side of their youngest child, a schoolgirl with bobbed hair, Mary Jane shoes and a winter coat. Standing behind them are their four sons, serious and smart in their tweed and ties, hair plastered carefully down. In the middle of the boys, her arms linked with the eldest two, is a glamorous young woman, half smiling, with pearls at her ears and neck, exuding confidence and perhaps a certain knowingness.

The year was 1933 and the family were the Walkers: Arthur and Dorothea, my maternal great-grandparents, and their children. Edward, aged twenty-four, tall and square-jawed, with a military moustache, was back on leave from India where he was serving with the Punjab Regiment. Beatrice – Bee – the girl in pearls, was still single at twenty-two but on the look-out for a husband. Walter, my maternal grandfather, aged twenty, looking proudly ahead, was about to follow Edward to India where he would join the 8th Gurkhas, his grandfather's old regiment. Then there is Peter, wearing Oxford bags instead of suit trousers, about to turn nineteen: he, too, would be sailing for India in a few months to work as a tea-planter. The fourth brother, Harold, was still a schoolboy, aged sixteen, although with his mind already made up that he would become a doctor. And last Ruth, fourteen years old and pony-mad, itching to get out of her formal clothes and back into her jodhpurs. Dorothea and Arthur look justly proud of their brood, savouring this moment of togetherness.

Within six years, war would engulf the Walker family and scatter them across the globe. While some remained in Blitz-battered Britain, others fought in India, Burma, Malaya and Italy. The war brought romance and marriage, but also widowhood, estrangement, infidelity and divorce.

It left one sibling crippled with lifelong pain but brought hard-won glory and success to others.

Of the six siblings, I knew Walter, my grandfather, best and got to know Ruth, the youngest, in the last decade of her life. The others I met only fleetingly, if at all. I knew something of Walter's war: unlike some veterans he was far from reticent about it and liked to talk of how he had fought and beaten the Japanese, whom he viewed with grudging respect. He had written his own memoir and been the subject of a biography, *Fighting General,* by the author and war correspondent Tom Pocock, which told of the battles he had fought, as commanding officer of a Gurkha battalion, in the hills, plains and valleys of India and Burma. I knew, too, that Peter had been held as a prisoner of the Japanese.

Ruth told me of her own experiences nursing the casualties of Dunkirk and the battle of Britain, and the impossibly romantic story of her love for her childhood sweetheart, of how war tore them apart and reunited them for a few snatched minutes at a railway station.

The more Ruth told me about her own and her siblings' lives, the more amazed I became that so much could have happened to one family. Every British family lived through the war, through the rationing, blackout and uncertainty that pervaded their lives for those six years. But for some families, the war enveloped them entirely: they did not simply witness and endure, they were thrown into its different theatres, as soldiers, doctors and nurses; victors and vanquished; prisoners and commanders. The Walkers were one such family.

When I began to tell people their story, the reaction was one of amazement. All this happened to a single family? How did their parents cope? What were they like? How did they all survive, against the odds?

I became determined to learn more of these great-aunts and -uncles, to get to know them posthumously, to colour in the characters of those black-and-white photographs, to explore the fates of the names on the family tree, the medal citations, in personal records and family stories.

I wanted to tell their story for its own sake, but also because it is the story of so many families who made sacrifices, whose parents waited anxiously for news, as Dorothea and Arthur did, from children near and far from home. I also wanted to tell the story of this vast and unprecedented conflict in a more intimate, personal way and to explore, through the Walkers' experiences, some of the less-known aspects of the war.

The Walkers were involved in some of its most famous, or infamous, episodes, from the devastation of the Blitz to the horror of the prisoner-of-war camps on the Death Railway. But they also took part in other events: battles of breathtaking brutality and extraordinary courage that rate few mentions in the history books; a guerrilla war in the jungle in which Allied soldiers joined forces with headhunters; pioneering plastic surgery to restore the faces and lives of maimed war victims closer to home.

We have read much of the upper classes at war – the Mitfords, the Ranfurlys, the Mountbattens – and also of the lives of working-class Britons, both soldiers and civilians. But what about 'the people in between', as Hilaire Belloc called them, the middle classes? The Walkers were solidly middle class. Like the Durrell family of Corfu fame, they were exiles of Empire, who had returned from years in India to live modestly in a semi-detached suburban villa. Their sons went to Blundell's, one of the country's oldest private schools, and became army officers, rather than 'other ranks'. The family mingled with the local gentry and bore a motto, *Nil desperandum* (Never despair), that would become only too apposite. In the fine social gradations of the time, they were perhaps upper-middle class, although the two daughters, Bee and Ruth, worked in a shop and a café respectively, which was definitely not upper-middle-class behaviour.

As I began to dig, I discovered letters, photograph albums, personnel records and even interviews that I had not known existed. In 1989, Walter had been interviewed about his military career by the author Charles Allen, for his book *The Savage Wars of Peace*, who passed the tapes to the Imperial War Museum; they were later digitised as part of the museum's online sound archive.

Most of us have abundant photographs of those we have loved but their voices are often lost. Even home videos tend to be more about action than chat. To hear his voice as clearly as if he'd been in the room with me, his familiar cadences and figures of speech – anything or anyone he admired was 'most marvellous,' while those he disliked were 'frightful' – was a joyous, unexpected moment of time travel. I could almost see his smile – he always managed to convey utter delight whenever I arrived at his house, even if he had seen me the day before – and feel his moustache brush my cheek as he kissed me. He was invariably immaculate and debonair, even in old age, his trousers pressed, his shirt ironed, a jaunty spotted handkerchief at his neck.

In 1998 Harold also gave an interview, about his time at St Thomas's Hospital during the war. Although I had never, to my knowledge, met Harold, his voice was familiar, similar to Walter's but with a gentle self-deprecation that contrasted with his brother's forceful, didactic delivery.

As well as those interviews, and my own with Ruth, I was lucky that most of them had a professional record of one kind or another: Ruth's wartime nursing record detailed every ward she had worked on, along with reports on her conduct, while Walter and Edward had records of their military service, and Peter had completed a liberation questionnaire giving the names and dates of the camps where he was held.

I was also able to trace some of their movements before and after the war using ships' passenger manifests, as well as marriage, birth and death certificates, via online subscription services. Bee proved the most elusive and divisive, leaving the lightest footprint, and contrasting opinions among the family between those who adored her and those who disliked her.

I have tried to maintain neutrality and objectivity, although history is written not just by the victors but by the survivors, so Ruth's perspective prevails over Bee's: I met Bee only once before her death in 1988. But elsewhere their own memories and stories are corroborated by the official records, or by the evidence of those they served with or were imprisoned alongside.

I talked to their children (and to Peter's widow), trawled through the archives, read the diaries and memoirs of those who had known them or lived and worked alongside them, and the war-crime affidavits of those who suffered in the same camps as Peter. I travelled to Burma to see where Walter fought, and to Thailand to see where Peter was held as a prisoner of war. I have been helped immeasurably by their families, who have unearthed hitherto hidden letters and records, and generously shared the stories their parents told them.

For some of the Walker siblings the war was, despite its pain and privation, a time of personal triumph. For others it brought unimaginable misery.

Throughout it they were sustained by a robust optimism and courage instilled by their upbringing and encapsulated in the family motto, *Nil desperandum*.

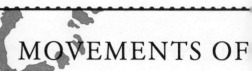

London

Tara, the Walkers'
family home

Lugo

THE
APENNINES

Cairo

Numerical sequence of
chronological movements for
each of the six Walkers

Bee   Peter

Edward   Ruth

Harold   Walter

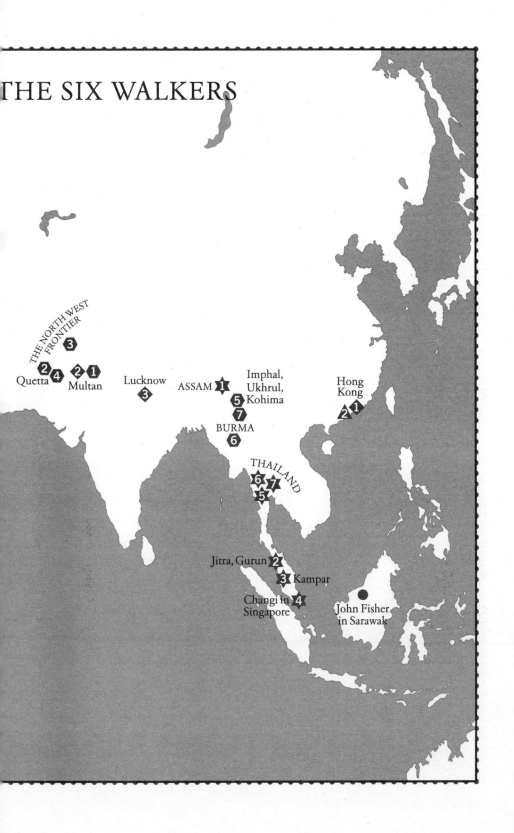

THE SIX WALKERS

THE NORTH WEST FRONTIER
3

2 4   2 1
Quetta   Multan

Lucknow
3

ASSAM 1

Imphal,
Ukhrul,
Kohima
5
7

BURMA
6

Hong
Kong
2 1

THAILAND
6 7
5

Jitra, Gurun 2

3 Kampar

Changi in
Singapore
4

John Fisher
in Sarawak

PART ONE

Before the War

I

'Six of us were more than enough'

———◆———

'TARA'. THE NAME conjures the rambling plantation house of *Gone with the Wind* fame, belonging to the O'Hara family. But while the O'Haras' Tara was a vast mansion set in hundreds of acres of the American Deep South, the Tara owned by my great-grandparents, Arthur and Dorothea, was a more modest affair, a semi-detached villa on the outskirts of Tiverton, a small town in rural Devon. They moved there in 1923 with their six children, Edward, or Eddie, Beatrice, or Bee, Walter, or Wally, Peter, Harold and Ruth, after a peripatetic decade when the upheavals of the Great War had caused them to move house frequently - no easy matter with a rapidly expanding brood. The children were aged from thirteen to six when they settled in Tiverton and it was here that they would grow up, the boys' shorts giving way to long trousers, the girls' smocks and long plaits to slacks and bobbed hair as they prepared to set out into the world.

From the outside, Tara seemed to be an ordinary suburban house. It was not grand but it was comfortable and spacious, with high ceilings, wide doorways and staircases. Its current owners have kept many of the original features - open a cupboard and you can see the wallpaper that would have been there in the Walkers' day - so it is easy to step back in time and imagine the house reverberating to the noise of six children: the clatter of rugby boots, the kitchen bell ringing to summon the maid, Bonzo the terrier barking as people walked past the window or chasing Fluff, the unimaginatively named cat, then the usual sibling teasing and badinage. Cricket bats and tennis rackets leaned against the wall in the porch - sporting trophies and team photos multiplied as the children grew up.

When Harold visited the house in the late 1990s he pointed out the cupboard in the kitchen where Arthur had hidden his secret stash of whisky, away from Dorothea's scrutiny. Or so he thought. In fact, according to Harold, Dorothea knew about it. Nothing much got past her.

Arthur and Dorothea named the house Tara in a nod to their first married home, a tea-planter's bungalow on the Tara tea estate in Assam, north-eastern India, where they had lived for five gloriously happy years. Tara means 'star' in Hindi and the house shone in their memories, so they tried to recreate something of their lives there by naming their suburban semi after it and filling it with keepsakes from India. As in the homes of many Raj retirees, mounted animal heads snarled incongruously from floral wallpaper, tiger and panther skins carpeted the drawing room and hall, and polo trophies gleamed on the mantelpiece.

In place of the small retinue of servants they had employed in India they had just one live-in maid, Irene, who cooked and cleaned for the family, and was allowed to use the bath once a week. Separate stairs led to her bedroom. Tara in Tiverton came with a long garden, stables and an orchard, four acres in all. A gardener, Venn, helped to tend the vegetable patch and the lawns. Arthur turned the stables into chicken sheds and sold hens, eggs and apples, which gave him a steady income, although not a large one.

'Tivvy', as locals called it, then and now, lay in the middle of farming country. Once a month the sheep and cows that grazed the billowing hills of north Devon were driven to market and it was there that Arthur sold his wares alongside local farmers. In the early evenings he liked to cycle to his local pub for a pint, sometimes wearing no jacket over his braces and looking much like a farmhand or labourer, to Dorothea's intense annoyance. She had been brought up in the smartest parts of Bristol and Cheltenham and, keenly aware of social strata, she found mortifying and inexplicable her husband's habit of donning a working man's clothing.

At least Arthur was a good sportsman: while in India his favoured sports had been shooting game and playing polo, in Tiverton he confined himself to tennis, which brought him into contact with the local gentry.

Dorothea was determined to make a successful life for her family in Tiverton. She had spent the last few years moving house almost constantly. Now once more she had a home of her own, but to keep it together and maintain a middle-class lifestyle on a shoestring with six children was a delicate balancing act, even for one as resourceful and determined as Dorothea. It was she who ruled the family home. 'She was a forceful character, a strict disciplinarian, a much sought-after organiser and ultra-efficient,' wrote Walter of his mother, making her sound more like a military commander than a rural housewife.

His father, by contrast, was hopelessly happy-go-lucky and easygoing. Like Mr Micawber of Charles Dickens's *David Copperfield*, Arthur was an eternal optimist, always hoping that something would 'turn up'. Even as a small boy, Walter was appalled by his father's improvidence: he himself seldom left anything to chance.

In 1914 when Arthur had left for the war, he had handed over the family finances to his wife and she remained in control from then on, budgeting carefully, scrupulously accounting for every penny, accepting relatives' help if it were offered. The Walkers were not poor – they could stretch to tennis and riding lessons, private education and domestic help – but money was tight and Dorothea became exasperated if Arthur bought the children iced buns as a treat and would round on him furiously. She was not entirely puritanical. Rather daringly for the 1920s, she rode a Royal Enfield ladies' motorcycle, travelling all over Devon to play in tennis and hockey matches, and would sometimes play cricket in the garden with her sons.

Like any mother of a large family, Dorothea was always busy. She had had to learn to cook when she came back from India and, with Irene, she churned out endless stews and puddings in Tara's homely kitchen, summoning the children for dinner with a gong. Her brood of six nearly became eight when she became pregnant with twins in the mid-1920s. The pregnancy was a surprise and not a welcome one. Finding the money and energy for yet more children was a daunting prospect, but the twins were stillborn. Ruth, perhaps echoing her mother's view, thought it was just as well: 'Six of us were more than enough.'

Resilient as she was, there must have been times when Dorothea yearned for the Assam Tara, for the song of the nightjars and hoopoes, the sweet, honeyed scent of the frangipani flowers, the purple-blue of the jacaranda trees and the vivid pink of bougainvillaea, the picnics and polo meets, stables filled with polo ponies and syces (grooms), not to mention a cook, bearer and ayah to take care of the domestic grind.

Unlike Arthur, who had spent some of his childhood and all his adult life thus far in Assam, Dorothea had only lived there for five years. She, too, had been born in India but when she was only four months old her father, Edward Barton Gardner, a surgeon-major in the Indian Army Medical Service, mounted his polo pony to play in what he promised his wife Catherine would be his last game. It was. He fell, breaking his neck, and Catherine had to return home to Cheltenham with Dorothea, her older sister Mabel and another baby on the way, born the following year. The widowed Catherine brought up her three daughters in Cheltenham, known as the 'Calcutta of the Cotswolds' for the large number of Raj retirees who settled there. The girls attended Cheltenham Ladies College, and grew into pretty, spirited young women, known as the 'Three Beauties of Cheltenham'. A portrait of Dorothea as a young woman reveals a pink-cheeked dark-haired doll-like beauty that belies the steel-cored matron she would become.

Like Dorothea, Arthur had also lost a parent at an early age. He was six when his mother, Maria, died from cholera in Assam, where her husband, Colonel Thomas Nicholls Walker, had been sent to fight in a war against the neighbouring Nagas. Nevertheless Arthur had fond memories of Assam and was determined to return there when he finished school in England.

He and his older brother Walter secured jobs with a tea company and set out for Upper Assam, where they were to open new plantations in what was then virgin jungle. Together they oversaw the destruction of the jungle, and all that lived in it, hacking down towering trees, ferns and sinuous creepers to make way for tea.

Tigers, roused by the devastation of their habitat, would sometimes spring from the trees surrounding the tea gardens, and planters would return home to their bungalows to find cobras curled up on their beds or in cupboards. Tea-planting was a tough, unpredictable existence. The labourers' work was backbreaking and debilitating, but the planters at least had time to relax, with hunting, polo and convivial evenings at the club in the town of Dibrugarh.

Arthur and Walter joined the local militia, the Assam Valley Light Horse, as many planters did, until in 1900, fired by patriotic fervour, they volunteered for the Boer War and sailed for South Africa. Both were decorated for bravery, but only one brother returned to Assam.

Arthur was wounded and invalided back home, but his brother was killed, defending an outpost against impossible odds.

During his absence in South Africa, Arthur lost his job on the Doom Dooma tea estate but he soon found another post with the Tara tea company and, in 1908, must have felt secure enough to return to England on leave. If he was not actively looking for a wife, he was certainly not averse to the idea of marriage. Six foot tall, aged thirty-five, powerfully built, a champion shot, brilliant polo player and war hero, he must have been quite a catch.

He met the twenty-two-year-old Dorothea in Cheltenham and surmised that, for all her china-doll prettiness and youth, she had the constitution and mettle to cope with the often lonely life of a tea-planter's wife. He proposed and was accepted.

Did he warn her that she would spend much of her time on her own while he was out on the plantation all day? If he did, it did not deter her. Perhaps she was intrigued to return to the land of her birth, and too self-sufficient to worry about loneliness. In any case, she was in love.

Their wedding took place on Tuesday, 22 September 1908, at the church of St Philip and St James, just around the corner from their house in Cheltenham, and was reported, the following Saturday, under the heading 'Interesting local weddings' in the *Cheltenham Chronicle* and the *Gloucester Graphic*.

The bride, it was noted, was 'attired in an elegant princess gown of pure white satin charmeuse, the corsage slightly draped, and finished with a lovely bertha [a decorative collar] of Honiton lace'. She was attended by five bridesmaids, including her two sisters. The paper printed an exhaustive list of gifts, with recipients' names, which included a pair of slippers and a tray cloth, but also Dresden china tea sets, silver salvers, a silver tea caddy, a silver fish slice and fork (most suitably given by a Mrs Spratt), a silver telegram form rack, silver shoehorn and button-hook and other Edwardian home essentials, such as silver menu holders, several silver bonbon baskets, a crumb scoop, asparagus tongs, 'd'oyleys' (doilies, though made of cloth rather than paper), muffineers (sugar shakers), silver jugs, a silver-headed whip, a gong – useful for summoning Arthur from the tea plantation – and several brooches set with diamonds, pearls and amethysts. There were a few practical gifts too, such as a travel clock, a barometer and a case of scissors.

How on earth did they transport all that half a world away to Upper Assam? And who carefully wrapped every glass and vase so that they would survive the journey, across oceans, along rivers, by train, cart and finally carried by coolies or mules? And how much of it remained intact by the time it reached Upper Assam? One fears for the Dresden china set.

The newlyweds did not head straight to India. First there was a honeymoon in Brighton and Paris, a bold choice for Arthur, who must have been feeling flush and confident in his future to take his bride to belle-époque Paris.

Dorothea had been a baby when she left India but her mother instructed her on the dos and don'ts of a memsahib, how to organise the kitmughar (butler), the bearer (a kind of valet for the sahib), a khansamah (cook) and a pani-wallah (water-carrier), the chowkeydars (watchmen), punkah-wallahs, mäter (sweeper), syce (groom) and, most importantly, an ayah to look after any children.

Their first baby was born not in Assam but in Cuttack, in the seaside state of Orissa (now Odisha), where Arthur's brother Samuel was a police officer. Dorothea's father had trained as a gynaecologist at St Thomas's Hospital in London, which perhaps influenced her to move within reach of medical help for the birth, rather than risk being stuck in the remote reaches of Upper Assam.

When the baby arrived, in November 1909, they named him Samuel, although he was later known by his middle name, Edward. Dorothea returned to England in time for her second child, Beatrice, to be born in Cheltenham, but she was back in Cuttack in November 1912 when Walter - Wally - named after Arthur's beloved brother, was born.

Even before the children could walk they were put on ponies and led about by grooms. A fine horseman, it was important to Arthur that his children rode well. Sometimes they would be allowed to watch him as he captained the Assam polo team - a photograph shows him, with a luxuriant moustache, having won the All India shield - hurtling up and down the field, mallet whirling, as his pony wheeled while Dorothea, perhaps, tried not to think of her father's death at polo. There were holidays in Cuttack, days out at the racecourse and evenings at the club, where immaculate servants served drinks on silver trays and memsahibs fanned themselves, trying not to scratch their mosquito bites.

In 1913 this idyllic life came to an abrupt end. Too many bouts of tropical fever, together with his Boer War wound, had weakened Arthur's constitution and he must have been advised, or perhaps Dorothea insisted, that he should leave Assam while he still could, rather than risk joining his mother in a local cemetery. With heavy hearts, he, Dorothea and their three children, Edward, Beatrice and Walter, packed their possessions and left the Tara tea garden for ever. It must have been a subdued voyage back to Britain, not the triumphant homecoming of a wealthy nabob that Arthur had envisaged as a younger man. He had no job or home to return to with his growing family.

Arriving in England, watching as their belongings were disgorged onto the chilly dockside, so grey and subdued in comparison to the brilliant colours and noisy whirl of India's ports, was always a shock to an expatriate. The small Walker children had known no other home than Assam, so the cold, clammy English air and the sedate, colourless streets of Cheltenham contrasted sadly with the warm, noisy technicolour of India.

Like many exiles of Empire, Arthur and Dorothea would have found their return a tough transition. They had left behind their home, the ayah who had been a second mother to their children, their other servants, their ponies and pets, their status and security. Their future was uncertain. At first they stayed with Dorothea's mother, Catherine, in Cheltenham, where a fourth child, Peter, was born in February 1914.

It was a very difficult birth, and when Peter finally emerged, he was weak and in distress, with part of his bowel protruding from his body, and he seemed unlikely to live. Dorothea later admitted, 'I didn't want to look at him because they thought he was going to die.' But Arthur, summoned to inspect his fragile son, said this was 'nonsense'. He is supposed to have poured a teaspoon of brandy down the baby's throat, which apparently revived him. It seemed as if the odds were stacked against Peter right from the start, yet then, as later, he clung tenaciously to life. A medical procedure restored his bowels to their correct position.

Six months after Peter's birth, Britain declared war on Germany. Arthur answered the call to arms once more, with three of his brothers, and was given a temporary commission as a lieutenant with the Oxfordshire and Buckinghamshire Light Infantry. In 1915 he was in Ypres, at the so-called 'Hellfire Corner': it was horribly exposed to German guns, and was reputedly 'the most dangerous corner on Earth'. While he was there Arthur fell seriously ill and was invalided home for major surgery.

Apart from a brief return to Ypres, Arthur spent the rest of the war on the home front, recruiting and supervising units of the Labour Corps. Dorothea and the children moved around the country, joining him when they could and otherwise living with her mother in Cheltenham.

Arthur had been brought up a Catholic and was one of nine children from his father's second marriage: his father, Lieutenant Colonel Thomas Nicholls Walker, sired more children with his third and fourth wives. Although Arthur was not quite as prolific as his father, he was keen to have a large family and didn't worry too much about how he would support them all. In January 1917 Dorothea gave birth to a fifth child, Arthur Harold, known as Harold, in Cheltenham.

Shortly afterwards, Arthur was posted to Devonport and must have taken to Devon's billowing green hills and narrow roads between high hedges - perhaps the lush green countryside recalled Assam - for he summoned Dorothea and the children to join him. It was there that Ruth was born in January 1919.

Dorothea and Arthur knew how fortunate they were: so many families were now fatherless and one of Arthur's brothers was in an 'institute for incurables' with shell-shock. But Arthur had survived and with 'the war to end all wars' over, they could put down roots and look forward to their sons and daughters growing up in more peaceful times.

First they needed a home to call their own. Arthur had small war and disability pensions and a new job with the Imperial War Graves Commission, but they did not bring in the kind of money that would enable him to educate six children privately, and to do otherwise was out of the question for a family such as theirs.

Then they discovered that Blundell's, one of the oldest public schools in the country, offered greatly reduced fees to boys whose parents lived in its local town of Tiverton. With Edward now at public-school age, this was incentive enough for Dorothea and Arthur to buy a house in the pretty market town.

Relieved that her sons' education was assured, Dorothea was determined not to let the family's genteel poverty affect the morale of the household. Her children remembered family life as cheerful, presided over by the genial 'Pops', as his family called Arthur, the house a whirlwind of children coming and going. His chickens and apples were a far cry from the acres of tea and his role as 'sahib' of a large plantation, with a workforce of several hundred, but he seemed content to have swapped whisky sodas at the club for a pint at the pub.

In some ways, he and Dorothea were an unlikely match, she the forceful, disciplined and somewhat snobbish matriarch, he the easygoing Everyman, but they complemented each other: she provided the firm cornerstone for family life, while he was the originator of jokes and treats.

Tara might have been a modest home compared with its Assam namesake, but it was a happy, settled household. It was from there that the children would venture forth to the far reaches of the Empire, just as the sun was beginning to set on it.

Before they went to Blundell's, Edward, Walter, Peter and Harold attended a preparatory school. Dorothea and Arthur picked St Petroc's in Bude, Cornwall, which offered plenty of sport and blustery seaside walks as well as academic preparation for public school.

While Edward adapted readily to boarding-school life Walter, normally the most conscientious of the brothers, rebelled. His school reports made depressing reading for his parents. Perhaps he was homesick but, if so, his unhappiness manifested itself in precocious misogyny: he simply refused to be taught by women.

Even from the distance of a century his stance is bizarre in one so young and at odds with other aspects of his character, such as his admiration for his strong, capable mother, with whom he had far more in common than his casual, improvident father. Whatever the reason, St Petroc's were not prepared to put up with Walter's behaviour and told his parents to find another school for him. Instead he was sent as a day boy to a prep school in Exeter, to which Peter followed him, catching the early train from Tiverton each morning.

It was a strict regime: 'stupid' mistakes were rewarded with a sharp clout on the back of the head by the headmaster, the Reverend Mr Bird, a fitness fanatic, who expected the boys to excel in football and cricket. Walter was not free of female teachers: his Latin teacher was 'a witch of a woman . . . ugly as sin', although she was, he conceded, a good teacher, who punished those who forgot their verbs by rapping their knuckles with the sharp edge of a ruler.

With the boys taken care of, Dorothea was faced with the problem of the girls' education. There was no equivalent of Blundell's and Dorothea's alma mater, Cheltenham Ladies College, was expensive and thus out of the question. At first, Bee went to school locally, but then Arthur's sister, Blanche, stepped in and paid for her and later Ruth to attend Thornton College, a convent in Buckinghamshire.

Dorothea was anxious: she had ensured that the children were brought up in the Church of England, not as Roman Catholics like Arthur. She worried that the nuns might try to convert her daughters and made the long journey up to Buckinghamshire regularly on her motorbike, a three-hundred-mile round trip, to see Ruth and assure herself that she was indeed attending Anglican services.

From the age of six Ruth had to take the train from Exeter to Waterloo, where she was met by a nun who took her across London and put her on a train out to Bletchley station, a few miles from the school. The journey must have been daunting enough but it was made more so by Peter, a keen practical joker, who warned Ruth to stay away from women wearing stockings as they were known to kidnap young girls and sell them as slaves. Poor Ruth took him seriously and looked with suspicion on all females in stockings, which was most of them. She was happy at Thornton College, though. She played netball and plenty of tennis, her favourite sport, and made friends easily.

When she came back to Tara for the school holidays, as the youngest of six she was alternately everyone's pet and the butt of their jokes and pranks. Mostly she could hold her own, but there were times when her brothers clearly overstepped the boundary between teasing and bullying. In her late eighties she was given 'A Grandparents' Book' in which to make a record of her life for her children and grandchildren, with formulaic but occasionally revealing questions and with spaces for her to write the answers. One question read, 'What do you particularly remember about your brothers and sisters from your childhood?' Her answer: 'Boys bullying me.' Walter was the best behaved, Harold the one she fought with most, Peter the naughtiest – and also her favourite. Everyone adored Peter. Despite their fights, she and Harold were closest in age and played doctors and nurses together, which turned out to be highly prescient.

When the boys left prep school they went to Blundell's, less than a mile's walk through the fields from Tara. Like most public schools, it had a strong military ethos, with an Officer Training Corps (OTC) and an 'army class' that prepared boys for entrance to the Royal Military College, Sandhurst.

With the branches of the Walker family tree filled with naval captains and army colonels who had gone east, it was a fair bet that at least some of Arthur's sons would serve abroad. Thomas Nicholls Walker, Arthur's father, had had an illustrious military career. He had fought through the Indian Mutiny in 1857-8* commanding the 'Forlorn Hope' at the Siege of Delhi, and was commended for his outstanding bravery. He went on to command the 44th Bengal Native Infantry, which became the 8th Gurkhas, and wrote a book about his military exploits recalling how, while breakfasting with a fellow officer during the siege of Delhi, they had spotted some enemy approaching. Taking up a rifle, his friend casually picked off four men. Then, Thomas wrote, 'He let me have some shot, and I accounted for three more.'

It sounds callous, as if he were shooting partridges, rather than men. He portrayed his experiences of war as a *Boys' Own* adventure tale, skimming over the brutal and bloody reality. It inspired his grandsons, Edward and Walter, who, by the time they reached Blundell's in the mid-1920s, were already dreaming of military glory.

At Blundell's, as at other schools, discipline was maintained by corporal punishment, and monitors (prefects), like Walter, were entitled to punish junior boys with the cane, which meant that occasionally he caned his younger brothers, Peter and Harold.

In one of Edward's school reports his headmaster wrote, 'I regret that he did not carry out his duties as monitor last term as well as I could have wished.' Edward was a genial, easygoing boy, much in his father's mould, which made him popular but perhaps reluctant to enforce discipline. Walter, by contrast, was quite prepared to make himself unpopular if it meant righting what he saw as a wrong.

Noting that day boys were treated as lesser beings by the boarders, who ribbed and sometimes bullied them, Walter took it upon himself as head of the school's day boys to sort out the school bullies in the old-fashioned way: with his fists.

---

* Known in India as the First War of Independence

Arthur had been keen that all the boys should be able to 'look after themselves'. To this end, he taught them all to box and coached them in the garden at Tara. Walter and later Harold proved determined pugilists and were soon winning school boxing competitions. Walter even enlisted a coach, a retired army sergeant, who kept up his training in the holidays and taught him to attack the moment the bell sounded and knock out his opponent in the first round.

The skills he learned in the boxing ring were now applied outside it. Any boarder who had the temerity to insult him, trip him up or ruffle his hair received 'a straight left to the nose or an uppercut to the jaw'. He despised the bullies, but he was not impressed by his fellow day boys, finding them a 'motley bunch of idle, unpatriotic, unkempt and "couldn't care less" type of youths. I decided to straighten them out . . .'

He set about his self-appointed task with ruthless energy. He ordered them not to let the boarders treat them with contempt or call them 'day bugs', and drove them hard to ensure that when they turned out on parade – every day boy was a member of the school's OTC – their drill was as immaculate as their uniform and shining boots.

The day boys' morale improved but Walter had, as he later admitted, overstepped the mark. The headmaster, Alexander Ross Wallace, a stern but enlightened man, summoned him to his study and explained the difference between driving and leading, later writing in Walter's report that he 'must not allow his zeal to outrun discretion'.

He did, however, prophesy that this keen young man, a 'tiger' on the rugby field and in the boxing ring, was a natural fit for the army and would go far: 'I regard him as in every way one of the most promising boys I have met and I foresee myself a very distinguished military career in front of him,' he wrote to Arthur. Wallace was a muscular Christian – he had been an Indian Army cavalry officer and civil servant and was later ordained – who ran his school much like a regiment. According to Walter, he was 'stern, strict, demanding the highest standards, yet approachable, a good sportsman who knew the name and character of every boy in the school'.

Walter admired him hugely – they stayed in touch until Wallace's death, fifty years later – and clearly drew inspiration from his example when he came to lead his own regiment. Just as Waterloo was, apocryphally, won on the playing fields of Eton, Walter's corner of the Second

World War was shaped by his time at Blundell's. When he left the school, the parents of the day boys he had so ruthlessly whipped into shape clubbed together to give him a silver cigarette case inscribed: 'I have earned you more friends than enemies.'

In the holidays, Ruth came home from Buckinghamshire and reunited with her brothers, swapping the confines of the convent for the boisterous, masculine environment of Tara, joining them in the treehouse that they called 'The Nest.' In summer, the boys played in cricket matches and tennis tournaments, and Ruth played tennis, too, while in the winter she and Walter hired ponies and went hunting with the Tiverton Foxhounds.

For Ruth, life with four brothers was never dull, but it had its challenges. Walter, seven years older than her, imported the school fagging system – younger boys had to run errands for older ones – into his home. Ruth became his fag-cum-valet: not only did she have to put toothpaste on his brush for him, but he ordered her to warm the loo seat in their outdoor privy before he would deign to use it.

If Dorothea was aware of it, she seldom intervened. But Ruth had one knight in shining armour – or, at least, in Blundell's uniform – who came to her rescue. John Fisher lived across town in a large house called the Mazry, with his widowed mother and sisters. He was the same age as Bee and was also a Blundell's day boy. Walter, two school years below him, was his fag. John was embraced by the Tara clan and was often to be found playing cricket or boxing in the garden with the brothers. Arthur treated him as a fifth son, perhaps recognising in John a kindred spirit: a good-natured, charming joker, with a gift for inspiring friendship and loyalty.

As Ruth recalled, 'He used to look after me from my four tormenting brothers, who used to tease me all the time and do terrible things to me.' This included locking her in cupboards and using her as a goalpost – the other was a tree – in their games of rugby and football. Once when her brothers were playing cowboys and Indians, they tied her to a tree and fired arrows at her. They had at least taken the precaution of placing rubber bungs on the tips to blunt them, but one arrow still cut her knee.

Seeing the blood stream down her leg and imagining their mother's reaction when she heard that they had been using their little sister for target practice, the boys panicked: 'We'll cut your throat if you tell Mother and Pop.' Harold offered her sweets as a bribe. She duly kept silent, but was savvy enough to use the incident to her advantage. For a time she gained influence by merely pointing to the scar on her knee, at which the brothers would hastily comply with whatever she demanded. She was duly promoted from goalpost to participant in the games. Harold gave her one of his precious sweets and the others became protective, showing concern if she fell over when playing.

The special treatment waned as the wound healed, but even so she still opted to play with her brothers rather than with girls of her own age, preferring the risks of being shot or sidelined when they held peeing contests to the more genteel activities then preferred by girls.

As the Tara clan grew up, the family photograph albums record trips to the beach, to Woolacombe and Bude, with groups of friends, athletic young men and long-legged girls in knitted bathing costumes and sunglasses, sometimes with Dorothea in dress, stockings and hat, seated on a deckchair in the background. Some of the young men in the photographs would not survive long into the next decade – the war took a heavy toll on Blundell's boys – but for now the skies above the beach were free of war clouds.

Ruth observed her siblings as they grew up and left Tara, returning home periodically on leave. She saw little of Edward, who was ten years older and, by 1928 when Ruth was nine, had already left home. Bee, the next eldest, remained at Tara for some years after leaving school, so Ruth had some companionship in the holidays although the sisters' relationship was often prickly. Bee, slender, pretty and much admired by her brothers' Blundell's friends, was infuriated when a tactless aunt declared, in her hearing, that Ruth would end up being prettier than her. 'From then on, she had the knives out for me,' said Ruth.

Despite such minor tensions, life rambled on happily as the twenties gave way to the thirties. Arthur would potter into town to place a sly bet on the horses or slip into a pub for a quiet pint, or cycle to Blundell's to watch his sons play cricket or rugby. He was an attentive, loving father, and both Peter and Harold told their families that they were his favourite son, suggesting that Arthur was skilled at making each child feel as though they were the centre of his world.

In spite of his disabilities Arthur remained a keen tennis player and played regularly with Sir John Amory, who lived at Knightshayes Court, a grand Victorian mansion overlooking the town and its lace factory, Heathcoat's, founded by the baronet's grandfather in 1916. The thriving industry protected Tiverton from the worst ravages of the depression that began in 1929. Demand for lace curtains increased as housing became more densely packed together in towns and people yearned for privacy from their neighbours and passersby.

Tiverton's population grew steadily and there were moves to improve the water and electricity supplies, plans for a new school, a new market and a new abattoir. It was an energetic, self-reliant town, run by a benevolent, liberal squirearchy, headed by the Heathcoat-Amory family, who provided housing and a pension scheme for the factory workers, while the local hospital was funded almost entirely by charitable donations. The National Health Service was still a long way off but Tivertonians were encouraged to join a local health-insurance scheme to which the better-off paid more than the low-waged.

Numerous committees and voluntary bodies kept the town running smoothly. Dorothea deployed her brisk efficiency as chair of the Mothers' Union, as well as organising tennis and hockey clubs for which she played. She was, according to Walter, a 'first-class' sportswoman, highly competitive and energetic. Her children would inherit her driven, ambitious nature in varying degrees, offset by Arthur's easy charm.

Beyond Tiverton, life in the surrounding countryside was hard. Prices for livestock and crops, which had been protected during the Great War, plummeted as Britain once again became more reliant on cheaper, imported food. In some areas, crops were left to rot in the fields as it was not economically viable to harvest them. Rural wages declined, and many young people chose to double their earnings by taking factory jobs instead of adopting the tough, impoverished existence of a farm worker.

With Arthur's eggs and fruit fetching lower prices at the market, money was tighter than ever at Tara, and Dorothea worried constantly about how she would keep the household going. Meanwhile the world into which her elder children were about to embark was changing.

In 1932 Sir Oswald Mosley formed the British Union of Fascists, exploiting the economic malaise and growing unemployment that followed the Wall Street Crash of 1929 with promises to help the working man, to fight against Communism and to uphold the British Empire. In Europe, the leader of the Italian Fascist party, Benito Mussolini, had become Il Duce, the country's all-powerful dictator, while on the far side of the world an extremist nationalist movement had taken hold in Japan. The peace that had prevailed for the past decade was looking shaky.

Notwithstanding the political ripples, the late twenties and early thirties were peaceful years for the Walkers, seen through the prism of the photo albums. There is Pop relaxing in his deckchair in the garden, the boys boxing with Venn, Dorothea and her daughters dressed up for a shopping trip to Exeter.

In a few years' time, war would take its toll on the family but, for the moment, they were still climbing life's ladders.

2

'The toast of the colony'

———❖———

I T WAS INEVITABLE that at least some of the Walker siblings would
head east. It was in their blood. Long before their grandfather had
fought in the Indian Mutiny of 1857, their ancestors had captained
merchant ships trading between England and the east, skirmishing with
French battleships and pushing the boundaries of Britain's growing empire.

By the late 1920s, the empire was no longer expanding and there
were burgeoning independence movements in India and Burma, but a
career in the military was still an attractive prospect for a young man.
Whatever the future held, the armed forces would still need officers and
men to defend Britain and her borders wherever they were drawn.

Having grown up on the tales of his grandfather's military adventures,
Edward decided to follow in his footsteps by joining his old regiment,
the 8th Gurkhas. The Gurkhas, from Nepal, had been part of the Indian
Army since 1815, famed for their loyalty and incredible courage in battle.
The Great War cemented their reputation: they won almost two thousand gallantry awards, including three Victoria Crosses. To command
such renowned warriors would be a privilege indeed. And a career in
the Indian rather than the British Army had many advantages: there
would be postings all around India and perhaps to Burma, Hong Kong
and Malaya, a far more exciting prospect for an adventurous and ambitious young man than a dreary round of exercises on Salisbury Plain
with the odd stint abroad.

There was also the chance of action in the ongoing war on India's
North-west Frontier against Pathan tribesmen, and a financial consider-
ation: while British Army officers required a healthy private income to
maintain themselves in the expected style, their Indian Army equivalents
could manage it on their pay alone.

In November 1927 Edward sat an exam for the Royal Military

Academy, Sandhurst, where young men fresh from public school, and a handful from grammar schools, spent fifteen months being drilled, lectured, screamed at and insulted, marching and riding, boxing and bicycling. If they survived the gruelling regime, and not all did, they would 'pass out' from Sandhurst as second lieutenants and join a regiment.

Before the exam, Edward had to fill in a 'form of particulars' stating his name, date and place of birth and, now utterly incongruous, 'whether of pure European descent', to which he wrote a confident 'Yes.' In the early days of the British in India it was not uncommon for British officers and civil servants to marry Indian women and while not quite encouraged, it was at least tolerated. The Indian Mutiny, though, had changed everything, hardening attitudes towards race, and by the early twentieth century admitting to a mixed-race grandmother could jeopardise your chances of being accepted as a prospective officer cadet.

Edward was reasonably academic but had a tendency to fall apart in exams, as his school reports noted. However, he passed the Sandhurst entrance exam and arrived there as an officer cadet for the summer term of 1928. Somehow, Arthur and Dorothea had managed to scrape together the fees of £300 – the equivalent of £18,000 today – more than twice the average annual wage of a skilled tradesman. But Dorothea was adamant that they could not afford to send any more boys to Sandhurst. Their next son would have to go into trade and earn his own money.

At Sandhurst, Edward overlapped with the actor David Niven, who arrived there a term later and recalled his early days as an officer cadet as 'sheer, undiluted hell', a relentless round of drills and punishments. The first ten weeks of the eighteen-month course were the most gruelling and interminable as cadets were not allowed out of the Sandhurst grounds. 'For the ten weeks on the square, we never stopped running, saluting, marching, drilling, climbing ropes, riding unmanageable chargers and polishing and burnishing everything in sight . . . boots, belts, chinstraps, buttons, bayonets and above all our rifles . . . "the soldier's best friend, mind",' Niven recalled in his memoir, *The Moon's a Balloon*.

Aside from lectures, drills and riding, much of the cadets' time was taken up with looking after their kit. They had to be immaculate at all times. The smallest speck of dandruff must not defile your collar, the brass buttons on your uniform and the buckles on your belt must be gleaming, your collar stiff with starch, your bedsheet straightened to the smoothness of marble. You had to wear a flat cap - known as a 'Gor Blimey' - at all times, even inside, except at meals and in bed. Cadets used bicycles to get around Sandhurst's extensive grounds but even that involved drill: you could not simply get on your bicycle but had to wait for the command 'Mount!' then swing one leg over and ride with a ramrod back, in tight formation, wheel to wheel.

Looking after the leather elements of their kit was a time-consuming task. Their boots and leather Sam Browne - the leather belt with an additional strap over the shoulder - did not only have to gleam but had to have a 'surface', meaning a very deep polish, so shiny that it gleamed with a light of its own. Until their leather was deemed to pass the eagle eye of the under officer, cadets were not allowed to leave the Sandhurst grounds, even at weekends. No cadet, however diligent, however furiously they spat, polished and burnished, ever had his leather passed for the first two months at least. Until then, every weekend was spent waxing, buffing and shining. It was a big moment when your leather was finally passed and you were free to go out on Saturdays and Sundays. The well-heeled cadets would head off to the races, or to London's West End to go dancing with girlfriends or, in Niven's case, for amorous adventures with a good-time girl named Nessie, the archetypal tart with a heart of gold. Edward remembered him as being 'very naughty'. Within a few years, Niven would leave the army for Hollywood, and Ruth would cycle into Tiverton to watch him on the screen at the Tivoli cinema. She had, she admitted, rather a crush on him.

Edward, like Niven, had an eye for the girls, but he did not have the funds from Dorothea and Arthur that would enable him to go cavorting in the West End. Nonetheless, he made friends easily and, although he was not marked out as a future star, he did well enough at Sandhurst. In his reports his company commander, Hugh Carlton Cumberbatch - a distant relative of the actor Benedict Cumberbatch - commented that Edward 'tries and works hard' and showed 'promise'.

The final hurdle was now to be accepted by the 1/8th Gurkhas. That his grandfather had been an illustrious former colonel of the regiment would certainly help his cause. However, his luck was out.

In the First World War, tall British officers, who stood sometimes more than a foot above their diminutive Nepalese soldiers, had been easily picked off by enemy snipers. To avoid this in future, an upper height limit of five foot ten was established for officers. Edward was the tallest of the Walker brothers at six foot one, a full three inches too tall, but he hoped this might be overlooked, given his strong family connection, and enlisted the help of several senior officers to plead his cause. Alas, it was in vain. His case went all the way to the commander-in-chief of the Indian Army, but the answer came back that 'The chief is very particular about the height rule in Gurkha battalions.' Edward had to find another battalion and settled for the 1/8th Punjab Regiment. He sailed for India in the autumn of 1929, the first of the Tara chicks to fly the coop.

Dorothea had been adamant that, with Edward going into the military, her second son, Walter, must go into trade and make some money. A relative worked for Imperial Tobacco and arranged for him to spend a day touring their cigarette factory in Bristol. Talking later of how his military career had begun, Walter told his interviewer Charles Allen about the visit: 'I saw the sort of job I'd have to do for the first two years, looking at cigarettes coming out of machines and so on, and I came back to my mother and I said, "This is not for me. I want to follow my grandfather and my elder brother into the army."'

Dorothea knew when she was beaten and, eventually, conceded defeat. 'Thank God for that,' was the response of Alexander Wallace, Walter's headmaster, echoing Walter. Wallace was in no doubt that the boy was made for the military, not for Civvy Street, and gave him a glowing report for his Sandhurst application. Walter passed the exam and sailed through the interview, awarded four hundred marks out of a possible four hundred.

Even before he arrived at Sandhurst he applied to join 1/8th Gurkhas. At five foot ten he was at the limit of the acceptable height, but there was only one vacancy for a new officer in the year that he would be eligible to join so competition would be stiff. Arthur swung into action and invited one of the regiment's senior officers to Devon to meet Walter for a round of golf, while another interviewed him more formally and pronounced himself impressed with the boy's character and ability, adding, 'It was nice to see that this young officer had clean fingernails.' I wonder how often the hopes of other candidates were dashed by grubby ones.

Somehow, Arthur and Dorothea raised the money to send another son to Sandhurst, perhaps with the help of a generous relative. When Walter arrived there in August 1931 he was looking forward to learning military tactics and crafts, such as map-reading or how to lay an ambush, and honing his marksmanship, already practised in the OTC at Blundell's. But he was amazed to discover that almost none of his time at Sandhurst would be spent acquiring military skills. True, there were occasional lessons on tactics but, to Walter's frustration, these were the failed tactics of the last war: the emphasis was on discipline, attrition and trenches as it was assumed that any future European war would be similarly static. It seemed that few lessons had been learned from the terrible waste of life on the Flanders battlefield.

John St John Baxter, who arrived at Sandhurst in the same intake as Walter and was to become a lifelong friend, was equally dumbfounded by the distinctly unmilitary nature of the course. Much later, he, too, was interviewed by the Imperial War Museum and said, 'I never fired a single weapon all the time I was at Sandhurst.' Baxter described how many cadets, including himself, saw the army as a means to an end: they wanted to do their job well, but they were keen to enjoy themselves at the same time. 'Whereas I think Walter Walker was rather the other way round – any sort of social life was unfortunate and just had to be. He was purely interested in anything to do with the army and training and so on.' So while other cadets slid off to the pub or to London for weekends, Walter spent almost all his spare time reading up on military tactics and sparring with the army's chief boxing instructor, 'Dusty' Miller.

Despite his dedication, even Walter got into trouble sometimes. He polished his leather for hours before the first inspection, only for his platoon commander to pronounce his boots 'bloody shit' and throw them out of the window onto the gravel below where they became pitted with holes. One Sunday, the elderly Duke of Connaught inspected the cadets on parade. Walter had taken the precaution of having his hair cut at the back and sides with electric clippers, so short that the white skin showed through. He was dumbfounded when the duke halted behind him and bellowed, 'Why has this gentleman cadet got long hair?'

It turned out that the sharp-eyed duke had spotted one single, tiny strand that the barber had missed, protruding below the bottom rim of his cap. For this heinous crime Walter was punished all the following weekend by being subjected to an endless round of drills and inspection, marching fast round and round the lake doing 'arms drill' on a hot summer's day.

At least he was never put on 'puttee parade', a barbaric punishment in which the victim was forced to run along the corridors, carrying a pack of sand on his back, while his fellow cadets lashed him with leather belts. It was only stopped when a cadet burst his appendix wound as he was being flogged.

It was not the brutality of the Sandhurst regime that annoyed Walter, but its futility. Despite the advent of tanks in the Great War, at Sandhurst cavalry still meant horses and the cadets spent endless hours in the saddle, a struggle for those who had not ridden before, if not for Walter, who hunted regularly. He clearly impressed his instructors as he was promoted to senior sergeant of his company.

At the end of 1932 he passed out of Sandhurst and readied himself to leave for India, the land of his birth. There was one last Christmas at Tara, although much of his time was spent preparing for departure, purchasing such essentials as '1 pillow, hospital pattern, hair, small' and '1 chair, officer's camp', a compass, binoculars and a revolver. New officers were also advised on what kind of 'mufti' – civilian clothing – was acceptable, reminded not to wear spurs or swords on board ship and to wait until they reached India to buy the mandatory sun helmet, although these had to be of the right sort. The wrong kind of pith helmet meant social death. Uniform had to be made to measure at Flights, the military outfitters, at great expense, forcing Dorothea to make further economies at home.

In January, before Walter departed for India and Ruth for boarding school, the Walkers gathered for a family photograph on the steps of Tara. Even Edward was there, on leave from India. Peter, too, would be heading abroad soon, leaving only the two girls and Harold at home.

Walter left Southampton on 8 February 1933 on the troopship *Somersetshire* for the six-week voyage to Karachi. All Indian Army officers had to spend one year with a British regiment posted in India before they joined an Indian Army regiment. Edward had chosen the King's Royal Rifle Corps but Walter opted for the Sherwood Foresters since his Uncle Sammy had served with them in the Great War. Moreover they were based at Multan in the north-west of India where Edward was now stationed with 1/8th Punjabs.

Other than family connections there was little to recommend Multan. It was famed for its dust, beggars and 120-degree heat. The 8th Punjabs' newsletter, with acid sarcasm, called it 'the glorious Riviera of the Western Punjab', and described how 'the early sun, the dust-laden air, the wonderful evening scene and the howling of the pies [stray dogs] all keep us here'.

Dorothea and Arthur had passed on the practical advice acquired from their own years in India, telling Walter, as they had warned Edward, of the furnace-like heat that would engulf him as soon as he disembarked from the ship, and of the ingenuity of the railway thieves, who would slip soundlessly through unlocked train windows and rob sleeping passengers.

But nothing could really prepare the newcomer. First, there was the tumult of the quayside at Karachi, teeming with labourers, who yelled and waved, touting for business as porters, spindly limbs belying extraordinary strength as they hoisted huge metal trunks onto their backs, while sweating policemen strove to keep order with whistles and the occasional thwack of a lathi – a heavy bamboo stick.

Walter, with John St John Baxter and two others also heading for Multan, found a carriage and settled down for the two-day-long journey north. In the restaurant car they met a jovial Englishman and his wife, who were also making for Multan, where he was the manager of Grindlays Bank. This friendly couple gave the young men a crash course in the dos and don'ts of living in India, and Walter looked forward to seeing more of them in Multan.

But it was not to be. So rigid was the social hierarchy and brutal snobbery to which the Raj clung, even in its dying days, that when Walter and his three companions arrived at the Sherwood Foresters' mess they were given a pile of calling cards and lectured by a senior subaltern on who to call upon, and in which order. Senior civil servants, clergy, doctors and police were all socially acceptable to officers of the Sherwood Foresters. The bank manager, being 'in trade', was not, and Walter was roundly rebuked for giving his card to a mere 'box-wallah'. Worse, his new pith helmet was deemed a size too large.

It was hardly an auspicious start. There was, however, compensation.

Each young officer was expected to employ a bearer, in Walter's case a kindly old Punjabi who not only took off his boots and unwound his puttees but squeezed his toothpaste onto the brush for him and held out his pyjamas at knee height. In the morning, he brought tea, hot water for shaving, Walter's uniform pressed and his boots polished. Within the space of weeks, they had gone from Sandhurst slaves to living like royalty.

The deficiencies in their Sandhurst training soon became sorely apparent. They had almost no experience of firing a rifle or light machine-gun, or throwing a grenade, and found to their embarrassment that they were expected to teach these skills to the soldiers in their platoon, tough, experienced men recruited from the minefields of Nottinghamshire and Derbyshire, some with thirty years' service. It was embarrassing at best, dangerous at worst: Walter and Baxter had to study the weapons manual. 'The two of us looking at our books, and saying, "Well, it looks as though you hold it this way," you see,' Baxter remembered. Determined to learn the military tactics that Sandhurst had failed to impart, Walter spent his days, and often his nights, map-reading, navigating and weapons training.

Another challenge was keeping the troops entertained, a euphemism for keeping them away from women and keeping down the rate of venereal disease (VD). There were concert parties, plays, games of tennis and hockey - rugby was impossible because the heat baked the ground as hard as concrete.

Although he was joining the Gurkhas, who spoke Gurkhali, Walter had also to learn Urdu since this was the official language of the Indian Army. He was determined to do better than his brother Edward, who had failed his Urdu exam several times. To this end, Walter spent his evenings with a *munshi* - teacher - even getting up at 2 a.m. for lessons before the 5 a.m. parade.

John St John Baxter's father was the commanding officer of 1/8th Punjabs and lived with his wife in married quarters in Multan. Opting for home comforts over the formality of the mess, Baxter moved in with his parents, and when he invited Walter to join him there, he gratefully accepted. One night in the Baxters' bungalow, Walter was studying late again for his Urdu exam when Baxter junior entered his room and froze in the doorway. 'There is a large cobra behind your chair with its head and body raised ready to strike,' he whispered. Walter sat still as a stone while Baxter alerted his father, who quickly fetched a curtain pole and felled the snake with one violent blow, finishing it off with two bullets as it writhed on the floor. Walter had remained motionless throughout the drama, to the approval of Colonel Baxter.

The colonel had one Walker brother living under his roof and another, Edward, under his command. Both young men impressed him. Baxter wrote in Edward's confidential report that he was 'an extremely loyal, zealous and hardworking officer whose all round efficiency is much above the average'. He was tactful in his dealing with superiors and subordinates and 'would go far in the service if he maintains his present high standard'.

Back in Tiverton, Dorothea turned her attention to her third son, Peter, who had now left Blundell's. While Walter, and later Harold, were school stars – both were monitors, both were champion boxers, and Harold even made the 1st XI cricket team – Peter was a steady sportsman, making his house team but no more, and never became a monitor. As the naughtiest of the brothers he was more of a poacher than a gamekeeper.

What struck people about Peter was his kindness and concern for others, so it was perhaps not surprising that he decided to become a doctor: with his ability to put others at ease he would have been well suited to the role of country practitioner. But Dorothea and Arthur blenched at the prospect of funding five years of medical school so Peter was told that he would have to find another career. It was Arthur who came up with the solution. He still had contacts in the tea business and thought Peter would do well to head to Assam, as he himself had done. Peter idolised his father and, of the four boys, was closest to him in temperament, gentle and genial but with a mischievous sense of humour, so it was fitting that he should follow in Arthur's footsteps. In November 1933, the Walkers waved goodbye to another son as Peter set off for India, travelling on the SS *Dumana*, to take up the post of tea-planter with the Eastern Assam Tea Company. He was nineteen and was about to embark on the happiest years of his life.

Now there was only one son at home, Harold, and two daughters. Ruth was still at school but Bee was now twenty-two, an eminently marriageable age. Two brothers serving in the Indian Army presented an ideal opportunity for her to spread her wings, see the world beyond their quiet corner of Devon, and perhaps even find a husband. India was the natural hunting ground for unmarried girls. For two centuries young women had sailed from Britain to India, where the supply of bachelors was plentiful. They were known as the Fishing Fleet, and those who failed to land a catch and returned home without a ring on their finger were cruelly dubbed the 'returned empties'. Bee was not averse to a spot of husband-hunting. However, the prospect of visiting her brothers in Multan, with its dust storms and broiling heat, cannot have held much appeal.

Then in January 1934 Edward's regiment was delivered from the purgatory of Multan and posted to Hong Kong. For ambitious soldiers Hong Kong was a frustrating posting: lack of funds meant that the army operated on a four-day week and, aside from a fortnight-long major training exercise once a year, their time was largely spent on sport, drills and socialising. For those who preferred socialising to soldiering, it was a dream posting.

Hong Kong in the thirties was a glamorous, exciting place to be. Ceded to Britain as one of the spoils of the Opium Wars nearly a century earlier, it had grown from tranquil backwater into a thriving cosmopolitan city where east and west met and mingled, in theory. In reality Europeans and Chinese were socially segregated. Even the wealthiest Chinese were barred from buying houses on the Peak, the most desirable location in the colony, and banned from the Hong Kong Club, the high temple of expatriate society.

Such iniquities might not have unduly troubled Edward or his brother officers of 1/8th Punjabs, who were simply delighted to have left Multan behind and to find themselves in what seemed to be a fairyland by comparison. Stately junks glided on the jade-green waters of the harbour, borne along by their spiky sails, hundreds of fishing sampans bobbing among them, while at night a million lights twinkled along the shore and were reflected in the water. The air was heavy with the scent of jasmine and frangipani.

There were parties and dinners in the Punjabs' officers' mess in Kowloon, on the mainland. So rigidly was tradition adhered to that, even if only one officer was dining in the mess at night, the regimental brass band had to turn out and play while the solitary diner had to wear full military regalia and observe all the mess customs, such as passing the port and Madeira to himself, then standing to toast His Majesty the King, which made for an absurd spectacle.

Edward was not quite twenty-five when he became engaged to a vivacious blonde named Marjorie Elizabeth Wilkinson, always known as Tiggy. The daughter of a senior judge, Hiram Parkes Wilkinson, she and her older sister Prudence – Prudie – had spent their early years in Shanghai and Northern Ireland. Theirs was a liberal, intellectual household: Hiram wrote academic papers on such recherché subjects as 'the Family in Classical China' and his daughters were clever and artistic. Prudie, a talented sculptor, went on to art school and to Cambridge after leaving their Scottish boarding school, while Tiggy's ambition was to become an actress. She had hoped to go to RADA – the Royal Academy of Dramatic Art – after leaving school but, to her intense dismay, her parents would not countenance it. In 1932, after several years of semi-retirement in Northern Ireland, Hiram was returning to Shanghai and Hong Kong to resume his legal career. He and his wife refused to let Tiggy remain in London, insisting that she accompany them when they sailed. Family legend has it that Tiggy had become involved with a married man, and her parents were anxious to get her away from him.

The Wilkinsons were based in Shanghai but spent some of the year in Hong Kong, with Hiram's work, and it was here that Tiggy met Edward. The romance was encouraged by Mrs Wilkinson, who thought that Edward, tall, handsome, charming, polo-playing and respectable, would be the ideal match for her flighty daughter, perhaps feeling that the sooner Tiggy was safely married, the better.

They had, on the surface, plenty in common. Both had been born in the east, then uprooted and taken 'home' to Britain. Both were sociable and good-looking. Tiggy was bubbly and bright; Edward was charming and popular. There were, however, some stark differences between them. The Wilkinsons and the Walkers were cut from different cloth. Hiram Wilkinson had been a high sheriff and a Supreme Court judge, while Arthur Walker was merely a retired army captain. The Wilkinsons were politically and socially liberal and had always looked down on the military, while the Walkers were deeply conservative and saw service in the military as a noble calling. Edward seldom read a book and had little interest in art, but Tiggy had grown up in a liberal intellectual household where books were written, not simply read.

Their discrepancies were brushed aside, along with their romantic pasts. Back in Tiverton Edward had had a girlfriend named Joan but they had never progressed to marriage, although he was still fond of her and even in old age spoke of her as the one who got away. But Joan was on the other side of the world, while Tiggy was in Hong Kong, lively, bright and attractive: what could possibly go wrong?

News of Edward's engagement was received at Tara with excitement. Here, at last, was an opportunity for Bee to head east: she would act as bridesmaid at the wedding. From the moment she picked her way across the ship's gangplank, she was besieged by suitors. Edward had hopes of matchmaking her with a regimental friend, Captain John Austin, but Bee quickly dismissed him as too short – she was tall and had in mind someone nearer to six foot.

Plenty of other young men lined up to take Edward's pretty sister out to tea at the Peninsula Hotel, or escort her on a sightseeing trip around the busy markets and steep ladder streets. Witty and charming, she was undoubtedly a catch, and one of her admirers from that time remembered her, with a wistful smile, some fifty years later, as the toast of the colony, with civilians and subalterns (junior officers, also known as 'snotties') competing for her favours. Bee used to recall proudly that she had been 'a snotties' delight', and perhaps it was the intoxicating glamour of Hong Kong compared with provincial Devon, or the thrill of being admired, that led her to accept not one but two marriage proposals – Ruth thought there might even have been a third engagement.

At least one lasted long enough for *The Times* to announce it in the Forthcoming Marriages column on 7 December 1934, followed by *Tatler*, two weeks later. 'The wedding is taking place at Hong Kong in February between Mr Oliver Egerton Christopher Marton . . . and Miss Beatrice Mary Colyear Walker, the elder daughter of Captain A. C. Walker and Mrs Walker of Tara, Tiverton, North Devon' ran the confident announcement. But evidently Bee got cold feet for no wedding took place. According to Ruth, her sister could not choose between her two fiancés and married neither. I could find no record of Mr Marton ever marrying: perhaps Bee broke his heart.

I wonder if Dorothea and Arthur were relieved to learn that she would not, after all, be marrying a man they had never met and making a new life out in Hong Kong. Or perhaps they were embarrassed by her change of heart, their having put the announcement in *The Times* and told their friends about the engagement. It must have been strange for someone as controlling as Dorothea to receive news of these *faits accomplis* six thousand miles away, to wonder whether her children were making the right choice of spouse, to know that it would be several years before she met a new family member.

Tiggy's father, Hiram, certainly sympathised, writing a kindly letter to Arthur and Dorothea, expressing his regret that they had been unable to attend their son Edward's wedding and assuring them that it had gone well. Following the church service, the newlyweds rode through Kowloon on a gun carriage, pulled by men from Edward's regiment, with the streets closed to traffic, thanks to Hiram's elevated position in Hong Kong society. 'We are indeed fortunate in having such a fine man as Edward as a son-in-law,' Hiram wrote to the Walkers, 'and they both seem very happy.' Beatrice, he added, was charming and 'looked very well'. He promised that his wife would send them photographs of the happy occasion, so at least they would be able to see what their new daughter-in-law looked like.

Two of these photographs survive. In the group photograph it is Bee who appears happiest, wearing a rather natty bridesmaid's outfit. She has even managed to relinquish her ever-present cigarette just long enough to be photographed with a bouquet. In the other, Tiggy and Edward are processing under an arch of swords, held aloft by officers of the 1/8th Punjabs. Edward looks proud, while Tiggy, in a stunning, slightly clinging satin dress, seems mildly perturbed at such a profoundly military spectacle, perhaps wondering what kind of life she was about to step into. Edward's regiment would move back to India in a couple of years' time, and home would be army quarters in a garrison town far from Hong Kong's bright lights, her parents and friends. She and Edward departed on a lengthy honeymoon, which included a trip to the Great Wall of China and a visit to Japan, which was becoming as well known for its militarism as its cherry blossom and beautiful mountains.

Not long after Bee returned to Tara, Harold left for London. Like Peter, he wanted to become a doctor, having been impressed by the actions of the local practitioner, who treated him when he was suffering from suspected appendicitis. Since his mother's father had trained at St Thomas's, he decided to apply there too. But, like Peter, he encountered a problem. His father wanted Harold to go into the army: Harold was a champion boxer, a keen sportsman and a school monitor, so what could have been a more natural fit? Or, failing that, why not the Church, since Harold had a fine tenor voice?

But Dorothea came to her son's rescue, putting her foot down and insisting that Harold should be allowed to pursue his chosen career if a way could be found to raise the funds for medical-school fees. It seems that, despite her insistence that medical school was out of reach of their children, it had become the lesser of two evils. Happily it transpired that Harold was eligible for a Kitchener scholarship. These bursaries, paid by the Lord Kitchener National Memorial Fund, founded after the field marshal's death in 1916, were available to officers' sons to help fund their higher education. With Arthur's war service and generations of Walkers who had served in the forces, Harold was more than eligible. It seems odd that Peter did not apply for this scholarship, but it is possible that the family discovered its existence too late, or Peter decided against it, perhaps not wishing to spend fifteen years in the military after he had qualified, which was the condition on which the scholarship was awarded to Harold. Harold opted for the Royal Navy and set off for St Thomas's in September 1935.

He had been a keen sportsman at Blundell's and even played cricket for Devon on occasion, so he was delighted to find that, for medical students at St Thomas's, proficiency on the rugby field and cricket pitch was deemed almost as important as their performance in the laboratory. One professor, a keen cricket fan, would help Harold with his practical work while quizzing him about cricket: 'How many runs did you make yesterday?' he would ask, as Harold was struggling with a procedure, before helpfully pointing out the best way to achieve it. The physiology professor, meanwhile, was a rugby aficionado and was impressed to hear that Harold played not only for the St Thomas's side but Harlequins too. Harold invited the hospital cricket team down to Tiverton to play Blundell's, and the rugby team to play the local Tiverton side. Ruth recalled that Tara reverberated to the boisterous camaraderie of the medical students who all stayed there.

Ruth had just left school and was working as a riding instructor, teaching Blundell's boys at the local stables. Arthur had taught her to ride – 'It was the only thing I could do better than my brothers' – but the Walkers did not have the money or space for horses of their own. The only way Ruth could get a day's hunting was to ride one horse and lead three others from the Tiverton stables to wherever the meet was, sometimes twelve miles away, then deliver them to whoever had hired them. In exchange she was allowed to ride one herself. At the end of the day she would lead the horses back to Tiverton, in the dark, a test of horsemanship and nerve.

At the end of 1936 John Fisher, the Walkers 'surrogate' son, and Ruth's white knight, returned to Tiverton after a four-year absence. After Blundell's he had had a spell as a vacuum-cleaner salesman but found it hard to muster any enthusiasm for it. In 1932 he had journeyed to Sarawak, Borneo. Sarawak was a curious colonial anomaly. It was not part of the British Empire but a private colony, ruled by the Brooke family since 1838 when James Brooke, a young English adventurer, had been given the territory as a reward for imposing peace on its warring peoples. His dynasty of 'white rajahs' governed Sarawak with a light touch via district officers and residents, who were encouraged to pursue a live-and-let-live approach. Christian missionaries were allowed to run schools but not to attempt to convert people, and the leaders of the Dayaks (indigenous people) had to be consulted on all decisions.

The Brookes, however, took a firm hand when it came to eradicating headhunting, practised by many Dayaks. It had been a rite of passage for boys becoming men, and men becoming fathers: the trophies were presented to wives who had just given birth. When they returned to their longhouses triumphantly, the heads were smoked and dried and placed on the longhouse's rafters from where they could look down on its inhabitants and bring them protection.

By the time John arrived, headhunting had been almost entirely stamped out, with a few exceptions. The *Sarawak Gazette* of 1 February 1936 reported that the government had paid five hundred dollars for the head of a murderer who had been on the run for some time.

John had been interviewed in London by the rajah's brother, Bertram Brooke, who judged candidates by how well they could hold their drink. Forewarned, John lined his stomach beforehand with sardine sandwiches and cod liver oil, and Brooke duly plied him with whisky, cocktails and champagne. 'Well done, my boy,' he told John, after several hours of drinking. 'You've got the job.' The two men shook hands and parted ways. As soon as Brooke was out of sight, John was copiously sick into a gutter. But it did not matter: he was on his way to Sarawak and to a life of adventure.

As a cadet in the Sarawak administration, John had to do stints in its various branches, including the postal service and the judiciary, supervising a chain gang and paying a reward to anyone who presented a dead crocodile: the reptiles menaced those who lived along the rivers. One man presented the same crocodile three times before John cottoned on to the fraud.

Life in the remoter reaches of the jungle was isolated but had its advantages. The rajah insisted that all his officers become fluent in the language of the people they served and to aid them in this he stipulated that they take a local mistress, known as a 'sleeping dictionary'. She would act as a housekeeper, lover and language teacher. John's 'dictionary' was a beautiful Malay girl named Ooni, who instructed him in Malay and other matters.

When John arrived back at Tara he was a different person from the unsuccessful vacuum-cleaner salesman who had left four years before. Bee, still single after her broken engagements, saw him with fresh eyes. He was not rich or handsome but he was tall and personable and, used to male adulation, she expected to add him to her roster of admirers.

John's gaze, however, fell in a different direction. Ruth was no longer the bob-haired schoolgirl he had rescued from her brothers but a confident young woman of seventeen. She could drive and had her job as riding instructor. She was generally dressed in tennis whites or jodhpurs, never a dress, and always seemed cheerful and engaging. She had even had a few boyfriends, including one named Michael, but had not had her first kiss.

On 4 February 1937 she turned eighteen and her mother organised a small party at Tara. Among the guests was John Fisher. To Dorothea's amazement, Ruth announced that for the party she would like to wear make-up and a dress. If she was hoping to attract someone's attention, it worked. By the end of the evening John Fisher had not only noticed her but had kissed her. Over the course of the spring and early summer their romance progressed. Their first official date took place at John's house and from then on they were almost inseparable.

John might not have been as handsome as one of Ruth's screen idols,

Clark Gable or David Niven, who had exchanged the army for Hollywood, but he was charming, with a gift for friendship and a subversive sense of humour, offset by innate kindness. Tales abound of his generous hospitality, love of leg-pulling, and his ability to solve almost any problem with the aid of whisky or pink gin.

It took a particular type of person to thrive in Sarawak's jungle outposts. The writer Somerset Maugham visited Sarawak and Malaya in the 1920s and depicted in his short stories the lonely misery of those who did not cope well with the isolation and took instead to drink or adultery, a portrayal that made him deeply unpopular in expatriate circles.

Women who married district officers and residents had, like tea-planters' wives, to be content in their own company since their husbands were occupied in their offices, and the nearest European neighbours might be several days' journey away. They also had to be resilient, open-minded and ready to get on with anyone, from bridge-playing rubber-planters to tattooed headmen, unfazed by the sight of a shrunken head grinning down from the rafters of a longhouse or a crocodile sunning itself on the riverbank.

John told Ruth of the land that he had fallen in love with, its blazing sunsets and jungles that teemed with life, from hornbill birds with their five-foot wingspan to pygmy elephants, orangutans and snakes that lodged in the rafters of the house, not bothering you as long as you did not bother them. He might even have shown her the tattoo he had been persuaded to have at a longhouse he had visited. Rather than matching the Dayaks' intricate and extensive tattoos, he had opted for a small fish on his left arm, in reference to his nickname, 'Fish'.

Ruth thrilled to these tales, reminiscent of her parents' stories of Assam. More importantly, she had adored John for as long as she could remember, so when he proposed she accepted without hesitation. Sarawak government officials were not granted permission to marry until they had served for eight years and John still had three to go, so they planned to wed in 1940 in Kuching's Anglican cathedral when Ruth would be twenty-one. She would travel out alone, with her trousseau, but this did not daunt her.

Dorothea and Arthur, thrilled that their surrogate son would soon be their son-in-law, readily gave their blessing. What neither they nor Ruth and John realised at the time was that Bee had harboured hopes of marrying him. She was now twenty-five: she could not stay in Tiverton for ever, and she had always been fond of John, who was the same age as her.

'John hadn't a clue about Bee,' Ruth recalled, with a chuckle, seventy years later, 'but she was very cross with me.' The only other person to object to the engagement was Harold. He liked John but was worried that Ruth was far too young to commit herself to marriage. They had fought as children but he was fond and protective of his younger sister. She, however, would not be deterred.

Before he left for Sarawak, John presented his fiancée with a diamond and sapphire engagement ring and a puppy, a dachshund named Jonathan, to keep her company for the next three years. He, of course, had his sleeping dictionary, Ooni, back in Sarawak.

The engagement photographs show the three in the Tara garden, John, Ruth and Jonathan the dog, blissfully unaware that their plans would be completely derailed by world events.

It was not long after this that Bee left Tiverton for London. After the excitement of Hong Kong, the appeal of provincial life, with its Saturday-night dances, tennis tournaments, films at the Tivoli cinema and agricultural shows, at which farmers' wives competed to become butter-making champions, had perhaps palled.

She began working in a clothes shop – her slender figure was ideal for modelling the dresses to the wealthy clientele – and sharing a flat in Belgravia with a girl friend. She told her family that she had been taken on as an assistant and model by a daring young designer named Norman Hartnell, who was, by 1937, London's leading designer, the favourite of George VI's consort, Queen Elizabeth. He designed the robes for her maids of honour at her husband's coronation that year and subsequently her dresses for her foreign tours. Later he would design for a trickier brief: her visits to bomb-hit areas in the Blitz, when she had to look regal but not extravagant when faced by people who had lost everything. But all that was to come. Far across the world Japanese forces had invaded China, capturing the international city of Shanghai, and war had broken out in Spain between the Fascist-backed Nationalists and the Republicans. Many people, though, were, like the new prime minister, Neville Chamberlain, still optimistic that peace would prevail and that another catastrophic war could be averted.

3

'You will soon enter a very dark tunnel'

———•———

WHILE HIS ELDEST and youngest siblings were embarking on marriage, Walter was too busy soldiering to give much thought to romance. At that stage, he said, he had 'no interest in the opposite sex whatsoever'. But that was about to change.

After his year in Multan, Walter travelled to the city of Quetta near the North West Frontier, where the British had been in conflict for more than a century with Pathan tribesmen. That savage war had given rise to Rudyard Kipling's gruesome advice to British soldiers to avoid capture at all costs:

> When you're wounded and left on Afghanistan's plains,
> And the women come out to cut up what remains,
> Jest roll to your rifle and blow out your brains,
> And go to your Gawd like a soldier.

Walter would soon be amid that conflict. Having completed his year with the Sherwood Foresters he joined his regiment, 1/8th Gurkhas, at Quetta, where they were preparing for their next stint on the Frontier.

He had his first close encounter with death not on the battlefield but in bed. On the night of 30 May 1935, after a bibulous evening in the officers' mess, he had decided to sleep outdoors to escape the sweltering heat. In the early hours of the next morning he awoke from a nightmare in which an express train was thundering towards him. Feeling the earth judder beneath him, he leaped into a cherry tree and watched as his bungalow swayed and rocked. It was one of the deadliest earthquakes in history and caused the deaths of between 30,000 and 60,000 people in the city.

During the rescue operation that followed, Walter trod on a sharp spike that entered his foot. Too stoic to seek help, he worked on as his foot became swollen and painful, but was eventually forced to go to hospital where doctors told him he had septicaemia and might die. Nursed devotedly by an officer's wife, he pulled through and soon returned to the grim business of excavating decomposing bodies from the rubble.

In May 1936 Walter returned home on leave, travelling by flying boat – air travel was considered so exotic that a local newspaper interviewed him on his arrival. His parents were thrilled to see him, complete with a clipped military moustache that he had been ordered to grow, but shocked at how thin and ill he appeared beneath the sunburn: shivering and feverish, he was diagnosed with malaria and spent the first six weeks of his six months' leave being nursed by Dorothea. As soon as he recovered, he bought a small Morris car in which he motored around the countryside to tennis tournaments and parties, and offered its use to Ruth while he was in India if she could pass the recently introduced driving test, which she did without difficulty.

Arriving back in India in January 1937, Walter dedicated himself to earning promotion and was soon made first lieutenant and adjutant of 1/8th Gurkhas, assisting the commanding officer in all aspects of running the regiment. Romance was still far from his mind: before his leave, he had met the daughter of the governor of Bombay, who had flirted determinedly with him, but he had resisted her charms. Then in Tiverton, the wife of the master of foxhounds had strenuously tried to matchmake him with her daughter to no avail. Walter seemed destined to remain a bachelor.

The regiment had now moved from Quetta to Shillong in Assam, at the other end of the state from Dibrugarh, where Peter was now living. It was known as 'the Scotland of the East' due to its cool climate, pine-forested hills and lakes. As the main hill station for Calcutta, it was a trawling ground for girls from the Fishing Fleet who frequented the Shillong Club, hoping to catch the eye of the officers of whichever regiment was stationed there, since they were expected to attend the club dances.

Walter considered these evenings a chore and avoided the dance-floor, preferring to take a whisky and soda and find a quiet corner with a book or periodical. While other officers surveyed the girls he remained oblivious to the wallflowers languishing at the sidelines and the pretty ones whose dance cards filled rapidly.

One, however, had noticed him. Tall, willowy and poised, Beryl Johnston was not a Fishing Fleet girl but lived with her parents on their tea plantation in Assam. She was a talented ballet dancer and, after leaving school, had taught at a prestigious dance academy in Cheltenham. The retiring principal had offered Beryl the chance to take it over but her parents considered such an occupation entirely unsuitable. They were also appalled to learn that she was being courted by a young man who worked in a bank, a mere box-wallah, and summoned her back to Assam. There, she was permitted, once more, to teach children dancing and to attend dances at the club, where she watched the young officers sauntering in. She thought them 'too pleased with themselves by half' and preferred to appear impervious to their charms. She considered the adjutant, Walter, to be the most handsome, but he was rather aloof and clearly did not dance.

One evening the club held a Red Cross ball. Walter had been reluctant to go but had been ordered to do so by his commanding officer. He settled himself in an armchair and prepared for another evening of sitting out the dancing with an out-of-date copy of the *Field*, flicking through the well-thumbed pages on fly fishing and gun dogs.

At some point he looked up and saw through a doorway an outstandingly beautiful girl. It was Beryl. She returned his gaze and, later in the evening, walked past him several times. Even Walter could see that she stood out from the Fishing Fleet girls, with her cool self-assurance and disarming smile. This was new territory for him. Until this point, flirting, or 'poodle-faking' as it was called then, had held no appeal. But this graceful girl intrigued him. Eventually he summoned the courage to abandon his armchair and ask her for the honour of the next dance. She told him she had promised it to another officer, but that she would ask him to excuse her.

Their first dance was not quite the stuff of fairytales. Rather than sweep her off her feet, Walter's dancing was disastrous. 'Have you ever danced before?' she asked him incredulously.

'No, never,' he replied, with some poetic licence. She offered to teach him and they danced the rest of the evening together. Walter's commanding officer, playing Cupid, discreetly ordered the others to whom she had promised dances not to claim them.

Of course I had heard the tale of how my grandparents met before, and read a brief account in Tom Pocock's biography of Walter. But it was only recently that I had the full story, in a letter that Walter wrote to my mother-in-law, Angela Walters. When my husband, Guy, and I got engaged back in 2000, my grandfather, as the family patriarch, wanted to get to know my future in-laws. He invited them to a lunch party and was charmed by them. He and my mother-in-law struck up a lively correspondence that continued until his death, three months after our wedding.

Reading the letters seventeen years later revealed much about him that I did not know – had never thought to ask him. He wrote about his family, and about his wartime experiences, often in gritty, guts-hanging-out detail (as well as venting his spleen on more current topics). But he touched on more surprising subjects, too, and displayed a romantic, deeply sentimental side. Our wedding had clearly stirred memories of his own courtship and nuptials more than sixty years earlier as, afterwards, he described to Angela the night he was shaken out of his monastic military existence. He was simply enraptured. 'No one has ever matched her beauty,' he wrote of Beryl. They made a good-looking couple, Walter lean, tanned and handsome, with dark hair and trim moustache, Beryl also dark-haired, with high cheekbones and long, long legs, resembling one of the prettier Mitford sisters.

Slipping away from the club at the end of the evening, they drove Beryl's father's car that she had borrowed to a nearby golf course, where they talked for so long that the car began to sink into the damp ground. Within three months they were engaged and he wrote home joyfully to tell Arthur and Dorothea the news.

His parents, far from rejoicing that he was to marry a fellow Assam planter's daughter, were furious. Dorothea's mother, Catherine, had known Beryl's grandmother in Cheltenham and the two women had disliked each other intensely. Most mothers, especially at a distance of five thousand miles, would simply accept that they had no influence over their son's choice of bride. But Dorothea had no qualms about interfering in her children's lives, particularly when it came to marriage. She had, by now, met Edward's wife as he and Tiggy had returned to England on leave in 1937. What Dorothea made of Tiggy is not recorded, but for her part Tiggy found her in-laws 'very middle class' and provincial, not as grand as Edward had led her to believe. There was one exception: Harold, now twenty, was back at Tara for his medical-school holidays and Tiggy, an irrepressible flirt, diverted herself by turning her attentions to him.

Determined not to allow Walter to marry a potentially unsuitable bride, Dorothea waded in, writing him a stiff letter, warning him not to go through with the marriage. She even wrote to Walter's commanding officer, who was on leave in England, insisting that he prevent it. The colonel agreed that, at twenty-four, Walter was too young to marry and, as he needed to have his commanding officer's permission to do so, Mrs Walker could rest assured that there was no question of the marriage being allowed to go ahead. But Walter was not to be defeated. With the CO still absent, he asked permission from the acting commanding officer, who had married young and, recognising a fellow romantic, granted it.

So, on 8 November 1938 Walter and Beryl were married in St John's Church, Calcutta, where the elite of expatriate society worshipped. Her sister Diana was her bridesmaid and Walter's best man was a friend from Blundell's who had also joined the Indian Army. In the wedding photograph Beryl looks ravishingly beautiful in a cream crêpe dress, with a long silk veil, while Walter, every button and buckle on his uniform polished to Sandhurst perfection, sword gleaming at his side, clasps her arm proudly, his other hand holding his pith helmet. None of Walter's family was present. Although Edward was back in India, he and Tiggy lived in Lucknow, too far to travel to Calcutta. Not even Peter made it, perhaps in deference to his mother.

Walter hoped to introduce his bride to his parents on his next leave in 1940, certain that Beryl's charm and sweetness would soon dispel any lingering disapproval that Dorothea harboured. In fact, they would not meet for nearly a decade.

The newlyweds spent an idyllic honeymoon in Puri, a beach resort on India's east coast. In the photographs Beryl, in a form-fitting bathing costume, and Walter in sunglasses and trunks, frolicking on the white sand and in the sea, look glamorous and sublimely happy, like 1930s Hollywood idols. Walter wrote an ecstatic postcard to Edward and Tiggy, describing their hotel as 'the most marvellous place' and promising to visit them en route to Quetta, where they were to begin married life.

Dorothea duly received photographs of Walter and Beryl, with Tiggy and Edward at Lucknow, and must have pored over them, trying to elicit any detail she could about her new daughter-in-law.

Three months after the wedding Walter's regiment was posted west again, to the frontier fortress of Razmak, in the heart of Waziristan, recently a part of the Afghan Empire and now the backdrop to 'the Great Game' – the struggle for regional dominance between Britain and Russia. Between Razmak and the fortress of Bannu to the north-east lay a sweep of rugged hills and valleys peopled by the Pathans. These warlike tribes had no wish to belong to any empire, Russian, British or Afghan, and fiercely repelled any incursions into their territory. The Frontier had been a war zone for nearly a hundred years since a British attempt at 'regime change' in Afghanistan had ended ignominiously and bloodily in the mountain passes.

Since then trouble had regularly flared up, with the Pathans making raids on British India to attack villages, army camps or police stations in search of weapons to take back to their mountain villages and copy in their own workshops. So successful were they that by 1939 they had a quarter of a million men armed with rifles, many of whom were deadly accurate sharpshooters. They would wait for columns on the move, laying ambushes in the hills that commanded the vulnerable road between Bannu and Razmak, descending on the unwary and slaughtering them mercilessly. The army's task was to turn the tables by raiding the villages and outposts from which the fighters operated, keeping the roads open and punishing the fighters and their entire communities in a brutal tit-for-tat war.

Since 1936, the tempo had increased. More troops were poured into the area, fortresses were built, heavy artillery brought in, but as other foreign armies would discover decades later, the guerrillas fighting on home territory proved themselves highly adaptable and resourceful foes.

Venturing out from the fortress into the inhospitable hills, the Gurkhas found themselves sniped almost constantly. As Walter wrote later, 'One grew used to the crack of rifle fire and the "tock dong" of bullets over one's head.' He was hardly inconspicuous: not only did his European face stand out from those of the men around him, but when he was put in command of one of the outlying forts he made a point of riding a white charger around it as a signal that he would not be intimidated. A friend from those days recalled with amused exasperation Walter's refusal to take cover even as the bullets zinged around their ears. Once, when they were opening the gates to the fort, as they did every morning, Walter mounted on his horse as usual, a bullet winged past his ear and the man next to him crumpled to the ground, dead. Somehow Walter always escaped being hit.

Forty years later, on a trip to Pakistan, he visited the area and was introduced to a village elder who had, in his younger days, been among those snipers on the hills. Walter recalled his time at the fortress, the horse he rode and the occasion on which he had nearly been hit. The old man's face broke into a grin. Through an interpreter, he told Walter that he had been the sniper: 'I was aiming for the man on the horse.'

One of Walter's regular duties was to lead raids on villages that were known to be manufacturing arms for use against the British. Often by the time they arrived the men had removed themselves and the weapons elsewhere. But the village women remained to ensure that the raiding party was given a hostile reception, hurling abuse and worse at the soldiers. At the head of a platoon of thirty-three Gurkhas, the women singled out Walter and would throw bucketfuls of urine and faeces into his face as he marched past. It was, as he wrote with understatement, 'a most unpleasant experience but one had to carry on with the job . . .'

The 'job' entailed searching every hut for arms, and then, with the approval of the political agent (a civilian intelligence officer), the women and children would be evacuated and the village burned down. Such treatment of civilians seems, through twenty-first-century eyes, barbaric as well as counter-productive. Much later in his military career, as a general, Walter made winning hearts and minds a central plank of his strategy. But for now, as a lieutenant, his was not to question why.

Wives and families could not join their men in such a dangerous posting. The nearest Beryl could get to the frontier was Bannu, which boasted a hotel known as 'the abandoned-wives hostel' where women whose husbands were fighting on the frontier could wait for them to snatch twenty-four hours' leave. Walter made it to Bannu only twice, so Beryl spent the early months of their marriage in Assam with her parents, digesting the realities of life as an army wife: frequent separations, with long and anxious waits for news.

Once she went to stay with Tiggy and Edward but it was a short visit. Beryl, still a blissfully happy newlywed, was shocked by Tiggy's relentless flirting with other men and mortified at having to witness the couple's frequent and furious rows. Desperate to escape without giving offence, she went to the nearest telegraph office and sent a telegram addressed to herself but purporting to come from her parents, urging her to come home instantly. She departed with relief.

In Assam, meanwhile, Peter had found his niche. His disappointment at being unable to study medicine had evaporated as soon as he arrived in November 1933 to take up his post on the Sealkotee tea estate in Upper Assam, a short distance from his parents' old home on the Tara estate.

His thatched and timbered planter's bungalow was not unlike the Devon cottages that nestled in the hillside villages around Tiverton, while the lush green slopes held a certain familiarity. His official title was assistant engineer so his primary responsibility was the factory where the picked leaves were crushed, fermented, oxidised and finally dried in hot ovens before being sorted and graded for export. Soon he was given responsibility for the wider plantation and spent his days riding to its far corners, checking on the tea pickers. Picking the young shoots was – and still is – done mainly by women, whose nimble fingers worked rapidly along the bushes, nipping off the leaves and dropping them into wicker baskets carried with straps around their heads. They moved along the rows, their brightly coloured clothes vivid against the dark green of the bushes. Children, too, were put to work, picking from the lower and younger tea bushes while men did the heavier tasks, such as hoeing the soil. It was hard, backbreaking work, poorly paid and not without its dangers.

As well as checking on the pickers, Peter had to inspect the bushes for any signs of disease. Once he was out on a far corner of the estate when, with a flash of amber and ebony and a furious snarl, a tiger sprang from its hiding place. A short while ago that land had been its jungle home. Now its habitat had been destroyed but it had been drawn back in search of food. In one bound it seized a tea picker, clamping its massive jaws around the man's head, and, in trying to drag away the screaming victim, pulled off his scalp. Peter did not relate what happened to the victim but it seems doubtful that he survived the encounter.

And, of course, there were close encounters with snakes. Peter returned to his bungalow one day to find that a cobra had crawled in to escape the heat. Sensing Peter's presence, it reared as a prelude to striking. Peter's reactions were fast: he whipped out his revolver and shot the snake before it could lunge.

At weekends, just as Arthur had, Peter led a life of leisure, playing polo and drinking at the club, sipping a chota peg – whisky and soda – and listening to the older planters regaling new arrivals with tales of the old days. If he had a few too many chota pegs, and then a few more, one of the club servants would see him to his horse. Occasionally he was too wobbly to mount, so the servant would drape him over the horse's back and give the animal a tap, at which it would start plodding home. It knew the way so well that it could deliver Peter to the steps of his bungalow. More wholesome were camping trips on the banks of the Brahmaputra River: in the photographs he sent home, Peter looks fit, happy and muscular, bare-chested in his shorts or a towel, pouring beer into a tankard and with a cigarette clenched between his lips. He was camping but he was hardly roughing it: on the back of one photo he writes that the tent on the right was the cookhouse and servants' quarters.

Young planters were advised to become friendly, but not too friendly, with senior planters' wives, who would be able to nurse them if they ever fell seriously ill, since the nearest major hospital was in Calcutta. But when Peter did fall ill it was not a planter's wife but nuns who came to his aid. What had begun as a dull ache in his lower abdomen developed rapidly into an agonising, sharp pain that left him doubled up.

Unable to reach a hospital, he managed to get to a nearby convent, where he asked the nuns for help. They could not remove his appendix but they could ease his pain if he was willing to undergo a rough and ready procedure that one of them had heard about, without an anaesthetic.

He agreed. It involved piercing his abdomen with a sharpened bamboo stick and sucking out the 'poison'. It sounds painful and highly unscientific, but when I consulted doctor friends they thought it would probably work by drawing off the pus and releasing some of the pressure. And, indeed, it did. Peter lasted long enough to get to hospital, where he was speedily operated on and his life saved.

It was not his only mishap. He was once bitten by a rabid dog and another time was pursued for miles by a swarm of hornets, having bumped his helmet against their nest while out riding. He rode furiously until he reached a pond and then leaped in. But for all these mis-adventures he was happy. As well as his polo ponies he had a dog and a pet otter, and found camaraderie in the Assam Valley Light Horse, his father's old volunteer unit. They may have been part-time soldiers but they took their training seriously and Peter became fit and strong as he marched up and down hills carrying heavy loads in the humid heat, little knowing that this would be ideal preparation for trials to come.

On one occasion he came across a fakir – holy man – who was telling fortunes and, out of curiosity, consulted him as to his future. The fakir studied him for a while, then made his pronouncement: 'You will soon enter a very dark tunnel,' he told him. 'Things will be very bad, you will suffer very greatly. But I can see light at the end. You will survive.'

Peter pushed the prediction to the back of his mind, but in years to come he would remember it and cling to the fakir's words: he would survive. It was his destiny to live, not die before his time.

Like Walter and Edward, he kept an eye on the news from Britain. Chamberlain's Munich summit provoked much discussion in the messes and clubs of India. Would it avert or precipitate war? Back in Devon the situation in Germany was already casting its shadow.

It was a depleted Walker family that gathered anxiously around the wireless to hear the news from Munich in September 1938. Ruth was now the only one of Arthur and Dorothea's children still at home. She kept herself busy as she waited for her wedding, playing in tennis tour-naments and motoring round the countryside in Walter's Morris. She even worked briefly as a waitress in a café in Ilfracombe, on the Devon coast, where the uniform included a red petticoat that had to be just – tantalisingly – visible beneath the girls' skirts.

Despite Neville Chamberlain's confident assertion that war had been averted, not everyone was convinced, and in towns and villages around the country preparations were being made in case the worst should happen. As stalwarts of the local community, Dorothea and Arthur volunteered for war work: she signed up as an Air Raid Precaution (ARP) warden while he became a special constable. Dorothea also took first-aid training, as befitted the secretary of the Tiverton and District

Nursing Association, and received a badge from the mayoress as recognition for distributing and fitting gas masks to around eight thousand people in the area.

Ruth enrolled in the Voluntary Aid Detachment (VAD) and also trained in first aid. Buoyed by winning the runner-up prize at a training session, and a medal for 'efficient service', she began to think seriously of becoming a nurse. Although the chairwoman of the Women's Institute urged girls to resist 'the glamour' of going away to drive ambulances or become a nurse, and stay in Devon to work on the land, Ruth was drawn to nursing. She wanted to see the world beyond Tiverton and, with the chances of getting to Sarawak for her wedding in 1940 receding rapidly, decided that nursing in London would provide a change of scene.

In the spring of 1939 another of Dorothea's homing pigeons returned. Peter came home on leave from the tea garden, the first time in six years that he had seen his family. Not that many of his siblings were around: Walter and Edward were in India, Bee and Harold in London. It was six years since Peter had left home as a nineteen-year-old, little more than a schoolboy. Now he was tanned and fit, with a moustache and the new confidence of a man in a position of leadership. Dorothea and Arthur were delighted to have their fourth son home, to hear his tales of Assam, the plantation, his polo ponies, the club, all the places and some of the people they had known so well. It was a happy few months, despite the talk of trouble ahead.

Peter picked up with old friends. There were outings to the beach at Bude, Woolacombe and Widemouth Bay. In the photographs Peter is in his swimming trunks, sitting on the beach arm in arm with a pretty girl named Alison, whom Ruth remembered as his girlfriend. Ruth was accompanied by Jonathan the dachshund and a friend called Michael, tanned, blond and almost god-like in his good looks.

Like most of us, Ruth tended to photograph the good times, the sunny days, so in her photograph album the summer of 1939 looks warm and idyllic, spent in a happy haze of ignorance of what was around the corner. But the Walkers, like most households, were well aware that the fragile peace brokered by Chamberlain might not hold. No one wanted to use the word 'war'. Blackout material was on sale and arrangements were made to billet evacuees from the cities in case of what was euphemistically called a 'national emergency'.

By the end of August, with sandbags in place around public buildings, gas masks issued and German soldiers massing along the Polish border, hopes of peace were dissolving rapidly. Even the women's editor of the *Tiverton Gazette* was anticipating rationing, advising her readers that 'one dress can look like three' with the addition of clip-on buttons, an interchangeable belt or a bolero jacket. Meanwhile Adjutant Jepson Jepson of the Salvation Army's Tiverton branch advised readers, in the storms and troubles ahead, to 'Hold fast to your faith – the lessons Jesus taught – never let them go, for you will be clinging to a rock that will weather any storm.'

On Friday, 1 September the long-planned evacuation from London began. The news caused some Tiverton householders to panic and converge on the grocers, anxious to secure supplies before the expected influx of child evacuees. In the event they did not arrive until some days later.

That Friday night the town had its first blackout. Special constables, like Arthur, had to inspect householders' and shopkeepers' blackout preparations, pointing out uncovered skylights or gaps in curtains. Those who had not bought blackout material hurriedly made do with cardboard and brown paper. One man had carefully blacked out every chink of light in his house, then undermined his efforts by lighting a large bonfire in his garden. An ARP warden told him to extinguish it immediately.

At 11.15 a.m. on 3 September, a gloriously sunny Sunday, the storm broke. The prime minister, Neville Chamberlain, announced on the wireless that Britain was now at war with Germany. Harold heard him in a flat close to St Thomas's, with another student and four 'masseuses' – female physiotherapists. They had scarcely had time to digest the news when the air-raid siren sounded and they had to hurry immediately to the underground shelter. Down in Tiverton, his family heard the news too. The word spread around the town as parishioners left church after Sunday services.

On 29 September 1939 the details of every household in England and Wales, adults and children, were entered into a register, much like a census but more detailed, giving names, ages, occupations and marital status of everyone living at each address. Forty-one million people signed the register, which was used as the basis for issuing ID cards and ration books.

Peter's entry reveals that he was living in a boarding-house in Blackheath, south-east London, perhaps while visiting the tea company's offices in London. Only two weeks earlier he had been arm in arm on the beach with Alison. Now those sunny picnics were over.

With barrage balloons rising over the city 'like great silver elephants on wire cables', as one Londoner described them, sandbags piled up outside public buildings, searchlights raking the sky at night, London must have felt even more alien to Peter, who had seldom been there before. He debated joining up in England, but with his passage back to India booked for 11 November he decided that he would return there and join the Indian Army if the war continued and spread.

In Tiverton, policemen were posting notices around town detailing call-up orders, where and when to report, for those already in the armed forces. Members of Territorial units and the artillery were ordered on parade. All in all, the people of Tiverton took the news coolly, at least on the surface. 'There was no excitement,' reported the *Gazette*. 'Tiverton went about its business with a calmness which was remarkable.' Behind closed doors it was another story as anxious families wondered what it would mean for them.

Ruth's mind was already made up: she would apply to St Thomas's Hospital to train as a nurse. Harold, of course, was already there. It was not a straightforward process. St Thomas's had a reputation for demanding not only excellence from its nurses but a certain level of 'breeding' too. 'Guy's to flirt, Barts to work, Thomas's if you're a lady,' as the saying went.

Ruth was summoned for an interview with the matron, Miss G. V. Hillyers. Dorothea had to accompany her so that Miss Hillyers could be sure she came from the right sort of background. Evidently Dorothea's family connection to St Thomas's helped to swing it for Ruth, along with her academic qualifications – she had a good brain and had left school having passed 'matriculation', not just the 'school certificate'. Miss Hillyers would have seen a confident, cheerful girl, practical and energetic, able to hold her own, thanks to four older brothers, although all was nearly lost when she somehow learned that Ruth had a sister who worked in a *shop*, which was considered quite beyond the pale. (Just as well she never discovered that Ruth had once worked as a waitress – not to mention the red petticoat.)

Despite this hiccup, Ruth was offered a place on the preliminary training scheme as a Nightingale nurse, as St Thomas's trainees were known. She had to buy her own uniform: a heavy navy cloak for going outdoors, a navy sash that crossed over the chest, a starched white cap, a dress with its collar starched till its edges were sharp, a long white apron that had to be kept spotless, black stockings and heavy black lace-up shoes.

The Nightingale School, where probationers began their training, had been evacuated to a large mansion in Shamley Green, Surrey, whose wealthy owners, Mr and Mrs Ward, had lent it to St Thomas's as a contribution to the war effort. It was here that Ruth arrived in November 1939, along with twenty other probationers in her 'set'. Her war was about to begin. A few days later, Peter set sail from Liverpool, leaving only Arthur and Dorothea at home.

In India, Edward and Walter heard the news of the war in Europe and wondered what it would mean for Dorothea, Arthur, Ruth, Harold and Bee in England. Would it eventually engulf the east?

The Walkers' lives had, for around two hundred years, revolved around the British Empire, building it, expanding it, defending it, their own careers and ambitions tied inextricably to its fortunes. It was now facing a struggle for survival. Would it emerge intact, broken or damaged? Would they?

PART TWO

The War at Home

4

'I'm going to cut your throat'

———•——

EVERYTHING HAD CHANGED and yet nothing had. In Tiverton,
Dorothea and Arthur observed the effects that Chamberlain's declaration had upon the town. As well as obvious signs of war, such as the
blackout blinds, there were more subtle changes too: some people sewed
luminous buttons on their coats so they could be seen at night now that
street lighting had gone. Many women stopped having their hair permed,
fearing that the two and half hours required might be cut short by the
undulating wail of the air-raid siren and they would be left half finished.
Heathcoat's factory began producing military textiles.

The streets were suddenly full of horses again as petrol rationing hit
home. A horse that might have fetched £55 in August 1939 was worth
£100 by October as horse-drawn delivery vans replaced lorries. And the
steaming piles they left on the streets were quickly scooped up, ideal for
use on vegetable patches once food was rationed, as was widely predicted.

In the *Tiverton Gazette*, advertisements for everyday products began
to make reference to the war: 'In times of abnormal nerve strain,
"Ovaltine" should be your constant stand-by,' ran one claim, while the
manufacturer of Carter's Little Liver Pills warned, 'War-time living upsets
your liver first.' Local retailers got in on the act too, reminding customers
to 'Secure your Winter Underwear before prices go up.'

The Dowager Lady Amory urged Tiverton women to get busy with
their needles to produce surgical stockings, nightshirts and day shirts for
the expected influx of wounded soldiers, and Dorothea was co-opted
onto the mayoress's working party for organising this 'great and noble
work'.

The evacuee children had begun arriving at Tiverton in early
September, clutching small suitcases and handkerchiefs hastily thrust into
their hands by their mothers. After a long, hot journey they were

marched, military-style, straight from the station to the cattle market where, as one recalled, 'It was all bustle as children were ushered into the pens. There was a nurse who checked all the children for nits and fleas.' The *Gazette* did not report this rather grim reception but instead noted that the new arrivals had been examined by a doctor and given refreshments.

Some were accompanied by their mothers, who complained vociferously about the quietness of the countryside, and a few returned to London the next day, prepared to face bombs rather than the tedium, as they saw it, of rural life. 'There is a great clamour for amusement among the women,' reported one local paper. The cinema, which had closed at the outbreak of war, reopened on Saturdays.

In time all of these precautions - the blackout blinds, the sandbags, the evacuation - began to look superfluous. The air raids did not materialise. Britain was at war but the fighting had not yet come to its shores. And as 1940 dawned and not a bomb had been dropped, many parents collected their children from their countryside billets and brought them home to the cities.

At Shamley Green in Surrey, Ruth was learning the basics of nursing. Sharing a dormitory in the sprawling arts-and-crafts mansion, she got to know the other girls in her set of twenty. Despite the Nightingales' reputation for being 'toffee-nosed', Ruth found many like-minded souls, some of whom remained her friends for half a century.

It was a military regime, not unlike the one her brothers had experienced at Sandhurst. The days began and ended with prayers, and lights out was at 10.30 p.m. They were punctuated by housework, practical demonstrations, lectures and unquestioning obedience to orders Sister issued - she could freeze your blood with a disapproving look.

They learned skills such as how to give blanket baths - washing patients who were bedridden by practising on life-size dummies of babies and women. There were no adult male dolls as that would be unseemly for young ladies. Instead, they were told that when washing male patients they should do the neutral areas of the body, such as the limbs, then hand the patient the flannel with the instruction 'Finish yourself off now.' A more sobering moment came when they learned how to lay out and wash a dead body, preparing it for the relatives to view, ensuring that in death, as in life, everything possible was done for the patient. In peacetime the majority of the bodies were of elderly patients but in war, with air raids expected, it was all too necessary that they practise on babies too.

Much of the training centred on housework and cleanliness. They were instructed on how to make beds, dust bed frames, disinfect and clean everything on a ward from bed springs to urine bottles. They had a half-day on Sunday and one full Sunday off every month, although even then they had to be back for chapel at 6 p.m. Any other free hours were spent in such wholesome activities as country dancing and amateur dramatics – clearly a favourite way of letting off steam, especially for Ruth. Her childhood ambition had been to be an actress and she loved the cinema. Like many young girls, she had imagined herself on the silver screen or the stage before plumping for a more practical career path, but her photograph albums include several scenes from plays put on during her training, a welcome few hours of make-believe before it was back to bedpans and bandaging.

Harold, too, indulged his thespian side. He had enjoyed performing in the choir at Blundell's. Now, at St Thomas's, he wrote and acted in a pantomime, complete with songs and in-jokes.

In the breaks between lessons at Shamley Green, Ruth and her friends could wander in the exquisite gardens, crunching across the frosty lawns to the large pond that was often frozen during the bitterly cold winter of 1939, or sit in one of the elegant drawing rooms knitting and chatting. There was a butler, housekeeper and housemaids, and the food was plentiful and delicious. Rationing began in January 1940, but at first only for bacon, butter and sugar. They were luckier than the set that had begun training at the very start of the war, when the preliminary training scheme was evacuated to the far less salubrious surroundings of Horton Mental Hospital in Epsom, before Mr and Mrs Ward's kind offer to share their house with twenty trainee nurses.

At the end of her two months at Shamley Green, Ruth took exams that would determine whether she could go on to St Thomas's as a probationer. They were tough and required some frantic swotting: it was said to be harder to get into St Thomas's for nurses' training than as a medical student. But Ruth passed and was deemed fit to graduate from dummies to real people as a Nightingale pro, as probationers were known.

On 26 January 1940 she arrived at the doors of St Thomas's Hospital, only the second time she had been there, carrying her suitcase with a spare uniform, a few other clothes and some home comforts. She had left her engagement ring, along with Jonathan the dachshund, at Tara for safe-keeping.

Probationers had to complete two months of preliminary training, followed by a further three years before they qualified as a nurse, then another year at St Thomas's before they were deemed a fully-fledged Nightingale nurse and awarded the coveted Nightingale badge.

The Nightingale School was named after Florence Nightingale, who had founded it in 1860 following her experiences in the Crimean War when the need for trained nurses became apparent. It was still run on the lines she had laid down, the day's structure inspired by the military regime she had observed in the Crimea.

Some of the more senior staff were old enough to remember when Miss Nightingale, as she was always referred to, never 'Florence', paid visits to the school to check that her regime was being adhered to. Miss Nightingale believed that the probationers should have their own rooms in the Nightingale Home.

Each morning the bell went at 6 a.m. They had to dress in the Nightingale uniform, stiff collars that, at first, rubbed their necks raw, heavy black leather belts in which they stashed their scissors (engraved with their names) and stiff cuffs that they had to remove from their sleeves whenever they were engaged in a messy task, but button on again immediately afterwards. After breakfast they would line up in their sets – mixing with other sets was not encouraged – and the home sister would inspect them before they went on duty. Fingernails had to be clean, hair tucked tidily away under the Nightingale cap, aprons starched, dresses ironed and spotless, the stiff black belt polished. One perk Miss Nightingale had allowed was that if they left their shoes outside their door at night they would be returned, polished, by the maids, who also made their beds and cleaned their rooms. Another was that on their days off they could have breakfast in bed, brought on a tray by a maid.

Ruth did not always pass Sister's scrutiny. Her hair, dark, thick and wavy, was inclined to escape from the starched cap, and her uniform somehow never stayed smooth: she was still, at heart, the Tiverton tomboy. But by the third month, her ward sister reported that Nurse Walker had taken the reprimands to heart and was 'tidier in her personal appearance'.

Once they had been inspected they would process out of the Nightingale Home in a crocodile, like schoolgirls, to the main hospital building, each peeling off to the ward on which she was working. As Big Ben struck eight o'clock, the sister of each ward would sweep in and hold prayers, the patients joining in. No allowances were made for patients of non-Christian religions. In fact, there were very few, and none would have dared to object. The one concession made to such patients was that if they died, the normal St Thomas's bedspread, with a cross woven into the pattern, was exchanged for a plain cover or blanket that was laid over the body.

After prayers, Sister would allocate everyone's tasks for the day. She was named after the ward on which she worked – Sister Elizabeth, Sister Male Surgical, Sister Albert. You could never call her by her actual name if you even knew it.

The medical work varied – there might be dressings to change or wounds to clean – but the probationers spent the majority of their time keeping every inch of the ward spotlessly clean. They began with bed-making and dusting. Windowsills, beds and bed frames, tables, lockers, windows and doors all had to be dusted, then 'hot dusted' with a cloth plunged into near-boiling water. Bottles (for urine), bedpans and basins had to be emptied and cleaned, every shelf polished, every sink rinsed, the floors swept and even buckets washed. Two hours later it all had to be dusted again, the beds remade and patients' ashtrays emptied. It is hard to decide which forms the greater contrast with today's hospitals: smoking on the ward or the meticulous, frequent cleaning. With no penicillin or other antibiotics available yet, cleanliness was the only weapon against germs.

The day continued like this, cleaning, dusting, bed-making, emptying bedpans and bottles, taking patients' temperatures every four hours, wheeling the beds of those suffering from TB or other chest problems onto the balcony for a dose of not-so-fresh London air (some even slept outside). Visitors were shooed out by 7.55 p.m., when the blackout curtains were closed and evening prayers said on the ward. The probationers trooped to the hospital chapel for yet more prayers at Compline – evening service – at which they were required to kneel. Sometimes a probationer toppled over, having dropped off from sheer exhaustion. The only real break in the day came at four in the afternoon when they had an hour for tea, brewed in their own individual teapots. At lights out, Ruth, like the others, had no trouble in falling asleep.

Many of the trainees were initially taken aback by the gruelling, grubby nature of the work, scrubbing bedposts and bedpans till they gleamed, their hands chapped and chilblained from constantly washing them under cold taps, all the time being exhorted to 'Hurry, hurry, hurry.' Not all lasted that first year, demoralised by the verbal lashings for being 'slow', 'stupid', or committing the crime of calling each other by their forenames instead of surnames (even less forgivable was letting slip their own forename to a patient).

Some girls came from far grander homes than Tara: among the 1939 Nightingale intake, there was a fair smattering of Honourables and Ladies, who had never had to do any domestic chores. The fictional Briony Tallis in Ian McEwan's wartime novel *Atonement* struggled as a Nightingale probationer with the gruelling physical demands of the routine, swaying on her feet with exhaustion, and Sister's regular reprimands for failing to execute orders with the precision and alacrity demanded.

But Ruth was used to obeying orders, whether issued by her brothers or by the nuns at her school. She was strong and fit from riding and tennis, while her training as a waitress, weaving in and out of tables laden with dishes, proved the perfect preparation for walking swiftly up and down the wards, always with good posture - Nightingales did not slouch - while carrying six full bedpans. She learned to pull the bedsheets tight so that they were icing smooth, and to remove any trace of dust, any speck of blanket fluff, or risk a verbal flaying.

Ruth's monthly reports were mainly complimentary: 'Nurse is good to her patients and is liked by them. She is fairly quick at her work but has not yet learnt to finish up as she goes along,' was the verdict for February 1940. By March 1940 she had shown 'marked improvement . . . She is interested and observant and very anxious to learn and gives an excellent report on her patients at night.'

On their afternoons off, Ruth and her friends would sometimes go to a matinee nearby in the West End. During the war, West End theatres offered free tickets to London's nurses and they were always given the best seats. That summer, before the Blitz began, *Me and My Girl* was playing at the Coliseum and *The Chocolate Soldier* at the Shaftesbury Theatre. A notice would go up outside Matron's office in the afternoon, informing the nurses which shows were offering tickets, and if any appealed to Ruth and her friends they would claim them. Some theatres insisted on evening dress being worn, so as soon as they finished their day shift they would hurry back to their rooms and hastily change before racing over Westminster Bridge to the West End. Sometimes they went to the cinema – the three-hour epic *Gone with the Wind,* starring one of Ruth's favourite actors, Clark Gable, was showing throughout that summer and autumn in West End cinemas. Occasionally they went dancing. There were tea dances at the Savoy Hotel, just across the river, and the Café de Paris in the West End held early-evening dances, which meant that they could be back in time for lights out.

If they were late getting back, the policemen outside St Thomas's would hold up the traffic so that they could cross the road quickly: St Thomas's served the Metropolitan Police so they were happy to do a favour for 'their' nurses, hailing them taxis and, later in the war, evicting any American servicemen who tried to share a taxi with them.

No Nightingale was permitted to marry while still in training. Few of the probationers had boyfriends and most of the time they were too tired for romance. Besides, Sister kept a watchful eye on them: not only were no male visitors allowed in the Nightingale Home, but they were forbidden to socialise with or talk to the medical students, even if they were their brothers and passed them in a corridor. Later in the war restrictions were relaxed to allow male visitors during daylight hours, but only under certain conditions. Ruth recalled that a matron put up a notice on the board instructing, 'If you invite male friends to your bedroom you must put the bed in the corridor.' Someone scrawled beneath the order the words: 'You can do it on the floor.'

Sometimes, in a corridor, Ruth would catch a glimpse of Harold hurrying past on his way to a lecture or to observe an operation, and they would have a quick, whispered conversation. In April, Ruth was transferred from Elizabeth Ward to a male surgical ward, which brought her into contact with him occasionally. Once they were both assisting at the same operation, Ruth as the 'dirty nurse', handling the used instruments and other equipment, Harold as the surgical dresser, in effect a junior surgeon, assisting at operations. But for the most part brother and sister saw little of each other.

Like other large London teaching hospitals, St Thomas's had begun preparing for war back in 1938, following the Munich crisis. Under the Emergency Medical Scheme each teaching hospital was allocated a number of other hospitals, psychiatric institutions and convalescent homes outside London to which to evacuate its patients when war began. St Thomas's had a network, known as a 'sector', of fifty-one hospitals spread around Surrey, Hampshire and south-west London, and as soon as war began, those institutions began to disperse their own patients elsewhere to make way for the influx from St Thomas's.

An advance guard of St Thomas's staff descended on those hospitals and at once began converting drawing rooms into wards, sometimes putting noses out of joint in their zeal. At Park Prewett Mental Hospital near Basingstoke, the staff were annoyed when a party of St Thomas's nurses swept through like locusts, snatching up utensils, food and other materials for their own use, while a group of medical students were so delighted to have left the strict supervision of St Thomas's behind that they proceeded to get roaring drunk and run riot through the hospital, breaking furniture and causing so much damage that they were banned from living on site.

Meanwhile, back at the mother hospital in London, an operating theatre was set up in the basement, safe, it was thought, from air raids, but so far this had not been tested. Sandbags crowded the entrances, windows were festooned with tape, lamps were dimmed and staff organised into fire-watching rotas.

The wards began to fill again as, in the absence of air raids, mothers and children who had been evacuated began to drift back from the country, so there was the usual stream of young patients who needed treating for childhood illnesses and accidents, all too common in the impoverished areas of Southwark and Lambeth on St Thomas's doorstep, and routine operations, such as appendix or tonsil removal and circumcision. War, or rather rationing, turned out to be the great leveller where health was concerned. Doctors and nurses noticed that the babies and young children they treated from the poorer parts of the city were becoming bigger and stronger. The pale, waif-like children of the hungry thirties were better fed than they had ever been in peacetime: rationing meant that poorer households, deemed 'priority classes', got a larger share, and with full employment, their parents could afford to look after them properly. Hitler had, inadvertently, improved the nation's health.

In April, just as the blossom burst forth in London's parks – now criss-crossed with trenches and allotments for vegetable growing – Ruth and her set were put on buses to Park Prewett where she was sent to work on the male surgical ward. The St Thomas's nurses who had spent the winter months there had found it a miserable place: bad food, rats and mice running around the ward in which they slept (converted into a nurses' dormitory) and uncomfortable straw pillows, but Ruth had fond memories of it. The workload was lighter than at St Thomas's, with many beds lying empty – for the moment.

There were forty-four male nurses left at Park Prewett, who had worked with the psychiatric patients – unmarried male nurses had been hastily dispatched elsewhere to remove mutual temptation – and they now acted as ward orderlies. The hospital was designed to accommodate a thousand mainly able-bodied patients. Now it had to be ready to take two thousand, some of whom would be acutely ill, unable to use stairs or even get out of bed unaided.

Administrative offices had to be hastily converted into theatres, the kitchens extended to cater for two thousand people; supplies of dressings and anaesthetics were stockpiled, operating theatres expanded, sheets boiled and ironed, beds made, bathrooms adapted for invalids. The first civilian blood banks had opened in 1939 and supplies of donated blood and blood plasma were brought to the hospital and refrigerated in readiness for transfusions. Blood was transported in refrigerated vans donated by Wall's, the ice-cream makers. Ice-cream manufacture became difficult after rationing was introduced and was banned altogether in 1942 until March 1945.

There were a few military patients already on the wards, recovering from complaints such as hernia or an accident, but at the end of April they were transferred elsewhere as their beds would be needed soon. As a nurse on the male surgical ward, Ruth knew that she would be dealing with battlefield casualties. But what type of wounds would they have? Would they have been gassed, blinded or burned?

Harold had also been transferred from St Thomas's. Medical students were in a reserved occupation, so he was not called up in January 1940 when two million young men were required to report for military service. By April the medical school was struggling to teach, with so few patients left on whom students could practise their skills, so the students were dispersed to sector hospitals. Harold went with five others to Kingston Hospital, where he lodged with a nearby family and spent three months learning anaesthetics and assisting in operations, but finding time for tennis matches, darts and golf.

As April drew to a close, the air of anticipation became more marked, more tense. Nurses and doctors crowded round wirelesses for the latest news from the Continent. It was troubling. The Phoney War had given way to a real one as the German Army invaded Norway and Denmark. British troops landed in Norway, and on the French and Belgian frontiers the men of the British Expeditionary Force (BEF), which had been steadily reinforced over recent months and was now half a million strong, braced themselves for the Germans' next move.

In the early hours of 10 May 1940, it came. German infantry divisions crossed the borders into Holland and Belgium. Over the following days they established bridgeheads in Dinant, Monthermé and Sedan to provide springboards into France, neatly bypassing the Maginot Line in which the French had placed such faith as a bulwark against invasion. They raced towards the Channel, and by 19 May were forty miles from Dunkirk, now the last remaining port available to the British. On the ground the BEF and her Allies tried desperately to hold back the advancing Germans. In the skies above, RAF pilots were trying to break up Luftwaffe fighter formations to prevent them from strafing and bombing the Allied troops below. But the Luftwaffe badly outnumbered the Allied aircraft, with 5,600 aircraft against their 3,000.

In just one week in May the RAF lost 205 planes over France and many fighter squadrons were all but destroyed. As a result, all RAF squadrons had to be withdrawn from the airfields of Belgium and France to avoid their wholesale destruction. Fighters were now being sent over daily from airfields in southern England, squadrons that were part of RAF Fighter Command, specifically designed to defend Britain. They were now entering the fray over France to defend the BEF from the Luftwaffe.

One such was 92 Squadron. On the evening of 23 May 1940, two of its Spitfires were shot down, one flown by Squadron Leader Roger Bushell, later to become famous as the leader of the Great Escape, and

Flying Officer John Gillies, son of the eminent plastic surgeon Sir Harold Delf Gillies, well known for his pioneering work in reconstructing the disfigured, burned faces of wounded servicemen in the Great War.

Gillies, a general surgeon in the Royal Army Medical Corps, had been horrified by the terrible facial injuries he saw in France and, with a French dental surgeon, began working on reconstructing faces that had been half destroyed by shells and shrapnel. Plastic surgery was not a recognised specialism in Britain: there was not a single plastic surgeon in the country. The focus on saving lives meant little attention had been paid to the need to rebuild ruined faces, with the result that many men were left so unrecognisably disfigured by their injuries that they did not want to live.

In 1916 Gillies had set up the first specialist reconstructive unit in Aldershot. He had to invent techniques for repairing burned and shattered faces using his own ingenuity and combing ancient texts for methods practised centuries earlier in India and Italy, where doctors had rebuilt the noses of patients who had lost them to 'honour' punishments, syphilis or fighting.

Perhaps Gillies's most famous invention was the tubed pedicle, which transferred new tissue from another part of the body to the face not merely by a skin graft, which might fail to take, but by a long flap of skin, rolled into a tube to stop it drying out and to reduce the chance of infection. The living tissue was joined to the site of the damage, keeping the blood supply intact.

The fleshy tubes, growing like pink roots from the abdomen up to the face, might have looked ungainly, even horrifying (one patient made a living as 'Elephant Man' in circuses between operations). But if all went well, after weeks or months the skin graft, fed by its umbilical cord, the pedicle, would 'take' on its new site. Men whose faces had been smashed to bloody pulp, jaws or noses taken clean off by a shell, would emerge, after months and years of painstaking surgery, during which time mirrors were banned from the wards, with facsimiles of the faces they had once had. Not perfect, but functional. By giving them back their faces, or something approaching what they had been, Gillies gave them back their lives.

At the end of the Great War the army no longer required his services, but as Britain's only plastic surgeon his skills were in constant demand, for treating the victims of traffic and other accidents, fires, and patients with cleft lips and palates. He balanced his books with private practice, performing breast enhancements, rhinoplasty and facelifts, until September 1939 when he put his private practice largely on hold as he prepared to operate on servicemen, and civilian victims of the expected air raids.

As consultant plastic surgeon to the army at home, Gillies set about organising plastic-surgery units. There were now three other qualified plastic surgeons in England and he decided that each should head their own dedicated unit. His protégé and cousin, Archibald McIndoe, treated RAF patients at the Queen Victoria Hospital in East Grinstead, another plastic surgeon set up a unit at Roehampton and a third at St Albans. For himself, Gillies selected Rooksdown House in the grounds of Park Prewett Hospital.

It was there that Ruth first met him. While assigned to the male surgical ward, she was sent over to Rooksdown to help Gillies's team as they began operating on some of the early casualties coming back across the Channel.

Ruth remembered Gillies as an avuncular, thoughtful man, 'Very nice, very kind,' although he had a temper that could erupt if his exacting standards were not met. But when it came to his patients' wellbeing, nothing was too much trouble. As a result, the unit had a noticeably happy atmosphere, despite the horrific nature of the injuries with which they often dealt.

On the morning of 24 May, Ruth noticed that Gillies was not his usual upbeat self as he went about his work on the ward and asked him outright whether something was wrong.

'My son has been killed,' he replied bleakly. Gillies had received the news only hours earlier that John was missing, presumed killed. His flight lieutenant later came to see Gillies and confirmed that John had crashed 'hopelessly'. There was no chance, it seemed, of survival. Gillies had operated on pilots before the war who had crashed during training accidents, and seen the horrific burns and other injuries caused when the plane burst into flames, so he could envisage more clearly than most the dreadful death that had awaited John as he plummeted to the ground. And yet, with an extraordinary effort of self-control, he managed to contain such thoughts and continue as normal, his hands as steady as ever as he operated.

Happily, it transpired that John Gillies had not been killed. Three weeks later, Gillies received a telephone call in the middle of the night with the news that John Gillies and Roger Bushell had successfully baled out of their planes, but had then been captured on the ground and taken to different prisoner-of-war camps. John Gillies survived the war but Bushell was executed, along with forty-nine other men, for his role in the Great Escape.

By the end of May 1940, Park Prewett and every other hospital in southern England was in a high state of readiness. Leave was cancelled, and there were no more empty beds, no more country walks or visits to the pub. Ruth remembered the rush to stock up on everything from blankets to blood. And then, one fine day in May, they came.

At ports across the south of England, military doctors inspected the wounded, directing them onto the lorries, trains and ambulances that would take them to the hospital most appropriate for their treatment. The 'Miracle of Dunkirk' had snatched 338,000 men from the jaws of annihilation. Lord Gort, the BEF's commander, had decided that, rather than engage in a futile counter-attack on the Germans, it would be better to preserve the army to fight another day. Fighting countless brave rearguard actions to hold off the enemy, the bulk of the British Army had made it to the harbour town of Dunkirk and from there they were evacuated by battleship and the famous little ships, manned by civilian sailors, that came to the rescue of the stranded soldiers, British, French, Polish, Dutch and Belgian. From 27 May to 4 June 1940 those vessels ferried them back to Britain under fire from the Luftwaffe.

At Park Prewett so many ambulances arrived at once that they were queuing nose to tail until they could get to the reception area. Other casualties arrived by train, from Southampton, Portsmouth and Plymouth, delivered straight to the back door by a special railway track installed from the main line. The walking wounded hobbled into the hospital, while the male nurses-turned-orderlies carried stretchers on which broken bodies lay beneath army-issue blankets encrusted with blood. Some men had languished for days on the beach before their wounds were treated. They were filthy, exhausted and crawling with lice. Some rambled incoherently or cried out in pain while others were ominously quiet.

Senior nurses and doctors inspected the casualties as they came off the lorries, rapidly classifying them into those who needed urgent treatment to save their lives, those who could wait, and those for whom there was no hope. The dying were put to bed and assigned a nurse who would sit with them, talk to them and hold their hand while they died.

Ruth, who had turned twenty-one a few months earlier, was the same age as many of the injured men. Some were even younger, boys of eighteen who had barely left their home town before they found themselves being strafed on the beaches of Dunkirk. They had seen their comrades ripped apart by bombs, or drowning as they slipped between boats, dragged down by uniforms heavy with water and oil.

She sat with those shattered shells of men, calming those whose breath was jagged with terror, listening to the last words of those who could still speak, talking to them in soothing tones. Having grown up with four brothers, she was never at a loss for conversation with young men, unlike some nurses who had had little experience of talking to the opposite sex.

With some, death came quietly: their breathing became ever shallower until it stopped, when she would gently close their eyes and say a prayer. Others struggled and cried out in fear and agony. Only a few months ago Ruth had practised on dummies at Shamley Green. Now, she was dealing with bodies of flesh and blood, still warm, whose hands she held as they took their last breath, some of them little more than schoolboys, asking for their mothers.

Carefully, methodically, Ruth performed the last offices, peeling away the blood-soaked bandages and tattered uniforms, sponging blood, oil and dirt off skin, combing hair and covering wounds with fresh bandages. The training helped, but lectures and textbooks cannot teach compassion and it was this quality, above all, that was needed and that Ruth gave her patients.

For the next few weeks rotas were ignored, days off forgotten, and the tennis courts, where Ruth had played in her off-duty hours, stood empty, their nets sagging. Every nurse worked extra hours tending the unending stream of patients, collapsing exhausted into bed each night, sometimes sleeping through even the shattering peal of the 6 a.m. wake-up bell when, following a hasty breakfast, they would be back on the wards once more. Some patients had festering wounds after lying on the beach for days, then on the deck of a rescue boat, splashed with sea spray. Ruth recalled how they were treated: 'The ones that needed to be operated on, we fed maggots into the wound, wrapped it in gauze, then plaster of Paris. It was wonderful. It saved hundreds of lives. Because they were all full of oil and dirt and goodness knows what.'

Unpleasant as this sounds, 'larval therapy' is a highly effective treatment of gangrenous wounds. Not only do the specially bred maggots eat the dead tissue so that it does not have to be cut away, they also release substances that kill harmful bacteria and stimulate the healing process. Although nowadays patients are often reluctant to try it, it is still used within the NHS and elsewhere because it is so effective in removing dead tissue, particularly with gangrene.

Other accounts of treating Dunkirk survivors refer to wounds crawling with maggots, implying that they were an unexpected presence caused by flies laying eggs on the wounds as the men waited on the beach. But at Park Prewett, according to Ruth, the maggots were medicinal, not accidental. Patients who were capable of washing and shaving were encouraged to do so, not just to save the nurses' time but to aid their mental recovery. Not every injury was immediately obvious, and some men were deeply traumatised by what they had seen and experienced during the retreat to Dunkirk.

One night while on duty on the male surgical ward, Ruth was working quietly on her patient notes while the men slept. She was alone but for her sleeping patients. Some moaned or groaned but for the most part they were quiet.

As she bent her head over her desk Ruth suddenly became aware of a man looming over her and looked up abruptly. The patient, standing in his pyjamas, was holding a cut-throat razor in his hand. Calmly, almost conversationally, he informed her, 'I'm going to cut your throat.'

All was still quiet on the ward. The patient was standing very close to her, although not touching her. There was an emergency bell with which she could summon help, but it was just out of her reach. Although she was frightened, Ruth forced herself to remain calm. With the man staring at her, a deceptively rational expression on his face as the sharp metal glinted in his hand, she tried not to let her own expression betray her fear. The man was clearly having a flashback to something that had happened in the last few days. Perhaps he thought she was a German and that his duty was to dispatch an 'enemy'.

She rapidly considered the options available to her. She could shout for help and hope to rouse nurses or doctors on nearby wards, but it would take them precious seconds to reach her and by then the man could have carried out his threat. She was smaller than him and unarmed. The other patients were asleep and, in any case, in no fit state to help her. Ruth glanced down and noticed that the man was barefoot. She had a flash of inspiration.

'I said "Major Jones" – or whatever his name was – "you haven't got your slippers on." He looked down and said, "Oh dear." And he put the cut-throat razor on the desk and went to get his slippers.'

Seizing her moment when he was far enough away, Ruth reached for the emergency bell. As soon as it rang, help came in the form of doctors and orderlies. Major Jones was restrained and removed from the ward. All cut-throat razors were later confiscated. Ruth's quick thinking had saved her.

Thirty miles away Harold, too, was dealing with the human debris of Dunkirk. He had moved on from Kingston Hospital to Pyrford Hospital, near Woking. Formerly a home for 'waifs and strays', it had been designated a hospital for injured servicemen. Here he studied orthopaedics under Rowley Bristow, one of the most celebrated and brilliant surgeons of his time. Under Bristow, Harold had learned how to treat the kind of wreckage that bullets, shells and shrapnel inflict upon human bodies and now readied himself to put theory into practice. He did not have long to wait.

As soon as the first ships began arriving at ports with their cargoes of wounded, Bristow went to meet them and select patients for the orthopaedic wards at Pyrford. For Harold, as he drily recalled, this was a time of 'valuable learning': he and his fellows took on far greater responsibilities than students would normally be given in peacetime. Hour after hour they worked in the operating theatres, setting shattered bones, stitching jagged wounds that had often hardened at the edges after several days in transit, which meant that all the dead flesh had to be cut away before healing could begin.

Despite the tempo of work, and having to attend lectures in his hours away from the operating theatre, Harold still found time for sport. 'How pleasant the Sector is,' wrote one of his fellow students at Pyrford, 'except on the rare wet days. Our tennis is no longer deplorable, golf is cheap and near . . . and the hospital is feeding us well.'

The opposite was true of Park Prewett, where the food was dreadful and the nurses had to supplement their diet with dandelion leaves. If they tried to save any food from their ration it was pilfered by the rats and mice that shared their living quarters.

As summer gave way to autumn, Ruth and Harold were transferred back to the mother hospital, St Thomas's. For Harold this was good news: only a handful of students had been selected to help keep the hospital going, and they would be getting the kind of hands-on surgical experience that they could never hope for in peacetime.

For Ruth, it was business as usual, this time on Albert Ward, emptying bedpans, heating Primus stoves to sterilise equipment, washing bandages and reassuring patients, all under the watchful eye of Sister Albert. The much-feared bombing of the capital had still not materialised. But that was about to change.

5

'This is a death I wouldn't have chosen'

B Y THE TIME Harold and Ruth saw their first casualties, flesh and bones pulverised by shell, noses and jaws shot away, on India's North West Frontier Walter had already seen at first hand what bullets and knives could do to the human body.

His first action under fire came in March 1940, when two Gurkha platoons under his command were attacked as they withdrew from a hilltop and one Gurkha fell wounded. Walter knew how vital it was to reach the casualty before the Pathans, only yards away, could get to him and set to work with their knives. Kipling had not exaggerated their brutality.

Several efforts to retrieve the man were met with a barrage of bullets, so Walter ordered his men to retake the ridge they had just vacated, pushing the Pathans back. A brief but bloody action ensued, Walter directing operations from a sangar (a kind of low stone wall used for defence in lieu of sandbags). Frequently he emerged to run between his men, covering the open ground as bullets zinged overhead, to give fresh orders, moving men forward and back to distract the enemy, while a party of volunteers went forward to try to rescue the wounded man before he bled to death.

As they did so, yet more enemy appeared, materialising out of the scrubby ground where they had lain concealed. Soon Walter and his men were being attacked not by one but by four enemy parties. A bullet smacked into the machine-gun next to him, sending a shower of metal splinters into his hand and into the eye of the machine-gunner. Another machine-gunner was hit and killed. What had begun as an orderly withdrawal had turned into a fierce firefight.

More men were hit, some badly, and Walter sent messages by runner, since there was no radio, asking for artillery fire to be brought down on the enemy. The valley erupted with the thunderous boom of shells while bullets ricocheted off the stones. Walter moved between his men, sometimes crawling, sometimes running as bullets flew around: one hit him in the hand, wounding him slightly. Eventually, the Pathans were driven back, and Walter was able to withdraw the rest of his men to Razmak, including the five wounded, and the dead man.

It had been the proverbial baptism of fire but Walter had kept calm, moving his men around the rugged hills, like pieces on a chessboard, anticipating the enemy's moves and making counter-moves. His commanding officer had been observing the 'show' from a distance, with a visiting brigadier. So impressed were they at Walter's calm conduct under heavy fire that he was recommended for a Military Cross. But it was not approved by the District Commander and Walter had to be content with a mention in dispatches. His commanding officer was indignant, telling Beryl, 'If anyone ever deserved the medal Walter did.'

Beryl, although disappointed for him, was grateful that her husband was alive. Too often, women at the 'abandoned-wives hostel' in Bannu, waiting for a snatched reunion with their husbands, received instead the news they dreaded: 'killed in action'. Usually they were spared the worst details of what had happened. One officer who had been wounded had to be left, as every attempt to rescue him resulted in further casualties. It was not until the next day that he could be safely recovered. Another Gurkha officer, the author John Masters, described in his memoir *Bugles and a Tiger* the sight that greeted the recovery party: 'He had been castrated and flayed, probably whilst still alive, and his skin lay pegged out on the rocks not far from the camp.'

A few months later, Walter saw such cruelty at first hand after an operation went badly wrong when he was appointed staff captain for the Razmak Brigade, a job that involved moving large numbers of men through hostile territory, an action fraught with danger. When entering a valley, the hills above it had first to be occupied to avoid them being used by the enemy, who would lie in wait and attack the column when it was at its most vulnerable. Only when the column was safely through the valley could the men on the heights withdraw speedily, avoiding any obvious route on which they might be ambushed.

That day, as the column snaked its way along the road, a party of men from an Indian regiment who had been holding a position on one mountain were given the order to withdraw. Hot, tired and thirsty, keen to get back to camp and confident that there was no enemy in the vicinity, they walked rather than ran down the mountain, choosing an easier way down a ravine rather than a safer but more circuitous route. It led them straight into an ambush.

The first that Walter knew of what had happened was when an exhausted Indian soldier staggered towards the column and blurted out that there had been a massacre. He was the sole survivor.

At once, a counter-attack was mounted to drive back the Pathans. When it was certain that they had withdrawn, Walter went forward with an armed escort to identify the dead soldiers so that their names and ranks were recorded, their regiments and relatives informed. He found a scene of unimaginable horror.

The soldiers lay dead in a welter of blood. They had been beheaded, castrated and had their eyes gouged out, possibly while they were still alive. The stench in 120-degree heat was unimaginable, the air thick with flies. It was a lesson that Walter never forgot. In the coming years, he recalled those mutilated bodies, the gluttonous flies, the earth darkened by blood, and drilled his men relentlessly in ambush tactics, making them repeat the exercise over and over again until he could be sure that no man under his command would lose their own life in such a needless and horrific manner.

Walter was immersed in the Frontier war, a savage, tit-for-tat conflict, for the next two years, all the time conscious that, brutal as the fighting was, it had become a sideshow to a far bigger and more critical conflict: the battle for Europe.

And in London Bee, Harold and Ruth were about to find themselves on the front line.

One of Harold's closest friends at St Thomas's was Peter Spilsbury. Spilsbury's father, the eminent pathologist Sir Bernard, had supplied the evidence that had clinched a number of high-profile murder cases over three decades, notably in the infamous 1919 case of Dr Crippen. (Subsequently, some of his evidence was judged to be flawed and he might have sent more than one innocent person to the gallows.) Peter Spilsbury was older than Harold and already a house surgeon, and he and Harold sometimes found themselves in the operating theatre together, with Harold acting as surgical dresser.

Life continued as normal at St Thomas's or, rather, normal for wartime, with sandbags around the hospital entrances and many wards closed to patients, used instead as nurses' dormitories. An editorial in the *St Thomas's Gazette* harrumphed at the 'ineffective and weary' flowers being planted in the beds around the hospital, which would have been better used to grow vegetables. With every front and back garden in London being turned into vegetable patches, and even Buckingham Palace gardeners evicting roses in favour of vegetables, it was a fair point.

Much of the day-to-day work of the hospital was now being outsourced to sector hospitals, including obstetric services: expectant mothers were put on buses for Park Prewett, where they and any accompanying children were systematically 'deloused' in one of the villas in the grounds before they were allowed onto a ward. It was a damning indictment of the living conditions in south London's overcrowded tenements and terraces, where a favourite children's game was, as a horrified middle-class observer noted, chasing rats.

At St Thomas's the medical students were formed into teams, each with an allotted post in the hospital at which they would assemble in case of a major incident. Each team would be assigned a responsibility: preparing casualties for surgery, acting as stretcher-bearers, treating the walking wounded, 'shock squads', for treating those with severe shock, or fire-watchers.

In the early months of the war everyone had sprung into action as soon as the air-raid siren sounded and rushed to their emergency posts, only to kick their heels for hours until they were stood down as the alarm turned out to be false. A year into the war, a more sanguine approach was taken. Unless the hospital authorities sounded an additional 'action stations' alarm, everyone carried on as normal to save on disruption and loss of sleep.

In her last few months at Park Prewett Ruth had seen and done things that the average peacetime nurse would never have experienced, certainly not in her first year. In peacetime there were, of course, tragedies – children hit by cars or burned in domestic fires, young men maimed and killed in industrial accidents - but, even so, few nurses had to deal with death, burns or mutilation on a daily basis with such young patients. There were some, not surprisingly, who simply could not cope, left quietly and were replaced. But most, like Ruth, stuck it out, and grew steadily more confident. Sister Albert was impressed, noting how conscientious and good-tempered Ruth was, with 'a great deal of common sense'. Such was the demand for nurses that VADs (volunteer nurses) were being hastily drafted into St Thomas's to be trained up as Nightingales. They could be spotted on empty wards being taught how to give injections to pillows.

Ruth had completed her first year of training and was given a room in Gassiot House, the nurses' accommodation block next to Westminster Bridge, where she was allowed slightly more independence than in Nightingale House. She still managed to find time for tennis when the weather was fine.

On 13 August, the day she travelled back to St Thomas's, the Luftwaffe had launched a major attack on airfields, aiming to put them out of action and neutralise the RAF before the planned German ground invasion. The offensive was codenamed Operation Adlerangriff, or 'Eagle Attack', and the start date was 'Adlertag', 'Eagle Day.' It did not go according to plan.

The Luftwaffe wanted to knock out Fighter Command's ground organisation but, due to faulty intelligence, many of the airfields they hit were not Fighter Command airfields and, in any case, by the following day, all had been repaired and were back in service.

Despite that failure, thanks to the RAF's robust air-defence system – the first time the Luftwaffe was coming up against a fully co-ordinated air defence system – Eagle Attack continued.

Then on 18 August, a Luftwaffe aircraft was shot down over London. Less than a week later, on the night of 24 August, German bombers appeared in the sky over central London and dropped bombs that killed nine people.

At St Thomas's some of the staff were watching from the roof as fires lit the London sky, and across the river, the iconic dome of St Paul's glowed blood red. The bombs were dropped in error while the planes were looking for military targets but they prompted swift retaliation by Bomber Command. The following night the RAF bombed Berlin, killing ten German civilians, and on three separate nights afterwards they struck again. Enraged, the Führer ordered a change of tactics, both in retaliation and because the Luftwaffe was not succeeding in destroying RAF airfields. Now London, its houses, factories and the morale of its citizens, would be the main target. The Blitz was indicative of panic within the Luftwaffe and Nazi High Command that the air battle was not going to plan.

On 7 September, on what became known as 'Black Saturday,' the Blitz began. The first raid started in the late afternoon. German bombers were seen flying in formation in broad daylight over London and began dropping their bombs.

Whistling and screaming as they plummeted, the bombs fell on factories, on a huge gasworks at Beckton, on the streets of North Woolwich, Canning Town, Silvertown and the docks. Within moments tremendous fires had sprung up, engulfing whole streets. Fire crews tried frantically to quench the flames as the deafening noise of gunfire signalled the valiant, if doomed, attempts of those on the ground to fight back. Queen Mary's Hospital in Newham was among the many buildings hit: six patients and two nurses were killed.

The daylight raid ended at around 6.15 p.m. Londoners emerged from their shelters to find their world in ruins: firemen were still battling to bring the fires under control and as the buildings blazed, chunks of masonry crashed to the ground. The toll of dead and injured could only be guessed at. They had barely had time to take in the devastation when, at around 8.30 p.m., the sirens wailed again: the bombers had returned. This time the bombs seemed even closer, falling with screeches and shattering 'crumps' as they exploded. One fell near St Thomas's, but little damage was done to the hospital. That first night of the Blitz, 436 people were killed, 1,600 seriously injured or maimed and many more traumatised. From that day forward, for fifty-seven nights, London was attacked again and again, day and night. There was no let-up until May 1941.

St Thomas's was an obvious target for bombers: it was large and right on the river, with the Houses of Parliament opposite and Waterloo station almost next door, and could easily be mistaken for a government building, or hit by bombs meant for Parliament. But Ruth did not remember worrying about it: she was simply too busy for such thoughts to intrude.

Harold was also sanguine at first. Despite their proximity to major targets, he and his friends remained optimistic: 'I don't think we really unduly worried every day that we'd get hit.' Everyone was, he remembered, 'very cheerful . . . amazingly cheerful and full of guts', although feelings towards the Germans had, he noticed, hardened into real hatred.

The day after the first raid of the Blitz, Sunday, 8 September, was fine, with not a cloud in the sky. Londoners were not yet sufficiently

Blitz-weary to know that cloudless skies were good for bombers. When the air-raid siren sounded that afternoon, some off-duty medical staff climbed the steps to a balcony overlooking the Thames. They spotted German bombers, flying in formation and accompanied by fighter-plane outriders in the east, so high in the sky they looked like mere specks of silver, too tiny to do any harm. And then the bombing began. They were aiming at the docks, where food and other essentials were unloaded.

Once again the London sky turned red with fire. A surgeon, watching from the balcony, observed that 'Every tall building looked as though it was on fire inside because all the windows reflected a red glow.' The Houses of Parliament were lit up with the light from the fire and the Thames took on a bloody hue, a scarlet streak through London that was easily visible from the air.

On Albert Ward, Ruth worked on despite the cr-r-r-rump and whistle of bombs outside. Bedpans still had to be carried, basins washed, patients given their cup of cocoa and blackout blinds drawn.

Like many St Thomas's staff, she had until this point taken an almost blasé approach to air-raid precautions, sleeping in her room as normal. Now that began to seem unwise. The hospital authorities had arranged for straw mattresses to be placed in the basement of Gassiot House and advised nurses and probationers to take their pillows, blankets, rugs and torches to sleep there, where they would be safer. Ruth was reluctant at first, fearing that she would get little sleep amid the rustling of straw mattresses and the fidgeting and coughing of her bedfellows, as well as the disturbing noise of rats scuttling along the pipes, and preferred to remain in her bedroom.

But as night fell, and the bombing continued, she had second thoughts. 'I'd had a bath and it was so noisy that I thought, I think I'll try the basement tonight,' she recalled. She bundled up her bedding and made her way down there. She was fully clothed, as instructed by Matron, although some nurses chose to ignore this order and traipsed down to the basement in silk nighties, dressing-gowns and slippers. Some disliked the idea of sheltering in basements, fearing they would be buried if the building above took a direct hit. A few nurses and physiotherapists (the 'masseuses') stayed in their rooms in Gassiot House, including an Australian physiotherapist named Barbara Mortimer Thomas, whom Ruth knew a little. Barbara was confident that, if need be, she could take shelter under the sturdy stone fireplace in her room.

The probationer nurses slept with their training sets, but most of those in Ruth's were on night duty as she had swapped shifts with another nurse. She lay listening to the ominous sound of aircraft overhead, the staccato 'ack-ack' of the anti-aircraft guns and the sickening boom of explosions that felt disturbingly close. Once again the docks were hit, the German bombers guided in by fires still blazing from the bombs of the night before.

Midnight came and went, then one o'clock. Ruth became increasingly desperate for sleep but while others dropped off, she lay reluctantly alert.

She was still awake when, at 2.30 a.m. (some accounts say 2.10 a.m.), there was a terrifying roar and the whole building rocked on its foundations. A massive bomb had fallen onto the north side of the hospital, causing the top three floors of Gassiot House to collapse in a tangled mess of masonry, water tanks and steel girders that bent and buckled. The hospital was plunged into total darkness, the only light coming from the fires that illuminated the London sky. The cacophony of thousands of windows shattering, with the boom and thud of masonry and other objects crashing to the ground, was indescribable.

Inside Gassiot House it felt as though the whole building was falling. Doors, window frames and great chunks of rubble were strewn everywhere, along with shattered glass.

In the pitch-dark basement, Ruth found herself alone. She became aware that the noise had receded. The roar of engines overhead could still be heard but the tumbling and crashing of falling masonry had abated. She called out, her mouth dry with dust from the rubble. No answer came. Had anyone else survived? The basement had been full, so where was everyone? She had lost her torch and could see nothing in the darkness. Reaching out with her hands, she felt hard steel: a girder or pipe had twisted and bent over her, shielding her from the falling rubble. If the building were to sway or receive a further shock, there was every chance that several tons of masonry and debris would come down on top of her. She dared not move.

In other parts of the basement, nurses were suffering similar dilemmas, trying to extricate themselves without dislodging masonry that might fall and injure or kill others who were trapped below, silent and invisible. Some began climbing out, making their way gingerly up the stairs, which had been partially buried under rubble. Many were barefoot, and as they crunched over the broken glass and twisted metal they cut their feet.

Those who went up the stairs first were the lucky ones as with every step they took they could not help nudging the loose rubble that tumbled down onto the nurses climbing up behind them, cutting and bruising their legs. Water from a broken pipe was gushing through a window into the ruins of the building but some of the nurses managed to climb through it. Ruth was unaware of this as she lay, not moving, praying that the rubble would not topple and bury her and that the walls would hold and not collapse inwards.

Harold, like Ruth, had slept above ground until that night. But after the bombing of the docks the medical students left their usual sleeping quarters in the private patients' home, long since emptied of patients, and set up mattresses in the basement of the main hospital building, where they hoped to snatch a few hours' sleep.

They were awakened by a shattering noise. Glass was flying in all directions as the hospital's several thousand windows were blown in by the bomb. A friend of Harold's, a student named Sam Maling, described in a letter to his family in New Zealand the 'stench of explosive and the dense choking cloud' that came down the corridor as they struggled into clothes or dressing-gowns.

Some had torches but many of those had been smashed by the concussion effect of the bomb. Anyway, it was thought too risky to use them in case the light was spotted by the bombers still overhead. Crunching over glass and debris, they made their way through a pall of dust until they reached their assembly point, where they were rapidly organised into teams. Some were sent to the wards, where windows had been blown in and beams had fallen from the ceiling, although the patients were miraculously unhurt. The students were put to work carrying them down several storeys on stretchers, exhausting work with the heavier ones. Other teams were told to make for Gassiot House where it was believed that people were trapped in the wreckage.

Sam Maling described what they found. 'What a scene! The sky was lit by the glare of many fires in London and against it we could see the shattered outline of the house. The top three floors had cascaded into the square in front of us, which was a great scree-heap of blocks of masonry, steel girders and general wreckage.' A vast iron water tank had been blown from the roof of Gassiot, hit another building, then crashed to the ground.

Cries were coming from the ruins of Gassiot House and someone quickly found ladders and began poking them through the windows towards the basement. Nurses who had been unable to reach either stairs or windows grasped them and began climbing to ground-floor level and through the shattered windows. Some of the students then climbed through the other way and began searching the ruins, calling for anyone who was still trapped. Time was of the essence. There was every chance that walls might collapse, burying anyone who remained inside.

Harold did not know where Ruth was, whether she had already escaped through a window or whether she was lying somewhere in the darkness, injured or dead.

Some had had a miraculous escape. A friend of Ruth's, Anne Cooper, had been blown clear of the building and was found, with another nurse, dazed but unhurt on Westminster Bridge.

Five other nurses were found stuck behind a wall. Heaving with all their strength, the students and house officers managed to shift a large piece of furniture that had been holding the wall up. It crumbled, releasing the nurses, who all seemed quite cheery as they climbed the ladder to where more students were waiting to haul them through a window.

Others were emerging from holes in the wall, their clothes torn, their hair grey with dust, cut and bruised, but with no serious injuries. Above the ground more students treated those whose feet had been cut as they clambered out, extracting glass and debris, then dressing the wounds. More shouts rose from the rubble, and Harold, with other medical students, helped out those who could walk, carrying any nurses who had bare feet and could not climb over the broken glass. Maling later wrote of having to carry a 'very' heavy' nurse on his back and out into the square. They had to fling themselves flat among the wreckage whenever the whine of a bomb sounded particularly close.

While the rescuers continued their search, shouting for survivors, Ruth lay in what was increasingly feeling like a tomb, oblivious of their efforts. She had tried calling but received no answer. She had lost her watch as well as her torch so she did not know how long she lay there. The heap of rubble that was trapping her had cut her off from the other survivors in the basement. She was entirely alone.

She forced herself to remain calm. And then she smelt burning and knew, with sinking certainty, she would die there. Having seen what fire had done the night before, turning the docks into an inferno that still smouldered twenty-four hours later, she knew that once the flames took hold of the building she would have no chance.

With a fatalism that many Blitz victims would display, she lay still and tried to resign herself to death, aged only twenty-one. As she put it, years later, with her usual phlegmatic understatement, 'I thought, "This is a death I wouldn't have chosen."' But perhaps rescue would reach her before the flames did. She began to pray. Just as she was beginning to think she might pass out from sheer exhaustion, she heard voices: 'Is there anyone down there?'

At once she began shouting, 'Help! Help me!' The voices came closer and she could make out the thin beams of torches piercing the darkness. And then, among the voices, with sweet relief she recognised Harold's.

'Are you all right? What condition are you in? We'll rescue you,' he called down to her.

But rescue would not be swift. Treading gingerly, so as not to dislodge more masonry and risk an avalanche that would bury Ruth more deeply, they edged towards a small opening in the rubble. She was a long way below them, the intervening space filled with precarious wreckage. She shouted up to them, explaining that a steel pipe or girder was protecting her and that their torches seemed a long way above. The ladder they had brought was not long enough to reach her so someone had to fetch another. As they shone their torches down, switching them off every time the planes went overhead, they puzzled over how to reach her without burying her. Someone returned with a second ladder and they tied them together. 'We can't come down to you, you'll have to climb out,' they told her.

Slowly, tentatively, they edged the ladder down through the gap. Ruth could see it now and was able to shout directions. Dust poured down and she tried not to imagine what would happen if they dislodged something more solid.

At last she managed to wriggle out from beneath the girder. Carefully, she gripped the bottom rung of the ladder and began half crawling, half climbing up. It was slow progress: she was tired and moved gingerly so as not to jolt the masonry. As she got further up the ladder she could see and hear the planes in the clear night sky, still droning menacingly overhead.

By the time she got to the top she was exhausted and grey with dust, her uniform torn and filthy, but there was Harold with outstretched arms. He and others helped her up the final rungs and, at last, she stepped onto the debris. 'I'll tell the parents you're all right,' Harold assured her. As they withdrew the ladder it nudged the girder, which crashed down, with all the rubble that had been resting on it. But it did not matter: Ruth was safe, no one else was down there and the building had not caught fire.

Ruth made her way through the rubble past the fire engines and rescue parties hurrying to and fro in darkness. The dust was settling but now the air was filled with millions of little lights, seemingly floating to the ground. It took her a while to realise they were feathers from pillows that had burst in the explosion and caught light, swirling to the ground like fireflies. It was, she remembered, an eerily beautiful sight. The Women's Voluntary Services (WVS) had arrived on the scene and were serving Bovril, tea and cocoa. Someone fetched Ruth a cup of tea and a sandwich. There was no point in going back to her room for clean clothes. It had gone, obliterated by the bomb, with all her possessions.

Elsewhere in Gassiot House other rescues were taking place, not all ending happily. There were still some nurses and physiotherapists who had not yet been accounted for. Later that morning, Harold was in the basement canteen when he overheard people whispering that his sister was missing. Mercifully, he knew this was not true since he had seen her emerge from the rubble a few hours earlier. But he needed to let his parents know that they were both safe before the news came out that a London hospital had been hit: the reports never specified which hospital since government policy was never to say exactly where the bombs had fallen. It was essential that the Luftwaffe should not know how accurate or otherwise their bombing had been.

It turned out that Nurse Walker was indeed missing – Nurse Cynthia Walker. Another nurse was also unaccounted for, as well as four physiotherapists.

Reporter Ritchie Calder of the *Daily Herald* newspaper watched the ARP teams and medical students continue to search through the debris of the Gassiot House basement and ground floor. It was impossible to climb up any further as some of the upper storeys had collapsed but others remained precariously, rooms cut in half leaving their interiors exposed, like stage-sets.

One rescue team, searching through the Treasurer's House, reported hearing noises from the third floor of the next-door building, Gassiot House. Someone was alive but trapped. There was nothing to be done in the dark, but at dawn the sister in charge of Gassiot led a rescue team up to the third floor of the Treasurer's House and pointed out a fireplace, suggesting they cut through it to what remained of the third floor next door. Barbara Mortimer Thomas was among the missing women. Sister knew that this was where her room was and recalled Barbara's belief that the fireplace would keep her safe from bombs.

They began boring a hole through the wall, working carefully so that they did not cause it to collapse. Finally, at 9 a.m., they broke through to the other side and were rewarded by the sight of Barbara. Like Ruth, and several other survivors that night, she had been saved by a huge steel girder that had crashed through the higher storeys and fallen across her room, breaking the force of the cascading masonry and debris. But enough of it had fallen on her to injure and trap her as she lay in bed, pinioned beneath the twisted wreckage of her room and bed frame, forty feet above ground level. She was conscious but in great pain.

Steadily, her rescuers chipped away at the hole, enlarging it until they could clamber through. The matron, Miss Hillyers, two sisters and a surgeon risked their lives to crawl through it and across the fragile floor to reach her. They managed to pass her food, hot drinks and even hot-water bottles to keep her warm as she was suffering from cold and shock, conscious that the floor beneath them might give way at any moment, sending them all down forty feet to their death.

A surgeon managed to reach her hand to give her an injection of morphine to ease her pain. Bravely, she told her rescuers not to bother about her. She had friends in the next-door room. 'Go through the bathroom and get the others before me,' she told them. No one told her that they were already dead.

At lunchtime she urged the ARP wardens, 'You boys go and get some lunch. I'm all right.' ARP workers managed to push some supports into the rubble to lift its weight off her. Meanwhile men were steadily erecting a huge scaffold, fifty feet high, to reach her, while the remains of the stricken building hung over them and the building next door threatened to collapse on top of them. Ritchie Calder was struck by their fearlessness: 'Clambering up the stanchions like monkeys, bolting the sections and flinging up clamps and catching them like jugglers. Doctors and nurses of the hospital watched in admiration.'

As dusk began to fall and the air-raid sirens set up their mournful wail again, the scaffolding had grown high enough to rescue her. The crowd below watched excitedly. 'We've won. She's out,' one man announced delightedly. His optimism was quickly shattered. A doctor who had crawled through wreckage to reach her shook his head sadly. 'She's dead.' At the moment of deliverance, her life had ebbed away. Shock had killed her. All they could do was to drape a red blanket over her body until it could be safely retrieved.

The other casualties were identified: three other physiotherapists and the two missing nurses, Sarah Durham and Cynthia Walker.

After her rescue, Ruth had made her way through the ruins of the hospital, oblivious to the rumours of her death or disappearance, to report to Matron. Her uniform was black and torn and her hair so thick with dust that it would take several days to wash out, but for once Matron did not chastise her. She told Ruth to get cleaned up, find a fresh uniform from somewhere and report for her shift as usual.

Ruth had been left with nothing but the tattered clothes she stood up in. She had to borrow spares from her ward sister, Sister Albert, who was nearly six feet tall. As Ruth was only five foot three, Sister Albert's uniform swamped her and had to be held up with safety pins. Later, she was given another uniform and some money to purchase a toothbrush, hairbrush, nightclothes and other essentials.

Albert Ward was out of action but plenty of patients, currently being moved to temporary wards in the basement, needed looking after. Some nurses, those who had been badly bruised or cut, were given a day or two of sick leave. But anyone who could get back to work did so, despite having been awake since 2.30 a.m. The normally stern sisters relaxed their strictness that day. Sister Albert was kindness itself, ensuring that Ruth was not given too much to do on the ward.

Ann Reeves, another probationer who had crawled out of the rubble of Gassiot House, recalled a large, bosomy sister of whom she had previously been terrified, giving her tea and reassuring her, '"It's all right my girl." It wasn't - everything was shaking and breaking and crashing all round. But she was comforting.'

There was, of course, no counselling, but Ruth felt there was no need. Getting back to work, she thought, was 'much the best thing'. Her mind was occupied by the needs of her patients, and morale was kept high by the camaraderie of her friends, who swapped their stories of escape and survival, and giggled about those who had crawled out of the carnage in their slips or nightdresses. As for those who had not survived, this was war and, for the moment, there was no time to grieve: everyone simply had to keep going.

Had the bomb fallen on any of the other hospital blocks, with wards full of patients, many more would have been killed. A number of the wards had been damaged and the electricity had been cut off so the X-ray department and lifts could not function. Also, the water and gas supplies were failing. It was clear that the hospital could not function as usual, and most of its patients would have to be moved elsewhere. Those who were well enough were sent home, others taken to the basement, and some evacuated to sector hospitals in Hampshire and Surrey over the coming days. The nurses worked tirelessly, settling patients into their new, makeshift wards, changing bandages and wiping brows when, just hours ago, they themselves were being bandaged and treated.

With extra patients arriving in the sector hospitals, more St Thomas's nurses would be required. Ruth was posted to Park Prewett, and that evening several Green Line buses, which were used as ambulances during the war, drew up at the hospital. Ruth, drooping with exhaustion, climbed onto one, clutching a bag with the few essentials she had been able to buy, and set off through the blacked-out streets of London for the Hampshire countryside.

Meanwhile, Harold and other medical students had been busy helping ferry patients to beds in the basement where, it was thought, they would be much safer than they would above ground. An operating theatre had been set up there and this was now pressed into action. Other areas of the basement were turned into permanent dormitories. With so much accommodation destroyed, they were crowded with professors and students, doctors, nurses and cleaners, sleeping head to toe, some on mattresses and the luckier ones on beds. The stringent rules forbidding students and nurses to talk to each other had evaporated overnight, replaced by mixed dormitories and sing-songs round the piano that someone had hauled into the basement. A stoic camaraderie prevailed and no one asked, 'When will the next bomb strike?' It was a matter of 'when', not 'if'. That much they knew.

6

'You'd better hope that he dies'

————

THE BOMBS CONTINUED to fall, some of them alarmingly close to St Thomas's, although the hospital was spared. The low grind of the bombers continued. The crump, crump of bombs exploding spelled doom for some other building, some other unfortunate people.

The night of Friday the thirteenth was unlucky for the hospital. One bomb hit a building where the maids lived, injuring several but luckily causing no fatalities. Miss Hillyers missed being obliterated by a bomb that dropped just yards in front of her: had she not paused to adjust her cap she would have been beneath it. Another bomb did not hit the hospital directly but fell close enough to damage buildings so badly that they had to be pulled down.

Harold was one of a number of students who had volunteered to remain at St Thomas's after the evacuation that had followed the first bomb. They treated a procession of air-raid victims, including ARP wardens, firemen and St Thomas's staff hurt by those first two direct hits. Day and night, the casualties were brought in: severed limbs, faces damaged and families shattered. There were also people hurt in traffic accidents in the blackout and run-of-the-mill cases, such as appendicitis and TB. The atmosphere was cheerful, but anger towards the Germans helped fuel the determination to continue as normal. Harold revelled in the extra responsibility, learning how to put in drips and perform blood transfusions.

'The experience was far in advance of anything we would have had as ordinary medical students in peacetime,' he recalled. Yet although he enjoyed the work, and the camaraderie, he felt intuitively that he would become a casualty of the Blitz. His premonition proved all too accurate.

On the evening of Sunday, 15 September, Harold had just been assisting, as surgical dresser, at an operation in the basement theatre alongside his friend Peter Spilsbury, as house surgeon. When it was over, Harold and Spilsbury had a cup of coffee and listened to the wireless, cheered by the news that the RAF had shot down a record number of German planes. They left the operating theatre just before 8.30 p.m. and were strolling towards a doorway, heading for College House, another part of the hospital.

In the sky above St Thomas's, a bomber released its load, sending one bomb spiralling downwards. With an ear-splitting, thunderous explosion it smashed through the main corridor of the hospital near the Central Hall, and fell straight into the basement, shattering and disembowelling the very fabric of the building and causing the collapse of two buildings, the Medical Outpatients block and the sitting room of College House. Huge chunks of masonry and rubble crashed into the basement corridor. Metal pipes and girders buckled and twisted, while filing cabinets, cupboards and radiators were flung into the air.

'It is said that you never see, hear or feel the one that gets you,' Harold wrote later. 'This is true . . .' He remembered nothing of the moment that the bomb hit. But the hospital secretary, who was nearby, described the impact: 'There was no warning scream of the bomb, only one terrific CRACK!, a blinding flash, and utter darkness. For a time I was conscious only of choking fumes and dust.'

The sounds of breaking glass, screaming and chaos filled the air. China and glass flew everywhere. A pipe had burst, sending hot water surging through the hospital canteen, over the feet of those trapped there, who became terrified that they would drown.

A flying piece of metal, probably a girder, had hit Peter Spilsbury, killing him instantly. Another piece of metal, or perhaps the same piece of debris, had hit Harold smack in the head, felling him and fracturing his skull. Now he lay unconscious, unaware that his friend was dead beside him.

Sam Maling had also been walking along the corridor and was about to turn into the X-ray department when he was deafened by a thunderous explosion and the lights went out, plunging everything into darkness. With a horrifying rumble the building began to fall about his head. A moment later, amid agonised screams and shrieks, came a penetrating, pungent smell of smoke, fumes and cordite.

Maling groped his way up to the ground floor to find that the hospital had been 'cut right in two'. Once again he rushed to rescue survivors. The theatre sister, Sister Forbes, was dead: the shockwaves of the blast had killed her instantly (by sucking the air out of the lungs without leaving any sign of injury on the body). Nurse Richardson had been badly injured and Maling helped carry her out but she later died.

The carnage was extraordinary. Of all the bombs that hit St Thomas's throughout the war - the hospital was hit ten times, including incendiary bombs and a V1 - the bomb on 15 September 1940 was the most destructive.

The dispensary was engulfed in flames, fuelled by the alcohol and acid stored there. Glass bottles burst in the heat. The dispensers managed to climb out of the window but not before acid, running freely across the floor, had burned into the soles of their boots. Worse, the gas mains had been hit and the leaking gas was blazing furiously, producing choking fumes. Glass and rubble were strewn everywhere. The fire brigade arrived and began training their hoses on the flames, not realising that bodies, both living and dead, were still lying under the rubble, including Harold. 'They almost drowned him,' according to Ruth.

Soon the water was six inches deep, with pillows and mattresses floating incongruously on it. When they trained their hoses on the dispensary, they inadvertently added fuel to the fire by washing the blazing spirits across the smashed corridor and into what had once been the outpatients department, setting this alight too.

Herbert Frewer, assistant clerk of the works, who knew the layout of the hospital better than almost anyone else, began organising a rescue team, which Maling joined, with his friend Dr Harry Norman. Within moments of the bomb hitting, with masonry still falling, the rescue work began, those who were unhurt quickly forming into teams. In places they had to wade through water that was two feet deep and mixed with concentrated sulphuric, nitric and hydrochloric acids.

Hearing screaming from the basement canteen, they entered and found a scene of devastation with china and glass flying everywhere. There were dozens of wounded, and ARP wardens began taking them into the X-ray department, which turned into a temporary first-aid post. Another operation had been about to begin when the bomb hit, on a policeman who needed his appendix removing urgently. With the basement operating theatre now in ruins a new theatre was hastily improvised

– the theatre sisters had to retrieve their instruments from several inches of water and re-sterilise them using a portable Primus stove since there was no electricity or gas, and the operation went ahead three hours after the blast, using emergency lamps as lights.

Amid the confusion it was a while before anyone realised that a few people were still unaccounted for. The rescue teams had already moved on to another part of the building when someone wondered what had happened to Harold Walker and Peter Spilsbury. Could they be in the collapsed area of the corridor that was blocked off by wreckage? Could anyone have survived the collapsing masonry and the chemical fumes?

Frewer thought it might be possible to tunnel a way through to the corridor. Under his direction the rescuers began crawling through the wreckage. Great chunks of brick and plaster were crashing constantly around them as, wriggling under pipes, through the mass of twisted debris and mangled medical instruments, iron bedsteads, pipes and brickwork, their clothes soaking, they felt their way in the darkness.

One of the rescue team described the 'strong smell of escaping gas while the ground was covered with liquid from the dispensary, which had been destroyed, most of which had caught fire. German planes were still circling overhead so that we could show no lights, and masonry was still falling from the smashed buildings above us.'

Frewer, Maling and Norman crawled forward, showered with dust, wriggling through the rubble, all too conscious that at any moment the direction of the fire could change and engulf them, the smell of gas adding to their discomfort. Eventually, someone managed to turn off the gas but the stench, mingled with the fumes from the dispensary liquids, made them choke.

The doctors carried phials of morphine in their pockets, knowing that anyone they found alive would be badly in need of pain relief. Frewer directed them towards a large girder that had slipped down from the top floor and was wedged between two walls, catching much of the debris on it. If anyone were to be found alive, he guessed, they would likely be under the girder.

He suggested to the rescuers that they tunnel underneath it, a task fraught with danger as every movement risked causing an avalanche of debris that could crash down, killing or burying them alive, if fire did not engulf them first.

According to Frewer, there were three survivors under the girder: Denis Nixon, the house physician, Harold and the assistant chaplain, the Reverend 'Dickie' Bird. The chaplain had been admiring the fish tank in the College House sitting room when the bomb hit. Harold's account, written fifty years later, describes how Bird was blasted, along with the rest of the room, onto the street and was rescued 'naked and hairless', but Frewer, writing not long after the event, states that Bird was also beneath the girder.

An elderly consultant, Sir Maurice Cassidy, watched the rescuers crawling forward as rubble rained down all around. As they crawled and climbed, they called out and were rewarded with a voice answering them in a low tone from the depths of the wreckage. They thought it was Harold and provided a cheery running commentary to reassure him as they edged forward, but in fact it was Bird, whose knee was soon spotted protruding from the rubble. He told them that Nixon was trapped somewhere nearby.

Harry Norman carefully cut away Bird's trousers and administered a morphine injection into the calf. Bird's body was pinned under huge blocks of masonry and there was no chance of extracting him until someone found jacks that could be used to heave them off.

Carefully they dug further down into the debris with their hands and found a head. It belonged to Denis Nixon. He was badly injured and in pain but Norman managed to inject morphine into his finger.

The building shook and trembled around them as they stabilised the casualties. After an hour, working with painstaking care, they managed to extract Nixon and Bird, getting them onto stretchers and out through the narrow tunnel they had created. For their bravery that night, Frewer, Norman and Maling were later awarded the George Medal.

At some stage later, a little further down the corridor, they discovered a motionless, partially buried body. It was Harold. He lay amid the broken glass, cut, bruised and burned, his face badly lacerated. They edged closer, felt for a pulse and found a faint one. Working steadily, switching off their torches whenever a plane was heard overhead, they managed to get him onto a stretcher and to the first-aid post for assessment.

He had gashes on his scalp that needed stitches but most worrying was the damage to his skull. He had a lineal fracture at the base, he was in a coma, and the prognosis was grim. If they could keep him stable, they might just save his life, but what kind of life would it be?

Peter Spilsbury's body was not discovered until the Tuesday when the rubble was at last cleared away. According to Ruth, he had been decapitated, but no references were made to his decapitation in the official accounts. Such details were sometimes kept quiet as they were bad for morale and disturbing for the families. Sociable, gregarious and well-liked, Spilsbury had been planning to join the Royal Army Medical Corps and then to follow in his father's footsteps by becoming a pathologist. But his future was now gone. His father, Sir Bernard Spilsbury, did not learn of his death until he opened a letter of condolence the following day or, according to some reports, when he arrived at the hospital in the morning. The shock all but destroyed him.

Another house surgeon, Colin Campbell, had also been killed, bringing the total to four dead and more than fifty injured among the hospital staff, some seriously. Others suffered from the less obvious effects of bomb blast, feeling dazed, as if coming round from an anaesthetic.

When Harold's condition was considered stable he was taken by ambulance to one of the sector hospitals in Woking. Ruth was contacted at Park Prewett by the specialist under whose care Harold was placed, a neurologist named Jack Elkington, known as the Elk, whose icy intolerance of anything less than perfectionism made him the scourge of nurses and medical students alike. He summoned Ruth to Woking so that he could explain her brother's situation.

There, he did not mince his words. The brain damage seemed likely to be severe. 'You'd better hope that he dies,' he told her, 'because if he lives he'll be a cabbage.'

Shocked, Ruth pressed him for a glimmer of hope, asking, 'Is your diagnosis complete or is there part of the brain that might recover?'

'There is always hope,' he told her, 'but at the moment I feel he is not going to make it.'

Ruth looked at Harold lying in the bed, and wondered how she would tell her parents that their youngest son was as good as dead.

Her answer was to take a more optimistic view than Elkington. Harold was, after all, a Walker, and Walkers did not give up. Observing the family motto - Nil desperandum - she telephoned her parents to tell them that Harold was alive, saved by a girder just as she had been, and omitting Elkington's gloomy prognosis. Where there was breath there was hope.

Ruth's optimism was rewarded. A week after the bomb had struck, Harold regained consciousness and, to Elkington's amazement, his brain appeared unaffected. He was bewildered to wake up in Woking, with no idea of how he had got there. He was, he told his interviewer in 1998, with some understatement, 'very surprised to know where I was and what had happened. If you've been unconscious for a week you wonder where you are.'

His head had been shaved and his scalp wounds had been stitched, but it would take a while for his skull to knit back together. His cuts and burns healed well. Photographs of him during his recovery show his head bandaged, and he is sporting a beard, since his wounds made shaving impossible. He was exceptionally lucky: no bones had been displaced and the only lasting effects he suffered were post-traumatic headaches and one episode of epilepsy.

For three months Harold lay on the ward at Woking with Dickie Bird and Denis Nixon. He and Nixon had played together on the hospital rugby team: neither would be going anywhere near a rugby pitch for some time, if ever, but their camaraderie kept their spirits up.

As the weeks dragged into months, Harold became desperate for something to pass the time. Studying was out of the question due to his headaches so instead he started knitting. He had taken a shine to one of the night nurses and, rather boldly, decided to knit her a pair of 'step-ins', a form of lingerie that was like a slip, but buttoned between the legs, forming a kind of loose-fitting vest-and-bloomers combination, an ambitious project for a novice knitter, and a rather intimate gift. However, to his disappointment he did not get to see whether they fitted her or not, as he confided to a hospital secretary some months later. If the nurse was Nightingale-trained she would have known that, if divulging her first name to a patient was forbidden, accepting the gift of hand-knitted underwear was out of the question.

Although Harold mourned the loss of his friend Peter Spilsbury, his survival left him not with 'survivor's guilt' but profound gratitude. He later told his family that he felt he had been spared for a reason and this belief spurred him on throughout his life and career.

Fifty years afterwards, Harold wrote about his injuries in the *St Thomas's Hospital Gazette*, partly to pay tribute to his friend Sam Maling, who had been too modest to mention in his own account of that night that he, Dr Norman and Herbert Frewer had been awarded the George Medal for their bravery, just as Harold never mentioned his own role in rescuing Ruth.

He wrote, too, to encourage young doctors or medical students to 'appreciate that many patients with similar injuries recover fully with good nursing, rest and the wise counsel of physicians and surgeons'. Never despair.

Meanwhile the Blitz continued. St Thomas's was hit again in October and showered with incendiary bombs twice in December, but there were no more casualties. The neighbourhood around the hospital was badly affected: two air-raid shelters suffered direct hits with tragic results and the hospital staff worked at full stretch to cope with a steady stream of people with catastrophic injuries: faces sliced by falling glass, limbs torn from bodies, families shattered by loss. Some were sent out to the sector hospitals, and it was often there that they began asking questions about what had happened to their relations and had to be told that they had not survived.

For the next three months Ruth visited Harold in Woking whenever she could get away from Park Prewett for a few hours. It was less easy for Dorothea and Arthur to make the long journey up from Tiverton due to petrol rationing, while all non-essential train travel was strongly discouraged. But at last, in time for Christmas 1940, Harold was allowed to go home to convalesce at Tara, where Dorothea cooked his favourite meals, as far as rationing would allow. Few of his local school friends were left at home: most had joined up or were working elsewhere. Many would not survive the war, and in later years he was saddened when he returned to Blundell's for reunions that he had few contemporaries with whom to reminisce: others were among the names carved on the memorial in the school chapel to the 172 Blundell's Old Boys who had lost their lives in the war.

Gradually Harold regained his strength, the headaches became fewer and less agonising, and he made plans to return to the hospital, as a student rather than a patient. He had six lost months to make up and would have to delay taking his final exams until the following year. Joining the navy was now impossible due to his injuries.

For Dorothea and Arthur, the delirious relief at their youngest two children surviving such close encounters with death gave way to some pondering. Tiverton felt very far away from London and the Home Counties where Ruth, Harold and Bee were all based. Dorothea felt the urge to hold her brood, or at least those still in England, a little closer. When life could be snatched away at any second, it made more sense to be nearby. If they were closer to London, Ruth, Harold and Bee could spend days off or weekends with them. Besides, although he was not yet seventy, Arthur was feeling his age. The chickens, the orchard and large garden were becoming too much for him to manage.

Arthur had spent some of his schooldays in Weybridge, Surrey, at St George's College, and now had a yearning to return there. It would be close at hand for London and for any of the St Thomas's sector hospitals where Ruth and Harold might be posted.

They sold Tara and its chickens and moved in with Dorothea's aunt in Exeter while they made enquiries about houses in Weybridge, seemingly undeterred that the town was firmly in the Luftwaffe's sights. On 4 September 1940 the Vickers factory, which produced Wellington bombers, had suffered a direct hit. Three bombs fell on the factory, killing 83 and injuring 419. But, then, nowhere was safe any longer.

By the spring of 1941, Harold was back at St Thomas's medical school or, rather, at one of its many offshoots. Following the bombings in September and October 1940 so much of St Thomas's lay in ruins that the medical school was moved to Godalming, Surrey. It took over a large manor house that had, until recently, housed a girls' boarding school down the road from the nearby boys' public school, Charterhouse. The girls had gone, withdrawn by parents worried at its proximity to London, leaving only the two headmistresses, Miss Popkin and Miss Dow, who were persuaded to stay on as housekeepers.

Into their quiet, genteel world burst a pack of rambunctious medical students, who were housed in the girls' dormitories, decorated with paintings of fairytales, their strapping frames overspilling the cot-like beds in which the girls had slept. Miss Popkin and Miss Dow's misgivings about medical students' wild reputation were not allayed by the students' habit of dashing in and out of bathrooms after a rugby match completely naked.

By the time Harold arrived, the ladies had long since resigned and the cots had been replaced by man-size beds. The medical school was presided over by a warden in the tall, rangy form of James Wyatt, a genial gynaecologist. Harold had missed his final exams while he was recuperating – they took place once a year – so he had to repeat some of his studies. Wyatt, kindly and avuncular, liked him and took him under his wing. His secretary, Pat Leicester, writing in *St Thomas's Hospital Gazette* in 1988, remembered Harold well.

She was an Australian and had never before come across public-school boys – many of the medical students were from such schools. As an avowed socialist, she was prepared to dislike them, but despite their boisterous behaviour she soon found her prejudice melting as she got to know them. Among them Harold stood out as 'a very nice lad . . . who was driving James [Wyatt] about for a time'. He confided in her about the step-ins he had knitted for the night nurse at Woking Hospital.

He had more luck on the romantic front with Wyatt's niece, a nurse named Jill, with whom Ruth was friendly. Harold and Jill became close and even talked of marriage. Although the romance eventually petered out, James Wyatt had a long-lasting influence on Harold. As Harold drove Wyatt around, Wyatt, puffing incessantly on Woodbine cigarettes that caused him to cough so convulsively that his pince-nez glasses regularly shot off the end of his nose, Wyatt inspired Harold with his enthusiasm for obstetrics and gynaecology.

While Harold was driving Wyatt around Surrey, Ruth was working in neighbouring Hampshire, once more with Harold Gillies, as a nurse on the plastic-surgery unit, filled with soldiers, sailors, civilians disfigured in air raids and pilots burned in the Battle of Britain, which had ended in October 1940. Although the majority of RAF patients were treated by McIndoe in East Grinstead, some came to Gillies at Rooksdown. There were also some unusual cases, such as the handsome SOE operative who was sent to Gillies to have his facial features changed so that the Gestapo would not recognise him on his return to occupied Europe.

Gillies often operated late into the night, so working for him was exhausting, but fascinating. For Ruth it was the most memorable part of her nursing career, and she remembered it with clarity and pride. Gillies still saw a few private patients at his London clinic, society women who, war or no war, wanted their wrinkles smoothed out, and an entertainer who desired a facelift before she departed overseas to entertain the troops. As one of his biographers recorded, these 'jaded ladies . . .

made a more useful contribution to the war effort than they knew', since it was through tweaking and pinching their facial skin and muscles that Gillies was able to refine his techniques for facial reconstruction.

Ruth was keenly aware that she was seeing medical history being made. She was put to work on skin grafting, then in its infancy, and described Gillies's method of creating a new piece of skin to patch over the raw flesh from which burned skin had peeled or been cut away. 'It was very elementary in those days. We used to have bits of gauze, Vaseline gauze, with little tiny squares, and he used to take a piece of skin off, and he used to put the piece of skin through a mincing machine and then with a little pair of tweezers we used to put a little bit in each square. And then it all grew together.'

This is known as 'pinch-grafting' and, although it is seldom used in plastic surgery today as it produces a somewhat unsightly checkerboard look, if a patient is very badly burned and a wide area needs to be covered with new skin a pinch-graft is the only real option. Nowadays much of the work of pinch-grafting is done by machine and the Vaseline gauze has been replaced by a paraffin gauze with a smaller density of holes, but the technique remains essentially the one that Gillies pioneered and Ruth carried out, requiring steady hands and even steadier nerves.

A major problem with burns injuries, then as now, is that they almost always become infected. Burns are, essentially, massive open wounds and therefore highly susceptible to infection. The infected sites produced foul-smelling green pus. The wards reeked of it. Even off duty one could smell it still in the nose and throat; it clung to your hair, and seemed to follow you around like a cloud.

When the wound became infected the graft could not be done. Grafting small areas of skin was relatively straightforward: to make new eyelids, small flaps of skin could be taken from the thighs or inner arms, and sewn on, but larger areas of skin did not 'take' so easily. The blood vessels might fail to connect and the skin would die.

Wherever possible, Gillies turned to his tried and tested tubed pedicle technique. Ruth described how he would make an incision in the wrist 'and you'd get a sort of piece of sausage growing, and it used to grow to about that size [about a foot and a half] and then you would get a long piece of skin which you'd flatten out and use to cover the wounds.'

The pedicles did not just look grotesque. With legs attached to wrists by pedicles, or two legs affixed to each other by a flap of skin, or an arm appended to a jaw, they also hampered patients' movements. Over the course of weeks, the tube would be detached at one end and gradually 'waltzed' up the body from the original site to the location where it was needed. Each time, the blood supply had to re-establish. The pedicles could not be too long as the blood supply was more likely to fail and the whole procedure would have to begin again.

Hands were a particular challenge: grafting skin around the bony contours of burned fingers was far harder than attaching it to flatter surfaces. Gillies, who was 'as full of ideas as a dog is of fleas', as one admiring colleague put it, had invented a solution. Ruth observed how he made 'a slit in their tummy, like a pocket, and the hand was put inside and then the tummy skin grew over the hands, and then you could cut it to make fingers'.

Those whose faces were badly burned could barely open their mouths to eat. The only food they could take was junket, a milky pudding, and fluids, fed into their mouths with teaspoons or tubes. Many were at Rooksdown for years – ten months was considered a short stay for military patients – so patients and nurses came to know each other well.

Ruth did not mind the long hours or the putrid smell, and she had the patience and precision required for skin-grafting. But the plastic-surgery unit could be heartbreaking. Despite Gillies's ingenuity and artistry, many of his patients would never again look as they once had. This was particularly hard for the young pilots of the RAF, and not all could come to terms with their disfigurement. According to Ruth, some of those who had been good-looking, 'all they wanted to do was get up again and kill themselves. They didn't want to be disfigured. We had to try and talk them out of it.'

It is a poignant thought: young men lying for month after month, bearing the agony of their injuries and the often worse agony of repeated operations, skin grafts and infections, with only one goal in mind: to return to the skies in the hope of being shot down. Some did return to flying, but others were too badly maimed to be able to grip a joystick, despite Gillies's endeavours. Did any retain their suicidal ambitions? Did they succeed? A nurse who worked at another plastic-surgery unit remembered, 'All too often, the man would be rehabilitated completely, he would go back to his squadron and the next thing you heard was that he'd been killed. It happened time and time again, and it was so, so sad.' Did some pilots deliberately fly to their deaths? It is hard to believe that anyone who had been through the horror of immolation in a cockpit would choose to go through that again, but perhaps their disfigurement spurred them on to take greater risks.

The plastic-surgery team worked as hard on repairing their patients' shattered morale as they did on their shattered bodies. 'One just had to be cheerful with them all the time,' Ruth remembered. Gillies ensured that every mirror was removed from the wards and ripped from the bathroom walls at Rooksdown. Only when he was satisfied with his handiwork, months or years later, would he allow a patient to see the results.

It sometimes proved too much for young men's wives, fiancées and parents to see the much-loved features of their boy so mangled that he was unrecognisable. Ruth and the other nurses tried hard to prepare them and reassure them that, given time and Gillies's ingenuity, they would once again recognise their boy, if not quite as he was before. But some simply could not cope with what they found. 'You had the tragedies,' she recalled. 'They were engaged . . . and then the girl couldn't take it or the wife couldn't take it. It's human nature...'

She would quietly lead them out of the ward and try to calm them down. A weeping mother or fiancée was devastatingly damaging not only to the morale of the patient but to that of all the others on the ward, who would wonder, Will my wife leave me? Will my fiancée reject me? Some refused to allow a loved one to visit, unwilling to see them flinch at the sight of their injuries.

Another nurse, Eileen Willis, remembered a mother visiting her twenty-year-old son at Rooksdown. She recalled, 'He was terribly badly burned, and I tried to tell her that he was very bad but they would do marvellous things. It would take time, though. But she said, "Let me see him." Well, of course, when she went in to him, her face just went chalk white and she burst into tears. I'm afraid I just burst into tears too . . .'

The sights, sounds, smells and, above all, the tragedies of the plastic-surgery ward took a toll on the nurses. Some found the seemingly endless suffering of their patients too agonising to witness and broke down. A few had to be transferred to other wards but Ruth found she could contain her emotions: with four older brothers and a no-nonsense mother, she had learned early on to hold them back. It was a time when the British stiff upper lip came into its own: if the patients read pity or horror on a nurse's face they would instantly know just how bad things were without the need of a mirror. And, on the whole, she remembered, 'Their spirits were very high.'

To reduce infection and to remove dead, rotting flesh, the burns patients were lowered with infinite care into lukewarm baths of saline solution. As well as helping with infection it gave them temporary relief from pain, but the real agony came when they were lifted out and the raw flesh was exposed. Equally agonising was the removal of the Vaseline gauze and, most painful of all, the harvesting of skin to be used in the grafts. Mostly, said Ruth, the patients were very brave and hardly ever cried, but occasionally a shriek would escape them.

As soon as patients were able to walk they were encouraged to get out and about, first in the grounds of Rooksdown, then further afield. Photographs of Rooksdown show men swathed in bandages, their faces invisible but for eye-holes, strolling in the gardens and relaxing on benches with nurses. Gillies was adamant that social rehabilitation was every bit as important as physical recovery. The deep fear of many patients was that they would not be able to go out in public without people recoiling from their appearance. Gillies enlisted Rooksdown's nurses and the people of Basingstoke to help them face their fears and reassure them that they were not freaks. He encouraged nurses like Ruth to accompany their patients, as soon as they could walk, to the local pub, the Swan, affectionately known as the Mucky Duck.

From time to time someone would go earlier in the day to warn the pub staff that Rooksdown residents would be arriving later in the evening. The blonde barmaid made a point of coming out from behind the bar to envelop them in her voluptuous embrace, tubed pedicles, forehead flaps and all. Gillies also urged the patients to go out and about in Basingstoke. Locals became used to the sight of men with what appeared to be mini elephants' trunks growing out of their jaws or with 'masks' of new skin grafted over their faces walking around town, or being pushed in Bath chairs. In Ruth's experience they were generally very accepting and did not stare, or at least not for too long. A few found the patients' appearance so distressing that they complained and urged the hospital not to let them out in public. Others, however, went out of their way to show their support, even welcoming them into their homes.

Another of Gillies's initiatives was to hold social evenings and dances in a pavilion in the hospital's grounds. He wrote, 'It is common to see a surgical patient dancing with a [patient with a] forehead flap and nurses dancing with [patients with] tubed pedicles.'

Ruth spent hour after hour with the patients, feeding and washing them, tending the skin grafts, reading to them or writing their letters for them if their hands were too damaged to hold a pen, chatting and attempting to bolster their morale by telling them that, even if they would never again be able to fly on active service, they could still contribute to the war by training other pilots.

Occasionally she had the difficult job of consoling those who had received the 'Dear John' letter they all dreaded from the wife or girl-friend who felt she could not cope with the injuries and was breaking things off. Sometimes a patient ended a marriage or engagement, feeling that it was unfair to his wife or fiancée to expect them to stand by a man who was so far removed from the one with whom they had fallen in love.

Ruth had her own heartbreak to draw on. When she had applied to St Thomas's she had made no mention of her engagement to John Fisher, since nurses had to leave the service when they married. But although she kept it quiet, the thought of their eventual marriage sustained her, a bright beacon of hope for life after the war. But then a letter arrived from Sarawak. In it John suggested they put their engagement on hold. Years later, she talked of it as a mutual decision, 'Because we didn't know what was going to happen to us.' As far as she was concerned, marriage to John was still on the horizon, but that horizon had become more distant.

When I asked her how she felt about this, she changed the subject deftly. As her son, Jonathan, told me, 'She had a good memory, but a selective one.' Ruth loved to chat about almost anything, he noted affectionately, but 'She never spoke about emotion.' None of her patients would have known that the cheerful girl who sat at their bedside, urging them to look to the future, telling them that life would get better, was silently nursing her own broken heart.

PART THREE

Retreat and Captivity

7

'Generals covered in medals recklessly squandered brave men's lives'

WHILE THEIR CIVILIAN brother and sisters were being bombed in Britain, Edward and Walter were still waiting in India to play their own part in the war. Both had watched in frustration as other regiments left to fight in North Africa and Europe, and although Walter had spent three years in action on the North West Frontier, that was not where the future of Europe was being decided. He and Edward both yearned to be part of the wider war. It would bring a greater chance of promotion, too, and a keen rivalry had sprung up between the brothers, both ambitious and eager to succeed. Edward was now acting major, a temporary wartime rank, carrying the role and responsibility of a major although officially still a captain, while Walter was a temporary captain although officially still a lieutenant.

As luck, and irony, would have it, the first of the Walker brothers to see action in the wider war was Peter, who had neither trained nor yearned to fight but found himself on the front line long before his soldier brothers. Peter had been in England on leave when war was declared. On his return to India he volunteered to go on the army reserve list to be called up, if needed, as an emergency commissioned officer. In 1940 the Indian Army began expanding rapidly to meet the demands of war and soon troopships were sailing west from India, taking men to the Middle East.

In December 1940, as the British began the Western Desert offensive against the Italians in North Africa, and the Indian Army came under pressure to supply more men and officers for the campaign, Peter left his polo ponies, pet otter and dog and journeyed two thousand miles from the Sealkotee tea estate to Bangalore Military College for officer-cadet training.

As he already spoke Hindustani and Assamese and had several years of military experience in the Assam Valley Light Horse, Peter was ideal officer material. He was physically tough and keen to serve alongside Edward in his regiment, 1/8th Punjabs. After four months at Officer Training School, Peter passed his Urdu exams and was commissioned as Second Lieutenant Walker into his brother's regiment.

The 1/8th Punjabs had spent much of 1940 training for the desert war, but instead in October 1940 they were ordered to paint over the desert camouflage on their vehicles, replacing it with jungle green: they were being sent to Malaya. Edward said goodbye to Tiggy and set sail with his men. The Punjabs were stationed in the state of Kedah in the north of the country, near the border with Thailand (which had been known until recently as Siam). If any attempt were made to attack Malaya by land, the invaders would have to come across that border, although such a possibility was barely countenanced. As recently as August 1940, the military planners back in Whitehall had played down the possibility of a war in the Far East, confidently pronouncing that Japan posed no threat to British interests there. War in the Middle East remained the priority where men and resources were concerned. Far East Command was the poor relation and would have to make do with whatever was left. The commander-in-chief of the Far East, Air Chief Marshal Sir Robert Brooke-Popham, was keenly aware that he simply did not have the wherewithal to withstand a Japanese attack and could only hope that it would never come.

Some defensive preparations were made to protect Malaya, which was one of the Empire's most profitable colonies, with its tin mines and rubber plantations. Airfields were hastily constructed up and down the Malayan peninsula in the expectation that the ageing RAF planes stationed there would be replaced or supplemented with the 336 modern aircraft that had been promised, but by the autumn of 1941 fewer than half had materialised.

Meanwhile there were reports that the Japanese were training troops in jungle warfare, a worrying sign given the jungle terrain at the centre of the Malayan peninsula. Informants in Saigon reported that a printing firm had been given an order to produce fifty thousand maps of Malaya with Japanese characters, and another to print Japanese–Malay pocket dictionaries. Japan was desperate for resources such as rubber, tin, timber and oil to fuel their territorial ambitions, and Malaya's thriving industries made it a prime target for a country with imperial plans.

The 1/8th Punjabs waited for guidance on whether or how they should prepare for war, but none came, so the commanding officer devised his own jungle-warfare training programme. Neither he nor anyone else knew how they would put it into action since the war plans that emanated sporadically from high command kept changing, each one contradicting the last.

In August 1941 Peter arrived in Malaya, one of a few 'first-class ECOs' (emergency commissioned officers), as the battalion newsletter referred to them, sent to replace experienced officers, including Edward, who had been posted elsewhere. He had returned to India at the end of 1940 to attend a six-month course at the Indian Army's Staff College at Quetta. So Peter would have no older brother looking out for him after all.

Attending Staff College marked out a young officer as someone destined for leadership and prepared him for how an army headquarters worked, how strategy was formed and filtered through the ranks – how, in short, to make war. Edward's early army career had been filled with promise and praise. He was efficient, capable, liked by his superiors and subordinates. He was polite without being oleaginous, approachable but not a pushover. He became lifelong friends with his brother officers and even former commanding officers, who all wrote him warm, affectionate letters, praising his loyalty, friendship and courage – as well as alluding to his love of a good time: 'What a party when we meet,' wrote one.

So Edward, like Walter, seemed destined to do well. In peacetime promotion was often slow to materialise, depending on older officers retiring and vacating the higher ranks in a regiment. But with the Indian Army undergoing a rapid expansion to meet the demands of war, regiments adding extra battalions requiring more men and officers, the prospects of promotion and leading his men in battle, the dream of every ambitious officer, had dramatically improved.

The six-month course at Quetta meant that he and Tiggy could live together after his absence in Malaya. It was a happy interlude. For the first six years of their marriage, Edward and Tiggy had been childless but at the end of 1940 Tiggy learned that she was pregnant. She later said that they had waited so long because Edward did not want children, but either he changed his mind or there was a happy 'accident'. In July 1941 she had her first child, Nicholas.

Edward was not there for the birth. A month earlier, he had been posted to the other side of India to take up the first of a series of staff jobs that would keep him in India for the next three years, and Tiggy was on her own when she went into labour. She had gone to the cinema to escape the summer heat within its cool confines when her contractions began. She managed to stagger outside to hail a tonga - a horse-drawn carriage - to take her to the military hospital, an uncomfortable and mildly terrifying journey to undertake on her own.

Tiggy had not made many friends among the other army wives. She had little in common with them: most came from conservative back-grounds, and if they had political opinions they kept them to themselves. Tiggy, by contrast, did not shrink from sharing her views, which were liberal bordering on subversive regarding the army and the Empire. She openly sympathised with the Indian independence movement, an unpopu-lar stance to take at army dinner parties, and delighted in stirring things up. She learned Urdu, which was viewed as extraordinary since most wives only learned enough to be able to issue orders to their servants. She preferred painting to watching polo and disliked the stifling dinner parties at which the men talked shop in acronyms while the wives made small-talk and what she called the 'narrow Raj atmosphere' of the army community, in which she now found herself adrift, held sway. She yearned for the liberal circles in which her family had moved in Shanghai and Hong Kong.

She must have envied her older sister, Prudie, who was living a wild, bohemian life in London, working as a sculptor while sharing her bed with a series of lovers, both male and female, following the breakdown of her marriage. Tiggy, by contrast, was stuck in a strait-laced society, with few kindred spirits and her husband some nine hundred miles away.

Walter and Beryl were also living in Quetta as Walter, too, had been selected for the Staff College course. However, this was of little comfort to Tiggy since she and Walter did not see eye to eye. Her liberal views were anathema to him, and the two sisters-in-law were not close either, particularly since Beryl's disastrous stay with her and Edward in Lucknow.

While his brothers were being groomed for greatness - or, at least, promotion - Peter was finding his feet as a lowly second lieutenant amid swirling rumours of war. After the glorious vistas of Assam, the jungles and rubber plantations of northern Malaya must have felt dark and oppressive to him. Troops stationed there month after month complained of 'rubberitis', a feeling of gloom caused by the cloying heat and relentless green walls of vegetation that surrounded them, along with leeches, gargantuan centipedes and every variety of snake. The Punjabs were supposed to be training on new vehicles and weapons, but the vehicles never arrived and there was not enough ammunition for the weapons due to the pressing demands of the campaigns in North Africa and elsewhere. The fall of France meant that Britain was fighting major land campaigns that she had never expected to fight alone and which demanded more men, machinery and other supplies.

Also, now that the Mediterranean was effectively closed to Allied shipping, vessels had to take the long route around Africa, causing delays. It was a frustrating time for them all, particularly Peter, who was appointed motor transport officer (MTO), but with very little transport to organise.

In December 1941 Peter and 1/8th Punjabs, as part of 11th Indian Division, were stationed at a road junction near the small town of Jitra just twenty miles south of the Thai border, when Japanese aeroplanes were first spotted circling overhead. It was the best defensive position in northern Malaya, and the key to holding the country, but they had not had time to prepare adequate defences as they kept being diverted to train for an operation that would, it was hoped, stop the Japanese in their tracks. This was a planned pre-emptive strike across the border into neutral Thailand, to stop the Japanese invading from that direction. The key to the success of the attack was speed: it must be launched at least twenty-four hours before the Japanese offensive began. Operation Matador depended on decisiveness.

On 4 December Peter's battalion was put on four hours' notice that they would be sent into Thailand. But no one gave the order for Matador. A day or so later they were told to be ready to move at two hours' notice: Japanese warships had been spotted in the Gulf of Siam. On 7 December, with Japanese aircraft carriers bearing towards Pearl Harbor and warships spotted in the Gulf of Siam, General Arthur Percival, the most senior officer in Malaya, conferred with his superior, Brooke-Popham.

Brooke-Popham, known as 'Pop-off' due to his habit of dozing in meetings, dithered. He had permission from London to launch Operation Matador only if he was absolutely sure that the Japanese were about to invade. But what if the Japanese warships seen heading towards the Malayan and Thai coasts were merely pottering around, not invading? What if he was responsible for starting a war with Japan?

While he hesitated, on the Malaya–Thailand border the 1/8th Punjabs waited in pelting rain for the signal to move across the border. Still no order came. At 10.30 p.m. on the night of 7 December word came that Operation Matador was being put on hold. The commanders on the ground begged for an actual decision. Was it on or off? They could not keep thousands of men standing to indefinitely.

The men were hungry, short of rations and tormented by leeches and mosquitoes. As he waited in the rain, his clothes soaked, boots sodden and starting to disintegrate, Peter would have felt the mix of excitement and gut-twisting trepidation experienced by many soldiers when facing battle for the first time. How would he react under fire? Would he live up to the examples of his father and grandfather? He had hoped that Edward would be at his side if he went to war but Edward and Walter were both miles away in peaceful India. The irony that he, a tea-planter, was about to go into battle while his two brothers, professional soldiers, were nowhere near the fighting was not lost on him.

Hour after hour they stood to. Dawn came and went with no orders. Only at 1 p.m. on 8 December did Major General David Murray-Lyon, commander of 11th Indian Division, learn that Matador was cancelled, and further confusion ensued when the cancellation itself was cancelled, only for it to be definitively cancelled again the following day. A smaller-scale raid into Thailand was launched instead to harass and delay the enemy and destroy a key road, but they did not manage to advance quickly enough and had to withdraw hurriedly across the border, having failed in their objectives.

They were unaware as yet that, in the early hours of 8 December, the Japanese had begun bombing Singapore. Nor did they know about the attacks on Pearl Harbor and Hong Kong, or even that the Japanese were already landing on the beaches of Kota Bharu on Malaya's east coast and meeting fierce resistance from the troops of 8th Indian Infantry Brigade.

The governor of Singapore's reaction to the landings was a laconic

'Well, I suppose you'll shove the little men off.' It would not prove so easy. Despite a brave but confused defence, the beaches were lost to the Japanese. By 10 December the enemy had seized several vital airfields.

Now the men of 11th Division, many of them fresh recruits like Peter, some mere teenagers, barely trained and untested in battle, held in their hands the fate of northern Malaya, on which depended the fate of the rest of the country and Singapore. Everything hinged on their defence of Jitra.

It was a bleak day for the British. The warships *Prince of Wales* and *Repulse* were sunk off the east coast of Malaya with the loss of 1,200 lives, and the RAF were forced to evacuate Alor Star airfield eleven miles south of Jitra, which had been bombed by the Japanese. No one told 11th Indian Division about the evacuation, even though one of the main reasons for holding Jitra was to protect that airfield.

Peter and his companions prepared for a battle in a position that was obsolete, with defences that were only half built, thanks to all the time they had spent standing to for Matador. They hurriedly filled empty petrol cans with soil in place of sandbags.

Efforts to halt the Japanese north of Jitra had failed and at 8 p.m. on the night of 11 December the unmistakable rumble of tanks and trucks, and the gleam of headlights through the gloom, announced the arrival of a Japanese column. The night erupted with the clatter of machine-guns and the boom of artillery fire as the advance guard of 5th Japanese Division, battle-hardened veterans of the savage war in China, began pounding the forward positions. Throughout the night confusion reigned as 'jitter' parties of Japanese raided the British-Indian lines, sniping, throwing firecrackers and screaming to throw the defenders off balance. When day dawned on 12 December Japanese soldiers came running towards them, wielding samurai swords and yelling terrifying war-cries.

A counter-attack was launched in which two companies of 1/8th Punjabs advanced towards the Japanese lines, only to be hit by friendly fire from another Indian regiment, who had mistaken them for Japanese. They regrouped and tried again, but immediately ran into heavy machine-gun and mortar fire. The commanding officer, the adjutant, a captain and twenty-eight Punjabis were all killed, their bodies crumpling into the glutinous mud. Some of the survivors tried to recover their colonel's body and were also slaughtered. The fighting lasted all that day.

Men's rifles became clogged with mud and ammunition was running low. By the time evening came and Murray-Lyon was at last given permission to withdraw from Jitra, the 11th Division was a shadow of its former self and 1/8th Punjabs had been reduced from five companies to three.

The battalion had lost its colonel, a shattering blow to its morale and organisation, as well as two other officers, leaving them severely short of officers. The defeat of 11th Indian Division by a far smaller force, a mere battalion, was an ignominious blow. Jitra had been deemed crucial to the defence of Malaya. Its loss was little short of a catastrophe.

As the historian Compton MacKenzie relates, writing in 1951, the men of 11th Indian Division had now been without sleep for a week: 'Muddied by swamps, soaked by streams, the 11th Indian Division needed rest as few troops have needed rest. There were no troops available to relieve it, and so it was called on to continue fighting and withdrawing for another lethal month.'

Peter had had his baptism of battle. Almost all the vehicles had been lost at Jitra so his role as motor transport officer was obsolete and he was attached to whichever company was most in need of an extra officer.

They slogged southwards. They had no food, except what they could find in villages. The enemy harassed them, sniping from the trees, and the Subedar Major – lynchpin of the battalion - was wounded in the stomach when he ventured into a village seeking food. The Japanese threw him into the river to drown. His loss was, as the regimental history noted, 'a further blow to the already battered battalion.'

It rained almost incessantly, and whenever the skies cleared they were dotted with Japanese planes. There was no sign of the RAF – 'Rare As Fairies', the soldiers complained - but this was no fault of the pilots, whose elderly Blenheim and Buffalo planes had proved no match for the Japanese Zeros.

The retreat down the Malayan peninsula brought them to Gurun, another strong defensive position if only they had had enough time to construct defences before the enemy came. But time was not on their side and all they could do was string up some wire, before the Japanese attack began at 3 p.m. on 14 December, with a merciless onslaught of mortars, shells, tank fire and air support. Men were being torn apart in bloody showers and confusion reigned. No one had expected to be fighting against tanks – the notion that they could get through Malaya's mangrove swamps and jungle had been scoffed at – but the tanks had simply bypassed the jungle and headed for the rubber plantations, cruising down the wide rows between the trees.

Night fell. In the darkness the Japanese managed to penetrate the positions of 6th Brigade, overrunning 1/8th Punjabs and their companions, the 2nd East Surrey Regiment. As the milky light of dawn filtered through the trees, they were down to their last ten rounds. Brigade Headquarters had been overrun and everyone in it killed, except the brigadier, who had managed to escape out of a window. The brigadier, Billy Lay, had been an impressive figure the day before, leading his men in a bold counter-attack, his pipe in his mouth. But now his reserves of courage seemed to have run dry, and he appeared panicky, swigging whisky from a hip flask, issuing wild orders. It was, wrote a survivor, Lieutenant George Chippington of the 1st Leicesters, in his memoir, too much like the last war, 'where generals covered in medals recklessly squandered brave men's lives'.

In pouring rain and jungle that tore their clothes to shreds it was difficult for the men of 11th Division to stick together. Some officers and men of 1/8th Punjabs became separated from the rest but managed to get to the coast and commandeer boats to the island of Penang, only to find that it had been abandoned by the British overnight, leaving the non-European residents to their fate at the hands of the Japanese.

The battalion history is a little unclear as to what happened next. A number of 1/8th Punjabs who had reached Penang remained there and were later taken prisoner by the Japanese. Others escaped by commandeering boats south, among them Captain Douglas Finlayson, a regular officer. Many years later Finlayson told his story to an interviewer from the Imperial War Museum, explaining that because he could sail he was given a boat and told to head south, then send boats back to Penang to take the rest of the men off the island and to Malaya's mainland to rejoin the fighting.

Finlayson and three East Surrey officers duly set sail, navigating with the aid of an AA road map. They landed in southern Malaya, reported to a reinforcements camp and were assigned to new units with whom they would continue fighting. Finlayson seemed certain that he had done his duty and followed orders and it is hard, hearing his account, to disagree.

But Peter felt that some of the regular officers had simply disappeared, while he and the remaining men of 1/8th Punjabs, along with other footsore, depleted battalions, were left to continue their retreat southwards, their boots disintegrating with their morale.

Eventually, hungry and exhausted, they reached the town of Kampar, where they joined another depleted battalion to form 1st Indian Infantry Battalion. It was a good defensive spot, atop a jungle-clad hill, and they were ordered to hold it at all costs. On 1 January 1942 the Japanese attacked. The men of 11th Indian Division had fought superbly with consummate bravery and endurance, holding off repeated attacks. The following day Captain John Graham of the 1/8th Punjabs led one company in an attack on Japanese positions, charging up the hill until a mortar blew his legs off below the knee. Kneeling on the shattered, bleeding stumps, he continued to urge his men on until he passed out from loss of blood. He died forty-eight hours later. Although the attack had succeeded, in the end the battle was lost. The Japanese, with their fresh troops and air support, could not be budged. Captain Graham was recommended for a Victoria Cross but it was not awarded, perhaps because the army did not like drawing attention to defeats.

It was the last major battle of the war for 1/8th Punjabs although there were other small bloody actions over the coming weeks. The Japanese history of the Malayan campaign states that they fought ninety-two battles: most of those actions were fought by the men of 11th Indian Division, to which Peter belonged.

Peter did not merit a mention in the history books, or even in the battalion's own account. He had not led a company into action or undertaken the kind of brave, battle-changing act that wins medals, or if he had there was no one to bear witness to it. But he had fought and had survived, and was the only British officer to serve with the battalion the whole way down the mainland of Malaya.

By the end of January there were just 150 men of 1/8th Punjabs left. Nearly three-quarters of their number had been killed, wounded or were absent. But Singapore was in sight: their five-hundred-mile retreat was over.

On the night of 30 January 1942 they crossed the Johore Strait, the narrow strip of sea separating mainland Malaya from the island of

Singapore. 1/8th Punjabs were acting as rearguard for the brigade and were in 'close contact' with the enemy, a military euphemism that fails to convey the brutal reality of grenades blowing men's feet off and bullets tearing into flesh, but they managed to get across the narrow causeway linking Malaya's mainland to Singapore before the engineers blew it up in an attempt to delay the Japanese. (In fact, the demolition was only partially successful and it was rapidly repaired by Japanese engineers.)

The Japanese Army had pushed the Allies off the Malayan mainland, wiped out their air force, destroyed the Royal Navy's best and biggest warships and overturned all the complacent predictions about shortsighted Japanese pilots and incompetent soldiers. And now here they were, having taken the whole of Malaya in a mere fifty-five days, a few miles from Singapore Island. The British had dubbed it Fortress Singapore because of its supposedly impregnable defences. These were about to be put to the test.

In Devon, Arthur and Dorothea read the news from Malaya with increasing consternation. Optimistic headlines claimed that the British were 'turning the tide' and that the 'Japanese joyride' down Malaya was slowing, thanks to the arrival of fresh troops to relieve weary, depleted regiments such as Peter's.

But anyone with a map could see how bad things really were, how every battle report came from further south than the last as the British were pushed steadily down the peninsula. Among the more optimistic tales of dogged defence and bold counter-strikes, reports of Japanese bombers 'screaming down from the skies' and 'mercilessly dive-bombing and machine-gunning our troops, supply convoys and communications' made chilling reading for anyone with a son or sweetheart in Malaya.

If the defenders of Malaya hoped to find some kind of sanctuary in 'Fortress' Singapore, with pillboxes and gun emplacements, bunkers, trenches and minefields, they were sorely disappointed.

For weeks the chief engineer of Malaya Command had been desperate to get on with building up defences on Singapore's northern shore. But his pleas had fallen on deaf ears. It would, he was told, be bad for civilian morale if they were seen to be preparing for an attack on Singapore. Besides, there was not enough civilian labour to build defences: all the available labourers were needed to repair the craters on the aerodromes caused by Japanese bombing, and to help in the docks of Keppel Harbour on the island's southern tip. So the beaches of the north coast had remained pristine, their white sand unsullied by pillboxes, searchlights, barbed wire or any other hindrance to an invading force.

On 20 January, Winston Churchill had sent a strongly worded signal: 'I want to make it absolutely clear that I expect every inch of ground to be defended, every scrap of material or defence to be blown to pieces to prevent capture by the enemy, and no question of surrender to be entertained until after protracted fighting among the ruins of Singapore city.'

This was all very well, but the streets of Singapore were now thronged with a civilian population of more than a million, doubled from its peacetime size by refugees from Malaya. A fight to the death would result in horrific civilian casualties. Moreover, the island had a limited water supply in the form of three reservoirs. If the enemy captured or destroyed these, neither military nor civilians could hold out for long.

Most civilians remained ignorant of this, and were optimistic that their 'Fortress' could withstand a siege, thanks to the 'impregnable' naval base at Sembawang on the north-east of the island, built at a cost of £60 million.

But now, in accordance with the scorched-earth policy, the naval base was already being destroyed by the British troops, its oil dumps set alight to deny them to the Japanese, sending vast black columns of smoke into the air that hung ominously over the island. The rationale for withdrawing what remained of the army to Singapore was to defend this base. So why was it happening if the base no longer existed? No one could answer that.

Still, General Percival made hurried plans to defend the island, with its seventy miles of coast along which the Japanese could land at any point. He had 70,000 men at his disposal, compared with the 30,000 of his opposite number General Yamashita, now just across the strait in Malaya. But numbers were not everything. The Japanese had tanks and aircraft while Singapore's defenders had none: even the remaining Brewster Buffalo aeroplanes were withdrawn from Sembawang airfield. Aircraft had to be saved to fight another day but men, it seemed, were expendable.

And the men who had fought through Malaya were exhausted and demoralised, officers and soldiers being rapidly switched to bolster battalions that had been decimated, leaving soldiers to be commanded by men they scarcely knew. This was the case for Peter's battalion, 1/8th Punjabs. Since their commanding officer had been killed at Jitra, what seemed like a lifetime earlier, other officers had replaced him, only to be killed or injured in their turn. A new commanding officer, Lieutenant Colonel Johns, arrived from India with 450 fresh troops, tripling the battalion's numbers. But the new troops were young, many only teenagers. They had not completed their training and were bewildered to find themselves thrust onto the front line.

There was a brief respite of sorts while the Japanese made their preparations to cross the strait and begin their assault on Singapore. The island was now under siege, although the censors refused to allow journalists to use the word, insisting that they refer to it as a 'besiegement' instead.

While Percival and his senior officers tried to work out where and when the Japanese would make their attack on Singapore, Peter, with the other men of 1/8th Punjab, was sent to Sembawang airfield near the crucial but now abandoned naval base. They were told they would have fourteen days before the Japanese arrived in which to reorganise themselves, construct defences, build gun positions and roll out barbed wire, trying to make up for the neglect of the last fourteen years of Singapore's defences.

In the event, they had only a week. On 8 February the invasion began. Percival had guessed that they would attack the north-east coast but the main thrust was on the north-west coast, beginning with a ferocious artillery barrage from across the strait in the morning, followed that night by a seaborne attack. The siege of Singapore was over. The battle had begun.

There is still an air base at Sembawang today. Surrounded by a high fence topped with rolls of barbed wire and a sign saying, 'Unauthorised Access Prohibited', its stern tone was somewhat undermined, when I visited, by a kingfisher perched on it.

It was hard to imagine the scene in February 1942, with mortars screaming, the air black with soot from the burning oil tanks of the naval base, men yelling in pain. With soldiers from the crack Japanese Imperial Guards Division just yards away, the Punjabs' casualties mounted. They lost their CO when he went to hospital with a sprained ankle –

perhaps Peter had him in mind, too, when he complained about senior officers deserting their men. If Captain Graham could fight on with bleeding stumps, could Lieutenant Colonel Johns not bandage his ankle and stay with them?

He was replaced by a major from another regiment but he was almost immediately hit by mortar fire. Another commanding officer was urgently needed, one who could rally the men. Peter was still a mere second lieutenant but he had two months of solid combat experience under his belt and knew the survivors of the Malayan battles well.

But he was not chosen. Instead an Indian officer, Lieutenant Tehl Singh, who had only just arrived in Singapore, was rapidly promoted to commanding officer. Not everyone was sure that this was a good idea. No one really knew him. Could his loyalty be assured? In other battalions some Indian officers and soldiers had deserted their units and joined a number of Indian prisoners of war who had been captured earlier in the campaign by the Japanese and persuaded to join a fighting force that became the Indian National Army. They believed that the INA would play an important role in liberating India from British rule, but the Japanese seem to have seen it largely as a propaganda tool.

Some of those soldiers were now in Singapore, enticing other Indians to leave the British side and join them. The following day, 12 February, the doubters seemed to have been proved right when Lieutenant Singh disappeared.

Another CO was hastily appointed: Douglas Finlayson, who had arrived in Singapore with 18th Division. Peter's feelings at being placed under the command first of the absconding Singh, then of a man whom he greatly disliked, must have been mixed at best. Finlayson had little time to rally his men before they were ordered into battle.

Perhaps it is understandable that, jittery after days of being shattered by shells and mortars, their commanding officers disappearing one after another, the frightened young soldiers of 1/8th, half trained, ill-equipped and utterly confused, had no stomach for battle. On 11 February, the regiment had retreated without being ordered to. The next day, with fear rippling through the ranks, three of the five companies turned and fled.

Those companies of 1/8th Punjabs were not the only ones to retreat without orders. Some units, feeling abandoned or buckling under the strain of constant battle, pulled back without orders, and there were reports of panicky troops deserting. Equally there were many instances of great bravery, by the regular army and local volunteer forces, of units that fought to the death. But General Percival failed to co-ordinate these disparate operations and, after the major defensive line that lay between the enemy and Singapore city was breached, the island was as good as lost.

On 10 February Churchill had sent another strongly worded telegraph, urging, 'The battle must be fought to the bitter end at all costs . . . The honour of the British Empire and the British Army is at stake.' Percival echoed him on 11 February, warning his army, 'It will be a lasting disgrace if we are defeated by an army of clever gangsters, many times inferior in numbers to our own.'

But Percival's words could not change the reality, which was that his counter-attacks had failed, and on 12 February he ordered a general retreat. All over the island, rubber and tin factories were set on fire to deny them to the Japanese. The acrid smell of burning rubber hung in the air as, on 13 February, General Percival held a conference with his senior commanders in his underground bunker at Fort Canning, in downtown Singapore.

With stocks of ammunition dwindling and the water supply about to fail – so many pipes had been shattered by shell – it was obvious that they could not hold out much longer. Percival had on his conscience the million civilians who had taken refuge in the crowded city. If he fought on, and the city was eventually overrun, how many would be killed or massacred in the bitter street fighting that would ensue?

In places the Japanese had overrun, massacres were already occurring. At the Alexandra Barracks Hospital, Japanese soldiers had bayoneted patients lying in their beds and the doctors who had tried to protect them. In all, 320 men and a female nurse were murdered. It was the first of many massacres on Singapore. Estimates vary wildly, but between 6,000 and 50,000 Singapore Chinese would be rounded up, beheaded or shot in the terror unleashed by the Japanese after the surrender, which was named 'soo ching' – 'purification by elimination'.

Discussions continued in the bunker, Percival arguing for a counter-attack and his subordinate officers pointing out that, with insufficient petrol, water, food and ammunition, victory was impossible.

The *Straits Times*, the Singapore newspaper that had now been taken over by the government, was still maintaining that 'Singapore must stand;

it SHALL stand' on its masthead as, on Sunday, 15 February, Percival bowed to the inevitable and, with his staff officers, walked up the hill to General Yamashita's headquarters bearing a white flag. The Australian commander General Gordon Bennett decided not to join his men in captivity but escaped Singapore by boat, later justifying this on the grounds that his skill and experience would be needed for future battles. His abandoned countrymen nicknamed their running shoes Gordon Bennetts.

An eerie silence fell over the city. In a few pockets inland, resistance continued as news of the surrender had not yet reached them. But at last the guns were quiet. The Fortress had fallen. It was, in Churchill's words, the 'worst disaster and largest capitulation in British history'. For Peter, and 130,000 other men taken prisoner in Singapore and during the course of the Malaya campaign, it was the beginning of their descent into Hell.

8

'Jolly sporting of them not
to shoot us up in the water!'

———◆———

ACROSS THE SOUTH China Sea, on the island of Borneo, another Japanese conquest had already reached its bloody climax.

The British government had undertaken in a treaty to defend Sarawak from foreign enemies, but the all-consuming needs of the war in Europe and Africa meant that only one battalion - a mere 600 men of 2/15th Punjab regiment - could be spared.

The Japanese had had their eye on north Borneo for years, coveting its abundant timber, rubber and oilfields. Sarawak, with its strategically important position in the South China Sea and governed, as they saw it, by a decadent lot of pink-gin-swilling British, with a mere handful of regular soldiers supplemented by local forces and volunteers, seemed a soft target.

Despite the British government's pledge to defend Sarawak, it had little chance of repelling a Japanese invasion with its small garrison and no air force or navy. As war began to look ever more likely, the rajah, Vyner Brooke, liquidated his personal holdings in the country and proceeded to Australia, via Malaya, on 'leave', deserting his people to face the Japanese without him. The rajah never got over the shame of having abandoned his kingdom in its hour of need. He made a belated attempt to return, but it came to nothing.

Meanwhile, in London his wife, the sex-obsessed Ranee Sylvia, concocted a harebrained plan to liberate Sarawak with a 'little band of men', which came to the attention of MI5. But, like Vyner's schemes, it amounted to nothing.

Coincidentally, John Fisher was also in Australia on leave when the news came through that the Japanese had landed on Sarawak on 16 December 1941. Three days later Japanese aeroplanes bombed Kuching, the planes diving low to machine-gun its terrified people as they ran for safety. On 24 December a strong Japanese invasion force seized Kuching and, after putting up a fierce fight, the garrison withdrew and made for the border with Dutch Borneo – the island was divided between the Dutch and the British.

Some civilians, including women and children, had also made the arduous trek south through the jungle to Dutch Borneo, but the Japanese were steadily closing in on them.

There were a number of Sarawak officials in Australia and they formed a government in exile. They began planning to rescue the refugees before the Japanese could get to them and even to mount guerrilla operations against the Japanese in Borneo. It would be a risky undertaking as by now Japanese warships, aircraft carriers and submarines were infesting the seas around the island and had even seized an airfield on its east coast. Nonetheless John and three other Sarawak officers volunteered for the mission, which was approved by General (later Field Marshal) Archibald Wavell, the Allies' commander-in-chief in South East Asia and India.

On 30 January they set off from Darwin on Australia's north coast in a Catalina seaplane belonging to Qantas Empire Airways. The flying boat, named Corio, was flown by Aubrey Koch, an experienced RAF-trained pilot. It carried thirteen passengers and five crew, and was scheduled to make its first landing at Koepang, on the western tip of Dutch Timor, before heading on to Borneo. Koch was careful to fly low, just 500 feet above the sea, hoping to avoid detection by any Japanese in the vicinity. It seemed that he had succeeded as he began to prepare for landing thirty-five miles from Koepang (now Kupang).

But then there was an unexpected noise. One of the crew, First Officer Victor Lyne, described hearing a 'rat-tat-tat . . . I wondered if something was wrong with the motor, but was not kept guessing long, because I saw tracer bullets flying past in front of the cockpit. We were still about fifteen miles from land.' Bullets were hitting the Corio's thin fuselage, ripping it and hitting the passengers and crew. Some slumped to the floor, instantly dead; others cried out in pain.

With several of his passengers and crew hit and bleeding, Koch worked desperately to keep his stricken craft airborne. He flew lower, zigzagging to try to evade the swarm of Japanese Zeros, seven of them now, diving and mobbing him. With no means of defending himself, Koch's only hope was to evade them by twisting and turning. He flew lower still, just skimming the tops of the waves, to try to shake off the Zeros and save his plane and passengers. Extraordinarily, he was performing these aerial acrobatics, swerving and diving frantically while bleeding freely from his left arm and leg where machine-gun bullets had torn into him. They were very close to land now, a mere four miles away. It seemed they might make it. But then one of the bullets must have hit a fuel tank as flames began to engulf not one but two engines. Koch realised he had no choice but to land his craft in the sea. Just as he was coming in to land, a huge wave appeared before the plane's nose. Koch tried to bring it up but the elevating equipment had been shot away, meaning it was unable to rise.

With a thunderous noise, the wounded Catalina struck the water nose first and broke into pieces. The wings were torn off and the body of the plane was wrenched in two, the tail protruding from the water. Koch and Lyne were flung from the cockpit. Other passengers were thrown clear of the cabin, but not all. Some survivors surfaced near the wreckage and grabbed mailbags to help them stay afloat. John Fisher had been hit in the hand and was bleeding from a bullet hole in one finger and from a gash in the back of his head. He also had two broken ribs.

As they swam about the wreckage, trying to find bits of debris to cling to that were not on fire, an ominous buzzing heralded the return of the Japanese Zeros, seemingly to finish off the survivors. As they dived low over the wreckage, the men in the water waited for the clatter of machine-gun bullets. But it did not come.

John turned to Koch, who now had a broken leg in addition to his other injuries, and was treading water nearby. 'Jolly sporting of them not to shoot us up in the water!' he remarked jovially, as if they were playing in a Sunday cricket match, rather than fighting for their lives.

They began striking out for shore but John quickly lost sight of the others. Hour upon hour they swam under the blistering sun, skin peeling, throats parched. After several weary hours, four men - Koch, Lyne, a Tasmanian named Westbrooke and another Sarawak civil servant, Moore - reached the shore. They waited, but no one else appeared. Several other people had survived the bullets and the impact of the crash and were last seen clinging to wreckage or mailbags. But now there was no sign of them. John Fisher was among those who seemed to have disappeared.

They had come ashore on the island of Pulau Menipo, across a narrow strait from Dutch Timor and apparently uninhabited. With its white sand and palm trees it might have been idyllic under other circumstances. Would anyone find them? And, if they did, would their rescuers be friend or foe?

After resting for a while, Moore began to walk along the beach in search of other survivors. He walked for more than a mile, maybe two, but could find no one. Despondent, he turned back. It was on his return journey that he heard something. Investigating, he found John Fisher lying on the sand. John had seen Moore go past and had tried to shout, but after several hours in the sea his throat was so dry and hoarse with salt that he could not make a sound. He was weak and in pain but still in good spirits. A shark had accompanied him during his four-hour swim to shore but, despite his wounds, it had refrained from attacking him. Finally, he was within yards of the shore and could almost feel the sand beneath his feet when a big wave took him back out to sea again.

Another man might have given up then, but John Fisher possessed almost superhuman optimism and determination. He set out once more, keeping his eyes on the shore. The agony of swimming with broken bones and throbbing, bleeding wounds can only be imagined but eventually he stumbled up the beach, collapsing in the shade of some palms. It was there that Moore found him, exhausted, his skin raw.

They were reunited and alive, but they had no means of summoning help, and although Moore and Westbrooke explored the small island, just 700 metres wide, they could find no source of water or food. Would they die, slowly, under the blistering sun, of heat, thirst and hunger? That first night the tropical rain came to their rescue and they were able to suck the water from the leaves of plants to slake their parched throats. At some point during his swim ashore, John had come across a mailbag that contained, among other things, aspirin tablets. They were undamaged by the seawater so they crushed them up and put them on their wounds, although as aspirin hinders rather than helps healing this was probably not very beneficial.

They stayed on the island for three nights, digging holes in the sand to sleep in at night while Moore and Westbrooke, who were uninjured, swam to Dutch Timor. After swimming across an alligator-infested river, Moore, helped by villagers, managed to reach Koepang. There the governor, after hearing his incredible tale, arranged for the Dutch air force to rescue his companions.

John Fisher was asked by an Australian reporter for his reaction when he saw the Dutch seaplane coming to rescue them. In the best British tradition of understatement, he responded, 'I'm afraid I thought in terms of Melbourne beer.'

After eight days in a Dutch hospital recovering from his injuries, John arrived back in Australia, along with the other survivors, and was admitted to hospital in Perth, suffering from flu brought on by his ordeal.

On 18 February 1942, little more than two weeks after the Catalina air crash, the Perth edition of the *Sydney Sun* newspaper reported that a wedding, due to take place that day in the Perth suburb of Claremont, had had to be postponed as the groom was ill with influenza. The groom was John Fisher, the bride the beautiful Baroness Isabella van Lawick, widow of a Dutch pilot from Surabaya, Java, whose plane had been lost over the sea some months earlier.

According to the newspaper report, John and Isabella had met on the boat to Australia, John travelling from Sarawak, Isabella from Surabaya with her two young sons, Hugo and Godert. Her husband had told her that if anything were to happen to him she should leave Surabaya as he feared that a Japanese invasion was imminent.

The wedding eventually took place on 28 February 1942 in the Perth suburb of Cottesloe, after John was discharged from hospital. The bride wore a simple short white dress, and the groom's best man was another Sarawak officer.

Ruth gave me a slightly different version of events, telling me that John had married Isabella to get her out of Java and that he had told her that, as he had a fiancée - Ruth - back in England, they would have to divorce after the war so that he could marry her. However, Isabella's son Godert, and the Perth newspapers, report that in fact it was a marriage born of love, not necessity. There was no need for any mercy-marriage to rescue Isabella from Java as she had already left when they met, and a marriage certificate was neither here nor there when it came to being evacuated.

Although Ruth preferred not to talk about emotion it is clear that, in the words of her son, John Fisher's marriage to Isabella 'broke her heart'. In her narrative, this heartbreak was mitigated by the fact that John still intended to marry her some day.

John and Isabella did not remain in Australia for long. The Japanese had begun bombing Darwin and other towns along Australia's northern coast, and there were fears that they would invade soon. Even Britain, now that the Blitz was over, seemed safer and, besides, John had no intention of sitting out the war in Australia as a civilian. He made up his mind to return to Britain and join the forces.

Following the abortive mission to Borneo, the civilians they had hoped to rescue remained trapped there. Some who had trekked to Dutch Borneo were murdered by Dayaks, while a party of men, women and children made it to the remote hill station of Long Nawang, where they were joined over several months by downed Dutch airmen and local military forces, swelling their numbers to around ninety Europeans and thirty-five Borneans. Then, in August 1942, a company of Japanese marines arrived, taking them by surprise. They executed the military refugees but left the women and children alive. Then, a month later, they, too, were put to death in the most sadistic way possible.

A witness from the Kenyah tribe saw what happened. The children were forced to climb up tall palm trees while the Japanese waited below with bayonets upturned. The children clung to the trees for as long as they could but eventually, exhaustion – or the Japanese shaking the trees – made their hands slip and they fell. They were impaled on the waiting bayonets. According to Ruth, who heard the story some years later, the mothers were made to watch their children suffer this horrific death. One woman was even forced to laugh and clap.

Had John succeeded in making it to Borneo, there was a good chance that he would not have made it out again and ended up executed, or at best imprisoned in appalling conditions in a Japanese internment camp, only to be killed later. Being shot down turned out to have been a bit of good fortune.

He hoped his luck would hold again when, in May 1942, he and Isabella sailed for England, taking their chances with Japanese and German submarines. Despite being followed by a U-boat at one point, the captain managed to shake it off and they arrived safely in England, one of the few ships to get through such dangerous waters without being torpedoed.

They docked in Liverpool on 7 June and made their way to Tiverton, where John introduced his new wife and two small stepsons to his mother. Having installed them in a house near his mother's, he reported to the nearest army recruiting office, signing on as a soldier with the Royal Army Service Corps.

Ruth was working at Hydestile hospital in Surrey, a hutted hospital that had become the major outpost for St Thomas's. Her reports describe her as reliable and conscientious, showing 'marked powers of leadership and teaching'. If she had learned of John's marriage she did a good job of hiding her feelings.

She at least had her parents nearby in Weybridge. Dorothea was working as a supervisor in the Vickers aeroplane factory, and was thrilled to be bringing home a pay packet for the first time in her life. But she and Arthur were deeply worried about Peter. They had heard nothing from him since the fall of Singapore and had no idea whether he was dead or alive.

Bee, at least, was in a happier frame of mind. She was in love. Earlier that year she had met an American working for the RAF in London. Elisha Gaddis Plum, known as Gaddis, was fourteen years older than Bee and a veteran of the Great War. He had joined the Royal Flying Corps (forerunner of the RAF) in 1918 after his application to join the America Air Service was rejected. Although not a natural pilot – he struggled to master the art of landing during training – Gaddis acquitted himself well in France, flying low over German lines to observe their artillery and later dropping supplies of ammunition to advancing troops. Sometimes he flew only a hundred feet above ground, under German artillery fire, until he could be sure of what the enemy's intentions were and report them to Headquarters. It was vital but relentless, dangerous work, although he was given spells of leave, which he spent with friends in the Monmouthshire countryside. It was there that he fell in love with Britain.

Back in France, the exhausting, perilous nature of his work took its toll on Gaddis: friends noticed that his usual ebullience and bonhomie were being sapped and he was starting to look gaunt and worn, but he had to keep going. On 10 November 1918 he was nearly brought down by German sniper fire near Carnières but managed to get back to his own lines. The following day, the Armistice was declared. Gaddis's luck and skill had enabled him to survive 'the war to end all wars.' He returned to New Jersey, where his family ran a printing and stationery firm and lived in some splendour in a twenty-five-room mansion. By 1940 he had taken over the paper firm and was involved in several other businesses. Since his father's death he had become head of the family but, at forty-two, was still a bachelor.

As a lifelong Anglophile, he was worried by what was happening across the Atlantic. Even though America had not joined the fight against Germany, he felt compelled to offer his services again. The Battle of Britain had not yet begun but it was clear that the war in the air would require an endless supply of pilots. Thousands of American citizens served with either the RAF or the Royal Canadian Air Force in the Second World War, a few, like Gaddis, veterans of the First World War. Because America was neutral they had to be smuggled to Britain via Canada and even forfeited their American citizenship (Congress issued them a blanket pardon in 1944), yet they made this sacrifice to help the British in their hour of need long before America entered the war.

At his own expense, Gaddis travelled across the dangerous waters of the Atlantic, sending his London friends a cable: 'AM COMING TO HELP COMPLETE THE JOB WE EVIDENTLY FAILED TO FINISH BEFORE STOP'. Aware that he might be too old to reprise his role as pilot, he planned to enlist as a gunner but, to his disappointment, he failed his RAF medical as his hearing was not good enough. A desk rather than a cockpit beckoned.

He was too ebullient to lick his wounds for long, and soon put his charm and business contacts to good use at the RAF's Equipment Branch in the Air Ministry in London. After America entered the war, following the Japanese attack on Pearl Harbor, those Americans who had enlisted in the British forces were given the option of transferring to the American forces but Gaddis preferred to stay with the RAF.

It may have been at the Air Ministry that he met Bee. She left no clues as to how she had spent the early years of the war. Her daughter, Mary, died some years ago and her son, Peter, said that she told several different tales about her war. She had mentioned being at Bletchley, the famous code-breaking station, but although Bletchley Park Roll of Honour does indeed include a Beatrice Mary Walker, it was not Bee but a namesake. She may have mixed up the war with her schooldays, when she did indeed go to Bletchley station, but the railway station rather than Station X, the Government Code and Cypher School.

She did mention that she had done some office work after leaving Norman Hartnell but was sacked because she was, as she confessed, 'hopeless'. In early 1941 all women who did not have dependants had to register for war work, and conscription of unmarried women aged twenty to thirty began in December that year. They had to choose between joining the services and working in industry. Wearing a hairnet and overalls in an ammunition factory was hardly Bee's style, so an office job certainly sounds more likely, possibly at the Air Ministry as a clerk or secretary: one version of events has it that she and Gaddis met at work.

Perhaps he was captivated by the bubbly, pretty girl with wondrous legs and an ineptitude for filing. For Bee, Gaddis clearly had something that none of her boyfriends or discarded fiancés had offered. Fourteen years older, he had sophistication, experience and wealth: Bee had always liked the finer things in life. Amid the grimness of blacked-out London, Gaddis must have seemed like a breath of fresh Atlantic air. In May 1942 they became engaged and three months later they married.

Thursday, 2 July was a dry, windy day. In Downing Street Winston Churchill was, once again, preparing to face down his enemies in the House of Commons. Britain had suffered a series of defeats in Asia and North Africa, with the loss of 50,000 men in the desert as casualties and prisoners, prompting the Conservative MPs Sir John Wardlaw-Milne and Roger Keyes, who was an admiral and former ally of Churchill, as well as the Liberal Sir Leslie Hore-Belisha, to propose a motion of no confidence in the embattled prime minister. The situation was not as desperate as it had been during his 'Darkest Hour' of 1940 but, as Churchill acknowledged in his own history of the war, the picture appeared bleak, or at least uncertain. 'All hung in the balance and after the surprising reverses we had sustained . . . who would predict how the scales would turn?'

Churchill's critics, including Labour's Aneurin Bevan, furiously attacked his handling of the war. Even Singapore, that supposedly inviolable fortress, the door to the whole of the east, had fallen. Churchill had made the crucial decisions. Now he would have to answer for them. 'We are at this moment in the presence of a recession of our hopes and prospects in the Middle East and in the Mediterranean unequalled since the fall of France,' he told the House.

And yet there were glimmers of hope. The German Navy had been defeated and eighty-five per cent of convoys were now crossing the Atlantic unscathed. Factory production had been stepped up: munitions and other war materiel were being produced at a phenomenal rate, while the tide was about to turn for the Allies in North Africa.

The MPs heeded Churchill's plea that they show their confidence in his government and voted by 475 votes to 25 against the motion of 'no confidence'. Not far from where Churchill was marshalling his famous oratorical powers, other preparations were taking place, just around the corner from the Savoy Hotel. The sixteenth-century King's Chapel of the Savoy (now the Queen's Chapel of the Savoy) is tucked discreetly away in a quiet courtyard just south of the Strand, a few yards but a world away from the noise and traffic of Waterloo Bridge. It is, and was, a private chapel of the sovereign and, under normal circumstances, only members of the Royal Victorian Order may, and could, marry there, unless they were parishioners. Bee and Gaddis fell into neither category but, as the current chaplain explained to me, his kindly wartime predecessor permitted couples to marry there even if they had no connection with it, allowing them to give a false local address in the register. Perhaps he felt that, since their married life might be all too brief, they should be allowed to begin it wherever they chose, and if that was in this serene yet splendid chapel, he would help them.

Why Bee and Gaddis chose it I do not know but the most likely reason is that it was a mere five-minute walk from the Air Ministry, meaning that Gaddis's colleagues could easily pop out to attend the service. None of his family could be there, of course, and many of hers were absent too. That was war.

Most brides look radiant but Bee was ravishingly beautiful. The pre-war Bee had a healthy, wholesome prettiness with her round cheeks and slim but sporty physique, as befitting the 'captain of games' she had been in her schooldays. Now, aged thirty-one, the apple cheeks of her Devon days had gone, revealing a mannequin's angular cheekbones, while age and rationing had transformed her figure from sporty to sylph-like.

She was no longer simply pretty but stunning in a floor-length bridal gown, an extravagantly scalloped couture creation, with a long bridal veil, a world away from the usual pictures of wartime brides wearing knee-length dresses or skirt suits, constrained as they were by clothes rationing: Bee had likely borrowed her dress from a pre-rationing bride. There had been no compromise on the engagement ring either: when Bee accepted Gaddis's proposal he had a family ring sent over from America, a ring so valuable that a representative of the Plum family had escorted it across the Atlantic, braving U-boats to do so.

Despite their gnawing worry over Peter's fate, everyone rose to the occasion, Dorothea and Arthur beaming for the cameras, and Ruth smiling on the arm of a portly RAF officer, one of Gaddis's colleagues. If any of the Walkers had had doubts about the wisdom of Bee marrying a much older man, an American at that, they were soon dispelled by Gaddis's jovial charm and his evident adoration of Bee. Although American servicemen had begun arriving in Britain earlier that year, there were still no more than a thousand in London. As yet they had not earned a reputation for being 'over-sexed, over-paid and over here'. In any case, Gaddis was no GI: he was a member of the British armed forces and a firm believer in the British Empire.

Dorothea had been worried about Bee's life in London. As far as she could make out, Bee ran with a racy set of friends, whose life revolved around nightclubs and parties. With Gaddis at her side, she would be exchanging the smoky clubs of Soho for domesticity. There would be no more broken engagements, no more uncertainty as to her future.

Bee would have financial security, too, thanks to the Plum family, and although Gaddis married in his RAF uniform, his desk job kept him safe from the kind of dangers faced by the poor, burned boys that Ruth had nursed at Park Prewett. Bee was unlikely to join the ranks of young war widows. All in all, it was an excellent match, and while Dorothea still viewed Walter's marriage with icy disapproval, she gave her whole-hearted blessing to Bee's.

9

'Never despair'

———————

WALTER WAS IN Quetta when he learned of Bee's marriage. He and Beryl were awaiting the birth of their first baby, due in September, and as Beryl's girth increased, the temperature edged steadily higher. Walter, by contrast, was thinner than ever, his already lean frame whittled by months of working under great strain. He, like Peter, had been involved in a fighting retreat.

In April 1942 his wish to fight against the Japanese, rather than the tribesmen of Waziristan, had at last been granted. He was posted to the staff of Major General Bill Slim, who had been tasked with trying to stem the inexorable Japanese advance in Burma.

Slim has been hailed as one of the greatest generals of all time: in 2013 he was voted the greatest British commander in history, jointly with the Duke of Wellington. But in April 1942 he was a little-known general fresh from the Middle East, stocky, square-jawed and from relatively humble origins; he had begun his military career as a private in the Territorial Army. Wounded and awarded the Military Cross in the Great War, he had served with the Gurkhas on the North West Frontier and, more recently, in the Middle East, rising to lieutenant general. He led from the front, was wounded again, and developed a well-deserved reputation for tenacity, aggression, strategic brilliance and resourcefulness – just the qualities required in a commander who would have to fight a campaign with both hands tied behind his back.

Bill Slim was plucked from relative obscurity to take command of an army already in retreat. Little thought had been given to defending Burma as it had been assumed that Singapore would be held and would protect it. But Singapore had fallen, leaving Burma weak, vulnerable and ready to fall too.

The Nationalist Chinese, under General Chiang Kai-shek, had been at war with the Japanese since 1937. They relied on military aid that came through Burma, along the Burma Road into south-west China. If the Japanese invasion cut this route, the Chinese Nationalist Army would be starved of supplies and the Japanese would be well placed to conquer the whole of China. Burma would also provide a buffer against any British counter-attack from India. An added bonus was the port of Rangoon (now Yangon), through which the Japanese could supply their armies in the region. And Burma was replete with vital natural resources from rice to teak, tungsten (a rare metal) and oil, all essential to keep their engine of war running. Conversely, if the British could keep Burma, they would deny these resources to the Japanese.

More ambitiously, if the Japanese conquered Burma it would also open up the gateway to India: the eventual goal was to invade India via Burma's north-west border into Assam. The Japanese anticipated that, once the Indians had seen the British defeated, they would rise up against them and help the Japanese bring down the Raj. 'Asia for the Asiatics' was the Japanese slogan, although it would soon ring hollow as the populations of Japanese-conquered territories discovered they had exchanged one lot of imperial masters for another, who would rule with terrible brutality.

This was the situation that Slim inherited: a British-led force was being out-manoeuvred, outflanked and pushed further and further back in retreat, only northwards rather than southwards, as had been the case in Malaya.

As in Malaya, the climate and terrain were against them. Slim described Burma as having 'some of the world's worst country, breeding the world's worst disease in the world's worst climate'. His headquarters lacked all the essentials that a headquarters relied on: wireless sets, signallers, stores, adequate transport and maps. Although he never appeared downcast he did admit to 'a sinking of the heart' as the grim reality of the situation became clear.

Slim commanded 1st Burma Corps, or Burcorps, as it swiftly became known. His immediate superior, General Harold Alexander, was in overall command of the Burma Army and was the chief strategist, but it was Slim who would fight the battles. His orders were to hold the capital, Rangoon, but by the time he landed in Burma, in March 1942, Rangoon had fallen. The only hope now was to hold northern Burma and preserve the army. Accordingly, Slim began withdrawing north, with thousands upon thousands of refugees.

When Walter arrived in Burma two weeks later, having made his way across India, he headed for Mandalay, where he hoped to get a lift on a convoy heading south to join Slim's headquarters. This was it: he was going to war, not for the first time since he had already been 'blooded' on the North West Frontier and had recently earned another mention in dispatches. But this would be different. He would be fighting against an enemy equipped with modern technology, not Victorian-era rifles, an enemy that had already defeated the Allies in Hong Kong, Borneo, the Philippines, the Dutch East Indies, Malaya and Singapore – from which there had been no news of Peter since the surrender.

Although as a staff officer (general staff officer grade 3) he would not be in the thick of the fighting, Walter would be in the army's nerve centre, observing command up close and playing a role in the vital decisions on which the fate of the army, and of Burma, pivoted. Slim would make the decisions, in consultation with his senior officers, but it was up to his staff to make sure that they happened, that bridges were blown, or built, that reinforcements were sent to the right position, that tanks and trucks had sufficient fuel – in short that the impulses travelled from the army's brain to the furthest extremities of its body.

Walter, impatient with the slow chugging of the train, grew further frustrated when it ground to a halt outside Mandalay and the guard could not explain why. He waited with increasing irritation, desperate not to miss the convoy. But when the train at last lurched forward and shuddered into the station, the reason for the delay became clear.

Mandalay was burning.

The Japanese had begun bombing the city in February but on 3 April, while Walter was restlessly sitting in the sidings, they had returned to drop incendiary bombs. In the ensuing firestorm, three-fifths of Mandalay's timber buildings were destroyed and two thousand of their inhabitants killed. The American journalist Clare Boothe Luce arrived two days later and wrote of the 'terrible stink' of the bodies that lay in the smouldering ruins and bobbed 'like rotten apples' in the still, green waters of the moat around Mandalay's fort.

Walter eventually caught up with Slim's headquarters on 16 April at the oilfields of Yenangyaung. The oil produced there was crucial to the

British war machine and would be equally helpful to that of the Japanese, so Slim had been ordered to defend them. But the day before Walter arrived Slim, realising he could no longer hold them, gave orders to destroy them. Cement was poured into the oil wells, machinery destroyed and stores of oil set alight, sending walls of flame five hundred feet tall soaring into the air, leaving baleful black clouds of smoke hanging, a toxic, choking canopy.

The headquarters consisted of a collection of trestle tables, notice-boards and trucks under a cluster of trees with some very harried-looking staff officers and, at its centre, Slim. With no air power and barely any intelligence available, Slim was stumbling in the dark, both metaphorically and literally: he had no way of knowing his enemy's intentions, and without the RAF he had to move at night or risk annihilation from the air. He was also constrained by the need for water. They were fighting in the dry-belt of Burma, in the dry season, with the temperature at 114 degrees. It was impossible to place troops too far from the few water sources available or their thirst would become incapacitating.

When Walter arrived he was immediately charged with helping to mount a counter-attack against the Japanese, who were trying to cut off Headquarters from the retreating troops. In the darkness and confusion, with almost no wirelesses to make contact with the troops, this was a tall order, but it succeeded.

They were not yet out of the woods. The Japanese were attempting to encircle Burma Division, one of Slim's two divisions, and its commander, General Scott, asked if he could break out under cover of darkness. His men were without water and if he waited they would be too weakened to fight. Slim ordered him to hang on a little longer while he tried to persuade his Chinese allies to mount an attack. It was a difficult, tense conversation, made harder because the two men were close friends whose children played together.

Emerging from his van, Slim prowled around Headquarters, seemingly sunk in thought. Walter was busy preparing orders for the coming action and Slim began studying the copy that was pinned to a board. Suddenly he frowned, strode over to Walter's table and exploded in fury. Walter, Slim pointed out, had failed to include the director of medical services in the distribution list. With battle imminent, that was an unforgivable error. Walter was utterly contrite and never forgot the lesson. Later, when instructing junior officers, he used this episode to illustrate the importance of attention to detail.

Burcorps managed to break out of Yenangyaung but many soldiers perished in the attack, some from enemy fire but others from thirst and heat exhaustion. Some of the wounded were piled on tanks but not all could be rescued. Some had to be left behind, and when an officer courageously returned to check on them he discovered that the Japanese had found them already. Every man had had his throat cut, or had been bayoneted. Elsewhere, men captured by the Japanese were hanged from trees and hacked to death.

Slim knew that holding on to any part of Burma was now impossible. All he could hope for was to preserve the remnants of his army to fight another day and delay the Japanese so that they would not reach India's border before the monsoon broke in May, when the paths through the mountainous border country into India would be all but impassable.

He would make no futile last stands since these could only result in Burcorps's annihilation. On 28 April, General Alexander ordered Burcorps's withdrawal to India, and on 30 April Mandalay was evacuated. At one minute before midnight, the road and rail bridge over the Irrawaddy was blown. The explosion, heard for many miles around, heralded the loss of Burma.

The withdrawal to India became the longest retreat in British military history, a harrowing exodus of a thousand miles through jungle, over mountains and across rivers. Vehicles became stuck in sand or swamps and had to be abandoned, rivers a mile wide had to be crossed without sufficient boats, and friendly Burmese villagers peacefully pushing bullock carts turned out to be Japanese soldiers in disguise with machine-guns hidden in the hay.

Most Burmese civilians were not villains but innocent victims of a war that had nothing to do with them. Entire villages, towns and cities were destroyed by Japanese bombers, their pretty houses collapsing like cards, their streets littered with the charred and bloated corpses of men, women and children who had had little idea what the fighting was about. And there were instances of villagers risking terrible reprisals from the Japanese to shelter stranded British soldiers.

Walter's primary role was to select a site for Headquarters every time they moved northwards, which was every couple of days. It was not easy: villages were too obvious, presenting an easy target for the Japanese Zeros. Trees provided good cover, but not small clusters of palms: jeep tracks could be seen leading to and from them. And the lack of maps, other than road maps, which did not feature contours, made it trickier still. So he would take a jeep and drive off into the unknown, hoping to encounter neither Japanese nor hostile locals. Usually he chose well, but on one occasion the Japanese took him by surprise, outflanking him by coming up the river in boats. A counter-attack had to be hastily mounted to prevent Headquarters being split from its army. Disaster was averted.

As they pressed on northwards the long, harrowing exodus from Burma took an appalling toll on men, mules and the 220,000 civilians who straggled along the same routes, children, the elderly and pregnant women among them. The majority were Indians who had settled in Burma at the instigation of the British and now had little option but to follow them out of the country. They clung to the army for protection from the enemy and from bandits, 'dacoits', who descended like carrion crows to prey upon these weakened, desperate people and any soldiers who became separated from their units, stabbing them to death.

Few provisions had been made for the exodus, particularly where the Indian refugees were concerned. With shocking discrimination, officials had established two different refugee routes, one for European and Anglo-Indians, another for Indians, which became known as the 'White and Black routes': the white route was shorter and easier, the black route a more arduous journey with fewer camps.

Staging posts along the way quickly became huge transit camps full of starving and desolate people, lacking food, water, medical care or the strength to bury their dead. Thousands perished from disease such as cholera and smallpox. Slim wrote of finding an Indian woman dying of smallpox at the side of a track, her tiny four-year-old son trying pathetically to feed her with milk. But despite his efforts she died and Slim and his staff persuaded another family to take the child on with them to India.

There had been an official evacuation by air, rail and road for European women and children, but not for Indians. (Some European families missed the official evacuation by air, rail and lorry and had to make their way on foot).

The governor of Burma attempted to defend the policy of prioritising European families on the grounds that if they were left behind they would likely become the victims of Japanese atrocities, as they had in Hong Kong, whereas the Japanese would be likely to treat fellow Asians decently. But this appalling apartheid left a bitter taste and consigned thousands of Indian refugees to a terrible ordeal, which many did not survive.

Some of the support staff attached to the army now deserted it, banded together into gangs and began looting, robbing and even murdering Burmese villagers.

The Japanese commander in Burma had been given his orders: to destroy Burcorps so completely that not a single soldier lived to return to India, while Slim was determined to bring out as many men alive as he could. One night in May, jitter parties of Japanese attacked Slim's headquarters. Their guard had mysteriously disappeared, so Walter and the rest of the staff had to stand to all night as the Japanese hurled grenades, screeched their war-cries and shouted taunts through the darkness.

At last the army crossed the Chindwin River, the last major river before the border with India. They had to leave behind hundreds of tanks, heavy guns and lorries that could not be transported across, along with the growing numbers of dead, too many to bury. One soldier asked how they would get from there to India. 'You walk, mate,' was the answer. 'You walk or you die.'

The last and final stretch of the trek into India led through the beautiful but formidable Kabaw Valley, a series of jungle-clad razor-sharp ridges and plunging ravines, each vertiginous descent followed by another painful ascent. On 12 May the monsoon broke, magnifying the misery of soldiers and civilians alike. Sheets of rain turned narrow paths into slippery quagmires along which they had to crawl, rather than risk sliding off the path and down the steep hillside to their deaths. Thorns tore and leeches fastened onto skin, blisters ballooned on swollen feet, while mosquitoes descended, bringing malaria. Chafed skin developed jungle sores. At night they lay down on the drenched earth, shivering with fever and cold, with nothing to cover them.

The only blessing was that the monsoon stopped the Japanese pursuit. They remained in Burma to survey the land that was now theirs and the spoils of war that the British had been forced to leave behind. It would take them a while to get the oil wells and other machinery working again, but it would be done.

Meanwhile soldiers and civilians stumbled and crawled onwards, past the bodies of refugees who had come the same way days or weeks earlier. Some had collapsed, never to rise again. Others had committed suicide and their bodies hung from trees, the smell of decomposition mixing sickeningly with the stench of excrement: dysentery and cholera were rife. Among the corpses were those of women clad in evening dresses and jewellery that they had worn rather than leave for the Japanese to find.

At last the survivors of Burcorps limped into India, gaunt, exhausted and malarial. Among Slim's staff, Walter was one of only half a dozen officers who were still on their feet. He no longer had his kit, which had disappeared somewhere along the Chindwin, with his Burmese batman. But he had his life.

Slim had saved his army from annihilation. More than thirteen thousand men had been lost, against four and a half thousand Japanese. But he had kept the army intact as a fighting force, and the morale of the fighting units remained high. Terrible as the retreat had been, they had reached what was, for now at least, a safe haven in India, unlike the army in which Peter had fought, which had nowhere left to retreat to once it had reached Singapore.

Walter was cheered to see a Gurkha battalion cross the border 'still marching in military formation and each man still carrying his rifle slung'.

Despite their extraordinary feat of endurance, no heroes' welcome awaited Burcorps in India. 'We thought we would be housed in clean, dry transit-camps to await leave,' wrote Walter, in his memoir fifty-five years later. 'This was not to be the case. Arriving at the frontier garrison town of Ranchi we were appalled to find the hospitals filled to overflowing and the comfortable transit-camps non-existent.'

The military establishment had done almost nothing to prepare for the arrival of thousands of sick, exhausted men. Instead, those who could still walk or limp were cursorily directed to camps on muddy slopes that already ran with excrement since the army units who had previously occupied them had not bothered to dig latrines. They were not even given tents, just rain sheets, inadequate protection against the ferocity of the monsoon.

Worse still was the attitude of certain Indian Army commanders towards the soldiers who had struggled out of Burma, behaving as if the defeat had been their fault, another ignominious disaster, like Singapore. It had not. They had succeeded in delaying the Japanese, holding off their invasion of India, beating off repeated Japanese efforts to deal the killer blow and annihilate the army. There had been no surrender.

Slim was furious. 'How much wiser,' he wrote in his memoir, *Defeat into Victory*, 'was the treatment of the troops who escaped from Dunkirk . . . they were received as if they had won a great victory, not suffered a disaster. My men had endured a longer ordeal with at least equal courage; they deserved an equal welcome.'

Even after Burcorps was officially disbanded on 20 May, its men continued to die from the ravages of the retreat, malaria, dysentery and exhaustion. Walter was one of the lucky few who were given leave and returned to Quetta, gaunt and sallow, but otherwise unscathed. The lessons he had learned by being at the tactical nerve centre of the army, seeing how decisions were made and how they played out, observing Slim's close attention to detail and genuine care for his men, and absorbing knowledge of the enemy would all come in useful soon. In the meantime he could relax into the routine of life at Quetta and await the arrival of his and Beryl's first baby.

One morning in September 1942 he was lecturing students at the Staff College about his experiences in Burma when 'I saw the adjutant peer through the window, grin and give what I took to be a rude gesture with two fingers of his right hand. I returned the signal but the adjutant shook his head and called out, "No, no! It's twins."'

Even in 1942, before the advent of ultrasound, it should have been possible for a doctor to tell that there were two heartbeats rather than one. But somehow this had been missed. After delivering one son, Beryl had had to shout for the departing doctor to return: 'There's another one coming.' The doctor's disbelief turned to amazement as a second son duly appeared. A short while later, Walter arrived breathlessly on his bicycle. 'The peaceful interlude had become idyllic,' he wrote.

Walter and Beryl named their twins Anthony and Nigel. Telegrams were duly dispatched to family back home, announcing the births, and

Dorothea and Arthur in Assam.

Tara, 1936.

The young Walkers in 1922.
Left to right: Ruth, Harold, Peter, Walter, Bee, Edward.

The Walker family at Tara, 1933.
Back row: Harold (aged 17), Walter (aged 20), Bee (aged 21), Edward (aged 23),
Peter (aged 18). Front row: Arthur, Ruth (aged 14), Dorothea.

Edward and Tiggy's wedding, Hong Kong 1934. Bee is second from right.

Peter with his Otter,
mid 1930s, Assam.

Harold and Bee at Tara, 1935.

Peter and Walter in Shillong, 1937.

Ruth and John Fisher on their engagement, Tara, 1937.

Bee, Arthur and Jonathan, Ruth's dachshund, Tara c.1937.

Peter, Alison and Ruth at Bude, 1939.

Walter and Beryl in Assam, 1938.

St Thomas's Hospital after the bomb on 15th September 1940
in which Harold was buried.

Harold convalescing in hospital after
the bombing of St Thomas's.

Ruth and two other fledgling
Nightingales, Shamley Green,
winter 1939.

Gurkhas manning
a post at Razmak
where Walter was
fighting in 1940.

Walter in his
sleeping quarters
on the Northwest
Frontier, 1940.

Gurkhas crossing
the Irrawaddy River
in Burma, 1945.

Bee and Gaddis's wedding in London, 1942.

The christening of Bee and Gaddis's daughter Mary, 1943.
Left to right: Harold, Arthur, Dorothea holding Mary, Bee, unknown friend,
Ruth, unknown friend, Gaddis.

Peter, shortly after his
liberation in 1945.

Edward with Tiggy and their sons
Nicholas and Hamish, 1944.

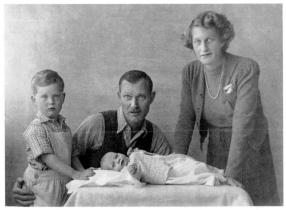

The Walkers and their spouses at Weybridge in the 1950s.
Standing: Peter, Walter, Beryl, Roy, John, Edward, Kay, Harold
Sitting: Nancy, Ruth, Dorothea, Bee, Linda.

congratulations poured in from near and far. None, however, came from Arthur and Dorothea, still smarting over Walter having gone against his mother's wishes to marry a bride of whom she did not approve. She could not bring herself to congratulate Beryl on the birth.

Her reaction hardly squares with Ruth's description of her mother as 'always very kind'. No doubt she was, most of the time, but she was clearly a woman who did not like to be disobeyed.

While his siblings were marrying, becoming parents and progressing in their careers, Peter's world had shrunk.

After the surrender on 15 February, the message went out to the units scattered around Singapore that they must lay down their arms and stack them neatly, ready to be handed over to the enemy. At first, some refused to believe it. Was it a trick? Even when it was confirmed, it seemed unreal. The Japanese appeared to be in no hurry to take delivery of their captives.

But the following day the British officers of Indian battalions were separated from their men, the Indians marched off to one camp, and the officers ordered to another at Changi on Singapore's east coast, with the officers and soldiers of British units. They had to march fifteen miles through Singapore's streets, clasping suitcases instead of rifles. Everywhere around the island, Union flags had been lowered and destroyed or hidden, replaced by the white flag with a red sphere at its centre: the Rising Sun of the Nippon Empire. Sikh policemen kept a watchful eye on the marching prisoners while Singaporeans looked on, confused. 'As though drugged with disillusionment,' as one British officer put it, 'their faces [were] strained, bewildered, enquiring, a you-seem-to-have-let-us-down kind of look.' Some were sympathetic and pressed food and water on the downcast prisoners. Others merely stared.

On they marched in the clammy humidity, the sound of tramping boots in the hushed streets a stark contrast to the cacophony of war. But evidence of fighting lay all around in the twisted, stinking corpses that no one had yet buried.

Finally they reached Changi, their home for the next eight months. Changi was not one but several camps, designed to accommodate around five thousand people, a fraction of the forty to fifty thousand demoralised men who now marched through its gates. Each division was allocated its own area and 11th Division, to which Peter belonged, was sent to Birdwood Camp, where Major General Billy Key, who had replaced Murray-Lyon as commander of 11th Division, was put in charge.

At Changi, the senior officers resumed command of their men and imposed military discipline on the camps. The men were given tasks, some essential, such as building latrines and digging drains, some seemingly designed to keep them busy and stop them brooding on the events of recent weeks. In Birdwood Camp, Key organised cricket, rugby, football and hockey on the cricket ground and ordered the men to dig vegetable gardens and tend them. Sweet potatoes, tapioca and pineapples all began to grow in orderly lines and Peter found satisfaction in tending the plants, just as his father had at Tara.

The Japanese had issued the PoWs with rice but the British Army cooks had no idea how to deal with it and the result was either a burned or soggy mess. Even when their technique improved, rice did not provide adequate vitamins, and the supplies of sardines, bully beef and jam that they had brought with them soon dwindled. A few daring individuals went beyond the wire by cover of dark to buy eggs and chickens from the locals but, as the months dragged by, the lack of vitamins and the diseases spread by flies resulted in dysentery spreading through the camp. Using the latrines soon took on a nightmarish aspect.

Even then, some senior officers clung stubbornly to protocol. A junior officer, John Coast, who wrote a famous memoir of his time as a prisoner of war, *Railroad of Death*, recounted how a 'rather pompous, fat major' gave him a verbal dressing down for his 'gross impertinence' in failing to greet him, a senior officer, in the latrines one morning as they both went about their business.

Food was not the only shortage. Medicine was also lacking, and hard-pressed doctors struggled to treat the wounded, as well as the swelling ranks of dysentery sufferers, without adequate drugs and equipment. Despite this, many of the men remained healthy for the first few months.

In Changi military camp a 'university' was set up: anyone with a hobby or particular expertise was encouraged to give lectures on subjects from law to medicine, engineering and agriculture. There were musical performances and singalongs, and the Roman Catholic and Church of England padres held services every Sunday.

Even so, the months crawled by. In August 1942 all prisoners of war above the rank of lieutenant colonel were shipped off to camps in Formosa, now Taiwan, leaving the lieutenant colonels in charge.

More and more men began to succumb to diseases that in peacetime would have been easily treatable. Then, in September 1942, came the 'Selarang Barracks Incident'. The Imperial Japanese Army (IJA) issued a document to all prisoners of war at Changi, which they were ordered to sign, promising that they would not attempt to escape. To British and Australian troops, who saw it as their duty to escape, this was unacceptable.

Four men, two Australian soldiers and two British privates, had tried to escape. The two Australians had managed to get hold of a boat, which they sailed in the direction of Colombo in Ceylon, now Sri Lanka, but after a voyage of more than a thousand miles they were picked up by a Japanese vessel and brought back to Singapore.

Apparently this escape attempt had prompted the Japanese to demand the no-escape pledge. To a man, the prisoners refused to sign. The Japanese reiterated their demand. Again the prisoners refused. Enraged, on 2 September the Japanese ordered every man in the Changi area to pack up his possessions and march to Selarang Barracks, a small area within Changi designed to house around 850 men. Now 17,000 prisoners of war were crammed onto the parade ground. Kitchen tents were set up there too. Each man had to commandeer a small area of ground on which to sit, cheek by jowl, with his fellow prisoners. Peter was among the thousands who sat under the blazing sun as the hours ticked by, then the days. Some men were perched on the roofs of the barrack huts. There was no room to move or to lie down. There were not enough taps, so water was scarce, as was food.

That same day, the four escapers were marched onto the beach and executed by firing squad. The Australian corporal begged for the life of his friend, a private, but the Japanese officers ignored him. The prisoners refused blindfolds and one of the British soldiers stood reading his Bible. The firing squad of Sikh soldiers were nervous, or incompetent, or both, for they fired wildly, the first two volleys simply wounding the men. 'Shoot straight! Why don't you shoot straight?' the Bible-bearing man begged them. But it took several more shots to finish them off. Reflecting on the bravery of the soldier who died still clutching his Bible, George Chippington wrote: 'We never know what lies within a man until he is put to the final test.'

On the Selarang Barracks square, word of the executions spread rapidly. So did flies, attracted by the hastily dug latrines. The smell was appalling, men sitting sandwiched together, streaming with sweat on the burning asphalt parade ground, or perched on roofs. Sentries posted around the barbed-wire fence threatened to shoot anyone who came close.

For four days and nights the prisoners sat in the open, alternately rained on and roasted by the sun. On the fourth day, the Japanese turned the screw by threatening to force the patients in the hospital, many of them dangerously ill, to join them. Told by the medical officers that this would result not only in patients dying but in a serious epidemic breaking out among the healthy men, the senior officers ordered the men to sign the form. As it was signed under duress it meant little, but it was enough to satisfy Japanese pride and the prisoners were allowed to return to their barracks.

The incident had revealed, if any doubt remained, the attitude of the Japanese towards prisoners of war: it was of contempt. Under their military code, any serviceman who allowed himself to be taken prisoner had forfeited any rights and could be treated as his captors saw fit. Some of the prisoners were put to work labouring on the docks, loading and unloading cargoes. It was a foretaste of what was to come.

Not long after the Selarang Barracks incident, Peter fell ill. On 19 October 1942 he was admitted to Roberts Hospital in Changi with bacillary dysentery. He was lucky: although the hospital was not well equipped by peacetime standards, it had some medicine and diagnostic equipment, including microscopes. Around 350 medical officers had been taken into captivity in South East Asia, and over the next three and a half years they saved numerous lives through their heroic efforts and ingenious solutions to the lack of drugs and equipment. For dysentery the treatment was relatively simple: starvation and doses of Epsom salts. One man lost four stone in a fortnight on this regime; others were too weak to pull through.

The doctors kept meticulous medical records using pencils, old exercise books, notepads or any scrap of paper they could scrounge. Each patient was recorded, with their date of birth, nationality, military unit, age, religion, medical condition and length of hospital stay; deaths are noted matter-of-factly in red pencil. Many of these records survive and you can look them up in the National Archives in Kew, which was where I learned that Second Lieutenant Peter Walker had spent ten days in Roberts Hospital, Changi.

The Dysentery Wing was located on the first floor of Barrack Block 151. There was a separate ward for officers: even in captivity military hierarchies were rigorously observed, at least for the time being. The room below had been converted into a chapel, St Luke's, and the sound of hymns being sung would float up to the dysentery patients, as they lay afflicted with painful abdominal cramps, vomiting and acute diarrhoea, unable to get to the lavatory without aid, slipping into and out of consciousness.

One of the dysentery patients, a talented artist named Stanley Warren, gave thanks for his recovery by painting murals depicting Biblical scenes to decorate the chapel. The murals were painted over but some twenty years later Warren restored them and the Changi Museum now displays replicas. The day I visited, the museum was thronged with chattering schoolgirls but when confronted with these beautiful murals, and the moving story behind them, even the liveliest fell silent.

Dysentery comes in two forms: bacillary, caused by bacteria, and amoebic, caused by a parasite. Bacillary cases would generally recover without drugs as long as the patient was given plenty of fluids to replace those lost, but amoebic dysentery required a more prolonged hospital stay. At Roberts Hospital, in those early days of captivity, the doctors had a pathology lab where they could study stool samples taken from the patients and identify which strain they had.

A bizarre, illicit trade soon developed among the patients: those who were confirmed amoebic cases would sell a stool sample to those who suspected that they had 'only' bacillary dysentery but wanted to avoid being discharged and sent straight back to work, either on one of the many camp 'fatigues', such as latrines maintenance, or on the docks.

The trade had been either undiscovered or ignored until the arrival of Captain R. C. B. Welsh from Kuala Lumpur, where he had previously been held, at about the same time as Peter was admitted. Within a few days of his arrival Welsh had put a stop to the stool trade by what he admitted were Gestapo tactics, getting a medical officer to record every 'motion' passed by each patient. He noted with satisfaction an immediate exit of malingerers. If some men hoped to gain a few extra days in bed to build up their strength they could hardly be blamed. They would soon need it for the trials that lay ahead.

I do not know whether Peter was aware of the 'stool trade' or even involved, but it seems unlikely. All his life he had a strong sense of justice and could be single-minded in his quest to right wrongs, big or small. Afterwards, he spoke bitterly of people who had behaved immorally, as he saw it, during the war and in captivity.

Peter might have been easygoing, like his father, but he also possessed Arthur's dauntless optimism, combined with a single-minded determination and stubbornness that probably came from his mother and would prove vital to his survival. Again and again, when hanging onto life seemed to be merely a futile, painful deferral of death, he would repeat the family motto, *Nil desperandum*, like a mantra. Some of the prisoners recited favourite poems or hymns in their blackest moments but for Peter it was two simple words: 'Never despair.'

By the time he was discharged from hospital, changes were already afoot at Changi. Back in May, three thousand men had been put onto trucks and then trains bound for Thailand. No more had been heard of them, but in June and then October more men were rounded up into groups to be sent north. Each group was given a letter, and in November it was the turn of Letter Party N, to which Peter had been allocated. He left Changi on 4 November having been promised, with his companions, that they were going somewhere with a better climate, plentiful food and good accommodation. They would all be healthier and happier.

Those who believed these assurances began to have their doubts when the men were loaded onto steel goods trucks at Singapore station. With around thirty crammed into each twenty-foot truck, there was barely room to sit or squat, let alone lie down. Sleep was all but impossible. For four days, the train jolted through the monotonous rubber country of Malaya, then the endless rice paddies of Thailand. When the sun shone, the truck became an oven, the metal nearly red hot, but when it rained they all got drenched. Sleep was impossible and there was no lavatory: when nature called, as it frequently did for the dysentery sufferers, there was nothing for it but to hang out of the doorway if they could get there. The floor of the truck was soon awash with urine and excrement. Water was scarce and food even scarcer. By the time the train drew into Thailand's Ban Pong station many were too weak to stand and several men were dead or died shortly afterwards.

Stretching their cramped, stiff legs, the survivors were marched a mile or so to Ban Pong transit camp, a mass of rickety bamboo huts in a sea of black mud. Even the hospital hut was flooded, water lapping beneath the bamboo slats of the huts in which they slept and flooding the latrines. Lieutenant Colonel Philip Toosey, who had arrived a few days before Peter, described the camp as 'the most filthy mess I have ever seen in my life'.

Peter shouldered his kit bag and made his way to the hut he had been allocated. Around the camp were the men who had left Changi in May. Several seemed to be ill, their limbs a mass of filthy sores and ulcers. Any illusions that persisted after their horrific journey now evaporated. They had not expected Utopia, but this was close to Hell.

PART FOUR

Triumph and Loss

10

'The very heart of Hell'

FOR MUCH OF his time at Changi, Peter had had little to do with the Japanese but as soon as he arrived in Thailand this changed. From the moment they stumbled from the rice trucks, they were under the scrutiny of the Japanese officers and guards. If any prisoner did anything to displease them, or sometimes for no reason at all, the Japanese would attack the luckless man with sticks, crowbars, boots, fists or bayonets.

Peter's years in the camps left him scarred in many ways, but the most visible were the bayonet marks on his back from where the guards had prodded him with the sharp blade shouting, '*Kurra kurra!*' ('Come on!') There were so many scars on his back that it was difficult to measure more than an inch between them, and the bayonets had left tiny holes up his neck too. Many of his wounds became ulcerated in the damp jungle climate and infested with maggots. Such wounds, at least, could be treated. Others would prove harder to heal.

The Korean guards, according to Peter, were even more brutal than the Japanese. The Japanese had colonised Korea in 1910 and conscripted Koreans into their army, but they despised them and treated them as the lowest of the low, frequently beating and slapping them, violence the Koreans took out on the prisoners of war.

At Ban Pong, the thousands of men arriving from Singapore were organised into work groups. Under the Geneva Convention, prisoners of war should not be expected to engage in any work that contributed to the war effort of their captors, or any work that was unsafe. The Japanese had signed but not ratified the convention and therefore saw no need to respect it. And in their view, anyone who was taken prisoner not only forfeited any rights but was deemed to have changed sides. So it was logical to put them to work for the Japanese since they were, in theory, now on their side. The prisoners were informed that they would now have to work for their keep. 'No work, no food.'

The work they had in mind was building a 258-mile-long railway between Burma and Thailand, to enable the Japanese to bring up materials and reinforcements to their forces in Burma and eventually beyond into India. The prisoners were now slaves in the service of the Nippon Empire.

Plans for a Thailand–Burma railway had begun long before the war. The British embassy in Bangkok had reported suspicious numbers of Japanese tourists coming to Thailand and photographing areas that later proved to be the route of the railway. The 'tourists' reported their findings to Tokyo. When the Americans defeated the Japanese Navy at the battle of Midway in June 1942, sinking four Japanese aircraft carriers, the Japanese knew they could no longer safely move men and supplies around by sea. Neither the Pacific nor the Indian Ocean was safe. With the next round of fighting likely to take place in Burma, they needed a secure means of moving men and materiel there from Japan and their other Asian possessions. That month, the order came from Tokyo for work to begin on the 'Thai–Burma Rail Link', joining the Thai and Burmese railway systems.

The planned route would stretch from Nong Pladuk station west of Bangkok to Thanbyuzayat in southern Burma. The Japanese engineers realised that the difficult terrain of dense jungle and mountain passes would make it impossible to use the kind of heavy construction machinery needed for building bridges and embankments, and digging tunnels. Even elephants, usually used for dragging logs and other heavy materials, would struggle on the steeper slopes. The only solution was to use human labour. The work would be dangerous and exhausting, but if the labour force could easily be replaced, it mattered little to the Japanese if labourers' lives were lost.

Originally they had planned to use Asian labourers and, indeed, the majority of the workforce were 'romusha', the Japanese word for labourers applied to the hundreds of thousands of men, women and even children recruited, often forcibly, from Java, Burma, Malaya and elsewhere. But with 200,000 prisoners now at their disposal, following their victories across Asia, the Japanese decided that putting them to work would solve the problem of what to do with them. Even before the war in South

East Asia began, the Japanese planners had decided to use prisoners of war as labour on the railway but they had anticipated using only 10,000. However, such was the demand for labour and the rate of attrition that 60,000 prisoners of war worked on the railway.

Peter was allocated to Work Group Two and sent to what became Group Two's base camp at Chungkai, around thirty miles from Ban Pong. He might have marched or, if he was among the lucky ones, gone by truck. Arriving at Chungkai, he found a putrid swamp of a camp. Rain had caused the latrines to overflow, their contents floating around the camp. The men were already viewing Changi, with its sanitary arrangements, huts and barracks, with nostalgia.

Peter was not at Chungkai for long before he and his companions were again told to start marching for their next destination, Wang Lan, seven miles away. It was a miserable march for exhausted, hungry men in pouring monsoon rain, and for some it was too much. Within a few days of arriving at Wang Lan, men were dying of dysentery and exhaustion.

In the Liberation Questionnaire that all surviving prisoners of war had to complete, Peter noted the various camps in which he had been held, with the dates and the names of the commanding officer in the camp, the British or Australian officers appointed to lead the prisoners. He struggled to fit the list of camps within the space allocated on the form, and to recall the dates of his many camp moves, and in some cases he must have made a guess. He estimated that he arrived in Wang Lan, or 'One Lung', as he wrote, in April 1942, when in fact he was still in Changi.

Confused, I consulted the Thailand–Burma Railway Centre in Kanchanaburi, Thailand, run by three cheerful and knowledgeable Australians, Rod Beattie, Terry Manttan and Andrew Snow, who have developed an impressive archive and encyclopaedic knowledge of the Death Railway, as it became known. Terry and Andrew's fathers were prisoners of war on the railway, while Rod is the author of a highly informative book about its history.

Within a few days they had emailed me details of Peter's movements, pieced together from Peter's own documents, including hospital records, and those of other men in Group Two. The 8,795 men of Group Two were split into working battalions of around six hundred men each and Peter was assigned to one of these. The leader of the camps where he spent the first five months of his time on the railway was Lieutenant Colonel Ted Swinton.

Swinton, commanding officer of the East Surrey Regiment, was fifty-three, a morally upright, somewhat stiff but courageous man who, according to the obituary in his regimental journal, always did what he thought was right, 'indifferent to the criticism of friend and foe alike'. He stood up to his captors whenever they mistreated the men under his command and was frequently slapped and beaten for his efforts. His men admired him, although some found his stubborn adherence to protocol exasperating.

One of Peter's companions in Group Two was Lieutenant Jim Richardson. Like Peter, Richardson was a wartime volunteer rather than a regular officer and he viewed Swinton as 'an unmitigated shit'. On one occasion, in the middle of the monsoon, Swinton noticed that Richardson's boots were without laces, this at a stage when many men had lost their footwear altogether, and berated him for 'letting down the officer class'. Richardson, who kept a secret diary that he typed up after the war, fumed that Swinton was a 'miserable, hide-bound regular, my particular bête-noir [sic]. Unfortunately he survived the war.'

On arrival at Wang Lan the 'other ranks', soldiers, not officers, were organised into working parties and sent out into the surrounding countryside to begin hewing a railroad out of the jungle. Issued with the most basic of tools, they were marched out of camp and after two miles were halted in the middle of dense bamboo, sixty feet high. With no mechanical diggers, the only way of removing the bamboo, roots and all, from the ground was by brute force.

The Japanese engineers supervised the prisoners as they hauled on ropes, heaving and pulling the bamboo as the engineers counted, '*Ichi, ni, san, shi* . . .' It was exhausting, debilitating work, fuelled only by a handful of cold rice for lunch. The sharp bamboo tore into the men's clothes and flesh, resulting in scratches and cuts that quickly became infected. They turned into tropical ulcers that grew at an alarming rate, eating away chunks of flesh the size of tennis balls. While the doctors still had a reasonable supply of drugs, the ulcers could often be healed, but when medicine became scarce the only remedy was agonising: scooping out the rotten, putrid flesh with a metal spoon. If this failed, the final recourse was amputation.

To begin with, the officers remained in camp while their men were sent out on working parties. The officers organised jobs around camp: cookhouses had to be built, latrines dug, water collected and boiled and huts constructed. But they did not get involved in railway building. It was simply unthinkable that officers would be made to work like 'coolies'.

A short while after their arrival in Wang Lan, though, Swinton was informed that the officers, too, must work on the railway. When he protested, citing the Geneva Convention, he was informed brusquely that the Imperial Japanese Army had not signed it. Swinton refused to back down but the following day the Japanese camp commandant ordered all the officers to be paraded in the camp square with the sick, hauled from their hospital beds. Still Swinton held his ground. The stand-off continued under the burning sun.

Jack Shuttle, a soldier in Swinton's own regiment, the East Surreys, described what happened next in his memoir, *Destination Kwai*: 'Suddenly a truck came careering down the rough track that had now been cut along the line from Chungkai, full of armed Japanese soldiers, which reversed into a position with the rear facing the ranks of officers. The covers opened and revealed a mounted machine-gun crew in the firing position and it was announced that if the orders were not obeyed they would open fire at once. At this stage it was felt prudent to agree . . .' Similar scenes were played out in other camps.

The officers were now formed into work parties, some specialising in bridge building, others in constructing culverts. A proportion of men remained in camp to carry out essential work, such as cooking, latrine maintenance, or working in the hospitals that were hastily constructed. But others were sent to the countryside on railway construction. It must have been humiliating in those class- and race-conscious times for a man like Peter, used to being in charge of labourers on the tea plantation, to find that he was now a slave in the service of a far-off emperor, at the mercy of overseers among whom this quality was in short supply.

For soldiers like Jack Shuttle, much as they admired Swinton's stand, it was a relief that the officers would now be joining in the work. They had felt aggrieved that the officers stayed in camp doing comparatively easy chores while they toiled all day in the rain and heat. Now they really were all in it together. Besides, as the Japanese kept reiterating, it was a case of 'no work, no food'. They supplied only enough rations for the working men: anyone who did not work was removed from the quota. As the food was pooled, there was less for everyone if the officers did not work.

Wang Lan was one of the better camps. Today nothing remains of it, except the railway line and a small station. Where the camp once stood an imposing modern villa has been built, but in 1942 the area was covered with thatched bamboo huts from which the men would emerge every morning for the hated '*tenko*', the headcount, which seemed to go on for ever while they stood in ranks under a furiously hot sun. The guards frequently lost count and had to begin again.

But the terrain was flat and there was a market nearby, which the prisoners were allowed to visit on the way back from work to the camp. Those with money or possessions to barter could buy extra food, such as duck eggs, bananas, peanuts and that mainstay of prisoner-of-war life: cigarettes.

At first the working day began at 9 a.m. with a 6 p.m. finish, but soon the hours increased, the prisoners' work became tougher and their captors more brutal. Not long after their arrival at Wang Lan, diphtheria broke out. This highly contagious bacterial infection first attacks the nose and throat. With the right anti-serum, most could have been cured but as it was not available, all that doctors could do was to scrape off the infected membrane that covered the back of the throat and cauterise it with potassium permanganate. It worked in about half the cases, but when it failed the bacteria spread into the bloodstream, infecting the heart muscle and damaging the kidneys and nervous system, often causing paralysis. Some recovered, others did not.

As well as diphtheria and tropical ulcers, men soon began to succumb to malaria, diarrhoea and dysentery. Malaria causes a high fever, chills, terrible tremors and convulsions, brain damage in the case of cerebral malaria, and often death. But the Japanese would not accept it as a legitimate reason to miss work. Men trembling and sweating with fever and weak as newborns were dragged from their sick beds and forced to march into the countryside to chop bamboo and heave heavy loads with no rest and little food. If they collapsed they were dragged to their feet and helped onward by their companions.

Small wonder that many died, as did the dysentery sufferers, dragged out to work while convulsed with painful stomach cramps. Walter wrote angrily in his memoir of the humiliation that Peter and his fellow prisoners had to endure: 'going on parade with dysentery and diarrhoea running down their legs'.

The Japanese medical officer in charge of Group Two was Lieutenant Nobusawa Hisashi. He was said to be a paediatrician in peacetime, but no one saw any evidence of his medical training and they nicknamed him 'the horse doctor'. He would accompany the engineers when they inspected the sick men, and laugh when they kicked or hit them.

As more men fell sick, those who were still standing had to work harder to make up for the shortfall. The first stage in construction was removing the bamboo and other vegetation, which was then carried away on men's backs. The next task was to build embankments and excavate cuttings. Again, this was done almost entirely by hand. The men would dig with their primitive tools, removing the soil and stone for others to carry away in baskets or sacks on their heads or backs, emptying them onto what became the embankment. They were, as they observed, like the slaves of the Egyptian pharaohs who laboured to build the Pyramids: whipped, abused, expendable.

As the embankment grew higher and steeper, so the men carrying the baskets had further to go, increasing the strain on their backs and aching limbs. All the time the Japanese engineers and guards would shout at them, berating them for their slowness and weakness and claiming that a Japanese soldier could do the work of ten 'no good' English soldiers. This was sometimes followed by a demonstration of Nippon superiority: the guard would grab a shovel and dig furiously for a few minutes, then sit down again.

When it rained, the prisoners' bare feet slipped in the mud – most of them had lost their boots by now – and whenever anyone fell, the nearest guard would pounce on him, beating him mercilessly with a heavy bamboo stick, wire whip, or the nearest tool to hand: a rifle butt, shovel or hammer. Often they would prod them with the sharpened end of a bayonet, hence the galaxy of scars on Peter's back.

When I read Richard Flanagan's Booker Prize-winning novel, *The Narrow Road to the Deep North*, based on his father's experiences as a prisoner of war on the Death Railway and featuring horrifically graphic descriptions of the sadism of Japanese and Korean guards, beating and kicking their captives to a bloody pulp, I wondered if Flanagan's father had been exceptionally unlucky. Surely it could not have been as bad everywhere on the railway.

But when I delved further into Peter's time on the railway, reading the memoirs and accounts left by men in the camps where he had been, as well as the affidavits given to war-crimes investigators after the war, it became apparent that such sadism was widespread. The engineers in charge of the project were under pressure to finish it, so they put pressure on the guards supervising the prisoners to increase the tempo of work, and the guards responded with brute force. If the guards spotted a man pausing to wipe the sweat from his eyes, or gather his strength before shouldering another heavy load, or swaying with exhaustion, they would spring at him and beat him energetically.

At first the work rate was reasonable: each man had to remove one cubic metre of earth per day. But this rate later increased so that men were staggering under absurdly heavy loads. It was bad enough when they were clearing soft earth, but as they moved northwards the ground underfoot turned to rock and they had to attack it with sledgehammers. One man held a long steel drill while his partner hit it with the hammer, until the hole was big enough for dynamite to be inserted. Then the rock would be blasted away and the rubble would have to be carried to other prisoners, who used hammers to smash the rocks into stones to provide ballast for the track. Each stage was backbreaking, each fraught with danger: the sledgehammer might slip and the man holding the drill would have his fingers broken, while men carrying huge loads of rock down steep, slippery hillsides frequently fell and broke limbs. Some guards would allow the injured man to be taken back to the camp hospital but others refused or even beat the victim.

In the early stages of his captivity, Peter told his family, he coped well. After his bout of dysentery in Changi he managed to remain off the sick list – or, at least, he was not deemed sick enough to be sent to hospital. By now most men had developed malaria and tropical ulcers but they simply had to soldier on. Swinton and the medical officers protested at the inhumanity and futility of dragging weak, ill men out to work and sometimes they were heeded, making the difference between life or death. But all too often it was a case of shooting the messenger or, rather, beating him. Doctors and senior officers were slapped, punched, beaten with bamboo sticks or sheathed swords, kicked to the ground, then kicked again. Sometimes the diminutive Japanese officer would call for a box to stand on in order to slap and punch the face of men who were nearly a foot taller. The height discrepancy seemed to increase their fury.

Peter had nothing but praise for the camp doctors, who worked tirelessly, risking their own health by caring for those with contagious diseases. The other people for whom he developed a profound respect were the Roman Catholics. He later said they never lost their morality, unlike some.

With the basics of life in short supply, it was hardly surprising that desperate men were sometimes driven to steal from each other. Blankets, which could mean the difference between life and death as they gave some protection from malarial mosquitoes, were regular targets for thieves, as were any possessions that could be sold or bartered for extra food. There were even instances of food being pilfered from the camp supplies and medicine being stolen from the camp hospitals to be sold for profit to local traders. Stealing from the Japanese was considered perfectly acceptable, if highly risky.

Several of the camps were sited on or near the River Maekluang. Its tributary, the Khwae Noi, became known later, erroneously, as the River Kwai. The river was their supply route, bringing bamboo, wood, iron and other materials to the working camps by barge. At the end of a long shift in the scalding heat, the prisoners delighted in being able to wash and swim in the river, at least in the dry season. But in the monsoon it bore disease, such as cholera, and the doctors prohibited bathing.

Some found solace in nature, watching clouds of gloriously gaudy butterflies flit through the jungle, glimpsing wild elephants and even the occasional tiger or otter. During the dry season, others marvelled at the splendour of the night sky, lying out under the stars to spot the Milky Way, galaxies that seemed almost at their feet. Some engaged in political debates or gave lectures about their area of expertise. One man took an accordion from camp to camp and was credited with boosting morale with his jaunty tunes.

That first Christmas in captivity, the prisoners paraded for *tenko* as usual in the morning, and collected their tools for the day's work. But then, a surprise: a *yasume*, a rest day, was announced. The men were allowed to return to their huts, bathe in the river or wander into Wang Lan market. There was little danger of any prisoner absconding: not only did they face the death penalty if caught, but with Thailand and neighbouring Burma and Malaya under Japanese occupation, there was nowhere to escape to. Later on, there were a few escape attempts but in almost every case the escapers were caught, brought back to camp and executed, sometimes after torture.

The prisoners lived on a meagre daily diet of 20 ounces of rice, 12 ounces of vegetables and small amounts of sugar and salt. This later fell to twelve ounces of rice and eight ounces of vegetables, then to a few spoonfuls of watery rice in the camps 'up country' near the Burma border.

Occasionally they added a tiny quantity of fresh meat to the stew, or peanuts, either bought or thrust on them by kindly Thais. But protein was generally in such short supply that all the men were soon suffering from the effects of malnutrition, making them vulnerable to other diseases. On Christmas Day the cooks baked bread from ground rice, spread with marmalade made from limes and tamarinds. In the evening there were sing-songs and thoughts turned to home.

For Peter, home was two places: there was Tiverton, his parents, brothers and sisters, cricket in the garden and trips to the beach with Alison. And then there was his other home at Sealkotee in Assam, his polo ponies, his dog and otter, the carefree pre-war existence of riotous nights at the club. He remembered the Indian fakir who had foretold that he would go through the very darkest of times but would survive. He clung to this prophecy, determined that he would get home, see Dorothea and Arthur again, then pick up the threads of his old life. Peter had a wealthy godfather, a Colonel Grimston, a friend from Arthur's days in the Assam Valley Light Horse, who had promised a chunk of his considerable fortune to Peter when he died. So while he cursed his bad luck at being a prisoner, Peter could at least look forward to financial security if he survived, as he was convinced he would.

When Peter talked of his time on the railway, a recurring theme was how fortunate he had been. He had several advantages over some of the other men around him. Having lived in India, he was used to the tropical climate and food, whereas those who had never had to eat rice before the surrender found it hard to digest, and could not stomach the local herbs and vegetables. He was lucky, too, in his physical build. He noticed that among the prisoners it was the big, burly blokes who suffered badly, their large frames withering on the near-starvation diet. It was, he said, 'lean little buggers like me that got through'. His five-foot-ten frame, his healthy, sporty, outdoor life in Tiverton and Assam, Blundell's, and the gruelling training with the Assam Valley Light Horse, carrying heavy weights up and down hills, now stood him in good stead.

And as an officer, from a middle-class household, Peter had never gone hungry, brought up on Dorothea's nourishing stews and strawberry puddings. By contrast many of the soldiers had grown up in poverty, and the years of malnourishment meant that their bodies lacked the reserves needed to withstand the near-starvation diet and gruelling phys-ical work. Officers, too, had more valuables to sell than most soldiers: a signet ring, fountain pen or watch could be sold or exchanged, in the early months, for vital extra food. Duck eggs, for example, could make the difference between life and death for men suffering from vitamin-deficiency diseases, like beriberi.

And officers were paid more than the soldiers. Early on in the railway construction, the Japanese announced magnanimously that all prisoners of war would be paid, thanks to the generosity of the Nippon Army, with each rank receiving the same pay as their Japanese equivalent, although after deductions were made for their 'board and lodging' the prisoners received only a fraction of this sum. For senior officers it was enough to buy extra food, but for the junior officers and soldiers the sums were paltry. To even things out the camp leaders introduced a kind of tax, with everyone contributing a similar proportion of their earnings to a communal fund from which eggs and other necessities were bought.

Peter also had age on his side. The prisoners ranged in age from nineteen to colonels in their fifties and sixties. Peter had just turned twenty-eight when he was taken prisoner and this put him in the age bracket that, in the view of one of his later camp leaders, Lieutenant Colonel Philip Toosey, gave him the best chance of survival. When asked, thirty years after the war, what made some men survive and others give up, Toosey replied: 'A man is at his toughest between the ages of twenty-eight and thirty-five. He's got the background, he's got some stability and he's got his full physical powers.'

Others believed in the power of friendship: having a friend to talk to or to look after you when you were sick, help you to the latrine, or feed you when you lay in hospital, could make the difference between life and death. But when a close friend died it was a shattering blow. Peter later said that almost all his friends in the camps died, one by one.

In some camps the prisoners befriended stray dogs. It was cathartic to stroke and snuggle up with a warm, affectionate creature at the end of each gruelling workday, even to share a scrap or two of precious rations, but the Japanese cottoned on to this as an opportunity to make the prisoners suffer. One of Peter's most bitter memories was seeing the guards take the dogs from the prisoners, toss them into the air and catch them on their bayonets, laughing as the creatures died in agony while the prisoners were forced to watch. After that, they learned to shoo the dogs away.

The working days at Wang Lan grew steadily longer as the targets set by the engineers for completion of each track section became more and more absurd. The prisoners had to continue working far into the night by the light of bonfires, whipped and beaten by guards in scenes reminiscent of depictions of Hell on the walls of medieval churches, in which humans were tormented in a fiery inferno by merciless demons. It felt, wrote George Chippington, as if 'I had, for a brief moment, looked into the face and even deep into the very heart of hell.'

One shift lasted for twenty-seven hours, but despite their exhaustion, the men returned to camp marching and singing to show their captors that their spirits were unbroken.

As their work progressed and their section of the railway met with that of the prisoners in the next group up the line, Group Two 'leap-frogged' forward. In February 1943 the prisoners at Wang Lan were informed that the next day they would leave for another camp.

They marched north, some eighteen miles, resting once overnight. Those who were weak with malaria or other illnesses had to be helped along by their friends. If not, the Japanese would have left them to die by the roadside. They reached their destination, Thakilen camp, the next day. It was pleasantly situated near the river but badly overcrowded.

It was here that they were placed under the command of a man who would torment them over the coming months: Lieutenant Kokubo Nagataro. A bully and a drunk, he delighted in humiliating the white men now in his power. Shortly after arriving at Thakilen he noticed that one of the Korean guards was friendly towards the prisoners. Kokubo turned on him and beat him brutally around the head with his clenched fist, only stopping when his arm became tired. From then on the guards, taking their lead from Kokubo, became increasingly vicious.

Years after the war, when Peter was saying goodnight to his two youngest sons and tucking them into bed, he recalled how, in the camps, he would tuck his blanket carefully in around his camp bed – or, rather, the bamboo slats that constituted a bed – not only to guard against mosquitoes but because sometimes a drunken Japanese officer would come into the prisoners' huts whirling a sword around.

It sounds like something out of Grimm's fairytales, a cautionary tale to deter children from getting out of bed at night, but after reading the war-crimes evidence, it seems likely that Peter was referring to Lieutenant Kokubo. Several prisoners of war described how, drunk and angry with the world – as well he might be since guarding prisoners of war was seen by the Japanese Army as a demeaning job for men with no real career prospects – Kokubo would stride around the camp and sometimes into the huts where the men slept, brandishing his sword. It was lucky that no one lost their hands or feet.

Once Kokubo stormed into a hut and woke the prisoners up, ordering an immediate *tenko*. One very proper lieutenant colonel insisted on dressing before he appeared on the parade ground. Kokubo took offence and launched a violent assault on the man, beating him to the ground. Every time the colonel stood up, Kokubo knocked him down again. The beating lasted at least fifteen minutes. Another time he made a British soldier kneel to attention while he raised his sword high in the air, before bringing it down with a sharp swipe. The spectators expected to see the man's head roll on the ground, but Kokubo instead swiped the top of his hair. Again he raised the sword and again brought it swinging down, but swiped clear of the neck. This cat-and-mouse toying went on for an agonising ten minutes, the soldier refusing to flinch. Eventually Kokubo stormed off. Such a magnificent display of bravery acted as a tonic on the prisoners: Kokubo had failed to break the spirit of the British soldier.

While being an officer had its advantages, it also brought risks. Officers felt a duty of protection towards the soldiers, so if a man in their working party was beaten, they often felt bound to intervene, although there was the chance that the angry guard would simply continue his attack with added ferocity, or turn on the officer instead. It was a risk that many willingly took.

One day while Peter was out on a working party, a guard sprang upon one of the men and attacked him, smashing the man's bony body with ferocity. As someone who valued loyalty and duty, and as an officer, Peter felt he had no choice but to step in.

Immediately the guard turned on Peter and beat him furiously. By the time they returned to camp, Peter was covered with welts and bruises but the guard had not finished with him yet. Walter recounted in his memoir the story that Peter told his family. He was 'tied to a stake with his head tilted upwards and made to stare into the sun. As the sun moved in the sky, so he was rotated on the stake.' He was ordered to keep his eyes open at all times, forcing him to stare full into the sun. If he closed his eyes for more than a second, he was beaten.

Hour after hour this continued, Peter's eyes burning painfully. By the time he was eventually cut free his head was a molten lump of pain and he could barely see. Such was the damage to his retinas that his eyes never recovered, and for the next few weeks his vision was so blurred that he lived in terror of accidentally chopping his fingers off with a hatchet as he hacked at the jungle.

Such cruel and elaborate punishments were not unusual on the railway. Some men were made to stand for hours in the burning sun holding a heavy rock high above their head. If they dropped the rock, or lowered it as their arms began to shake, they were beaten and the punishment would start again. Other men had a drum filled with water or rocks hung around their necks with wire that cut cruelly into their skin. One officer, who, like Peter, had intervened to stop a beating, was tied to a stake and burned alive. Reading the affidavits, what is astonishing is not that so many died but that so many survived.

The only respite from railway building was to become ill enough to be sent back to one of the larger camps, such as Chungkai, where there were hospitals with better equipment than those in the jungle camps. The equipment was not provided by the Japanese but by the prisoners, who set up workshops in which medical tools were made from scraps they could find or scrounge: stolen petrol drums were made into steel sterilisers, false legs were carved from wood, bicycle tubing and old bottles became blood-transfusion apparatus. Such ingenuity saved countless lives.

In March 1943, still in poor health, Peter left Thakilen and was sent back to Chungkai camp while Swinton and the rest of the group pressed on further north to Wang Pho South, where they were to build a wooden viaduct into a steep cliff side. Peter was lucky to avoid this move further north as it heralded a new and even darker era for the men working on the railway. In March 1943, with the British beginning to make incursions into Burma, the deadline for the railway's completion was brought forward to August of that year from December. This heralded the notorious seven-month 'speedo' period. Working conditions deteriorated rapidly, along with the health of the prisoners, as the engineers rushed to finish the project in time. Eight-hour days became twelve-hour days, then eighteen-hour days, and some men had to work for thirty hours without a break.

In the early months, from July 1942 to February 1943, the death toll among the prisoners of war was 418. From March to May 1943, as the tempo became more intense, the number of deaths rose to a thousand. From June to October that year, with the rains adding to their misery and bringing more disease, a horrific toll of 7,304 deaths was reached, of which more than half were British. Australian, Dutch and American prisoners of war made up the total.

Many of the deaths came from cholera, that most dreaded of diseases. The epidemic began in July 1943 and spread horror among the prisoners and the Japanese alike. A man could be perfectly healthy at breakfast and dead by lunch, his life sucked from him by the dreadful racking spasms that emptied his body of its vital fluids. Doctors battled to control it but the Japanese solution to cholera in the up-country camps, where no medicine was available, was simply to send the victims to Chungkai along the river, piling them onto barges where they lay emaciated and semi-conscious, wasted husks of men.

When they arrived at Chungkai many were already beyond saving. Cholera was so contagious that, as soon as he was confirmed as dead, the victim was burned on a pyre to prevent his bodily fluids causing contamination. His ashes were then interred in the ever-expanding camp cemetery. At the height of the epidemic, padres were conducting fifteen burials a day. Peter would have taken part in the cremation and burial parties – everyone took a turn – piling up bamboo to make a pyre, then standing back as the fire became hotter. Disturbingly, as the flames took hold, the sinews of the corpse tightened, causing it to 'sit up' and appear to move or twitch as though still alive.

Once the cholera epidemic was brought under control at Chungkai

- although it continued further up the railway - conditions at the camp improved thanks in large part to the efforts of the new camp commandant, Colonel Cary Owtram, who arrived there in June 1943. Cary made contact with a local trader, Sirivejjabhandu Boonpong, who supplied the camp with food and other goods. At great personal risk he also smuggled in vital medicines and other essentials. He became the prisoners' lifeline.

By September 1943 Peter had regained sufficient strength to be declared fit for work again. He was sent north to catch up with Group Two, who were now 200 kilometres north, near the Burma border. Here he was put back to work on railway construction, in the worst terrain imaginable, mountainous jungle so dense that the sky was barely visible, with lacerating thorns that tore at naked flesh. The 'speedo' period was still under way and the engineers were being berated by the Japanese high command for not having completed the railway by August. The prisoners would have to work harder, faster and ceaselessly.

As more men fell sick the rations allocated to the camp were cut further and further. Such an inadequate diet meant that the sick could not recover, and the 'well' men were overworked and fell sick, too, in a vicious, sadistic cycle.

Peter arrived at Krian Krai camp, 50 kilometres south of the Burma border, on 7 September 1943 to work on the final stretch of railway that would eventually meet the track coming south from Burma. This, wrote a man who was there at the same time as Peter, was 'a very bad camp' even by the standards of the railway line. During September and early October 1943, conditions were at their worst. With the engineers ordering that every man must work on the railway at Krian Krai, constructing a vast wooden trestle bridge, no one could be spared for hut building, so they had to sleep in thin tents, in fact tent linings, so ripped and flimsy that the rain and mud rushed through them. No drains had been dug, so the whole camp was a filthy swamp.

Each morning the men shuffled out of the camp on blistered feet, their legs riddled with ulcers, slipping and sliding in the glutinous mud, their bellies and limbs swollen with beriberi. At night their feet itched and felt as if they were on fire, a syndrome christened 'burning feet' and, like beriberi, caused by malnutrition.

The first task was cutting down the towering trees, which were then dragged to the location of the bridge by elephants. But when the slopes were too steep for the elephants, men had to take over, staggering under the weight of the enormous logs, which were then fashioned into piles – huge poles with sharpened ends that would form the bridge supports. These were hauled into place with ropes and hammered into the ground, using heavy metal weights. The enormous weights were pulled upwards by several men using ropes, then released onto the pile to drive it home.

It was dangerous, gruelling work that resulted in many accidents, some fatal, as exhausted, malarial men worked for fifteen or eighteen hours at a time. Every day they would parade, often in lashing rain, as the guards, supervised by the engineers, strode up and down the prisoners' lines, kicking their ulcerated shins, slapping their faces.

The hated Lieutenant Kokubo was in overall charge of administering the camps around Krian Krai but he left the prisoners largely to the mercy of three Korean guards, the senior of whom was twenty-one-year-old Fumimoto Tetsuichi. Fumimoto harboured a vindictive hatred for white men, especially officers. 'I am only a poor yellow coolie. You are haughty British officers but now you are my prisoners and I can do just what I like with you,' he gloated.

He was ordered by the senior engineer in charge to produce a certain number of men for work each day. If he could not find enough fit men he simply forced the sick to work. Men so crippled with dysentery and beriberi that they could not walk were forced to crawl a mile to the work site. If they were unable to work when they got there, they were beaten or simply left to die.

Some prisoners developed trench foot, while their tropical ulcers rotted and smelt so putrid that even the engineers sometimes sent them back to camp, out of disgust rather than kindness. In conditions of such utter misery some men talked of escape, but it was impossible. Others thought about jumping from the top of a cliff or a bridge for a quick death: surely anything was better than this agonising, miserable existence. Usually their friends talked them out of it, but some men's mental health was as broken as their bodies and they had to be confined to cages for their own safety, lest they run amok and attack a guard. In a neighbouring camp one deranged British officer became convinced that he was Jesus.

One day at Krian Krai a train pulled up on the nearest stretch of completed track. One of the carriages remained there overnight. It contained a group of young women, 'Jo Jo girls', whose purpose was to provide sexual services for the Japanese camp personnel. These women, forced or duped into sex slavery, infected with venereal disease and horribly mistreated, now showed tremendous compassion and bravery by passing money and cigarettes to the prisoners through the carriage window.

Yasume, days off, were now a distant memory. The prisoners had to work for fourteen weeks, fifteen hours a day, without any break. As well as beriberi, tropical ulcers, malaria and dengue fever, most were suffering skin diseases: dermatitis made their skin raw and blistered; scabies mites burrowed under the surface of their skin, causing it to itch so violently that they scratched themselves raw, causing more infection. Pellagra, caused by vitamin deficiency, brought the 'four Ds': dermatitis, diarrhoea, dementia and death.

The death rate was a shocking 22 per cent among British prisoners of war on the railway, compared with 3.5 per cent of those held by the Germans. Of the 30,131 British captives employed in the railway's construction and maintenance, 6,648 died, and the worst months during the whole three-and-a-half-year period were the latter half of 1943. A myth grew up that one prisoner of war died for every sleeper laid but this, as Rod Beattie has pointed out, is incorrect. There were 750,000 sleepers laid, and the total number of deaths among those working on it was 97,652, still a horrific tally.

The death rate among the Asian labourers was even more shocking than that of the prisoners of war: 56 per cent in the case of the Malay labourers, 44 per cent among the Burmese. As many of the Japanese records for the Asian labourers did not survive, the figures are approximate, but it is estimated that around 42,000 Malays and 40,000 Burmese died, as well as Javanese, Singaporean Chinese and Aminese.

In the prisoner-of-war camps, the mournful notes of the Last Post, played on a bugle, echoed again and again through the jungle. Soon the men knew the words of the funeral service by heart. Exhausted men summoned their remaining strength to dig graves into which they lowered the wasted remains of their companions.

When Peter talked of this period he said it felt as if he and his companions might as well have vanished from the surface of the earth. Deep in the jungle, no one except the Japanese knew where they were, or whether they were dead or alive. Peter's parents had been notified at the end of July 1942 that he had been taken prisoner in Singapore. In January 1943 the War Office got in touch again, notifying Arthur and Dorothea that their son was interned in Malaya, although by then he had been in Thailand for two months. Although the Japanese made the prisoners fill in postcards to be sent to their relatives in 1942 these often gathered dust in camp offices for months, and many relatives did not receive them until 1944, by which time the sender had often died. Peter's records suggest that January 1943 was the last time the Walkers received any news of him. From then on they did not know whether he was dead or alive.

The answer was somewhere in between. It was a half-life, an existence so bleak that it could not be called living. Hunger gnawed, keeping the prisoners from sleep in the few hours of rest they were permitted. Some caught snakes, rats, lizards and maggots: protein was vital for survival and no one could afford to be picky about where it came from. Peter sometimes ate bark from the trees.

But even picking leaves or bark could constitute a crime in the eyes of the ever-unpredictable guards and provoke a beating. Almost anything could be construed as an offence, if the guard was in the wrong mood. Failure to salute a guard was always punishable by beating. Another heinous transgression was failing to salute the Nippon flag wherever it was hung. Peter made this error once and was put in a 'no good house', as the Japanese called it: a cage made of bamboo, roughly five foot by five foot, with a corrugated-tin roof, in which it was impossible for a European man to stand up, while the roof turned it into an oven in the midday sun. This was not uncommon: some men were put in these cages for hours, some for days and, in one horrific case, weeks. There was no window, no latrine, barely any room to move. The guards urinated in his rice, but he had no choice but to eat it. Peter was not sure how long he was in there but when he was released he could barely move.

Peter's captors did not see this treatment as unfair or inhumane. Indeed, they used the cages to punish their own men, just as they beat and slapped them for trivial offences. Violence was an accepted means of discipline in the Imperial Japanese Army.

By October, Peter must have fallen ill again as he was sent to hospital at a camp 24 kilometres from Krian Krai, known simply as 226 Kilo

Camp. An indefatigable medical officer, Captain Alfie Roy, ran the camp hospital, working miracles in a bamboo hut with almost no medicine or equipment.

No medical records exist for the hospital at 226 Kilo, but it may have been at this camp that Peter had what was probably his closest encounter with death. He told his family that at one camp hospital he became so ill that he fell unconscious. He was later informed that harried orderlies, arriving to take away a corpse for cremation and burial, assumed that his wasted, motionless body was the corpse and carried it away towards the funeral pyre.

Just as someone was about to put a match to the bamboo, a member of the burial party noticed that the foot of the 'corpse' was moving slightly. Peter was hastily removed from the pyre and taken back to the hospital. He talked on several occasions about this horrifying incident, when death seemed to have its claws into him and Providence once again came to his rescue. He remained grateful ever after for his lucky escape.

At the end of October 1943 the two rail tracks from north and south finally met near a camp called Konkoita, and an elaborate ceremony was held at which a Japanese general drove a golden spike into an ebony sleeper and the first train crossed the joining point. The Japanese press were on hand to capture this great achievement of the Nippon Empire and a handful of the most robust-looking prisoners, who had worked in camp jobs rather than on the railway, were handpicked for the cameras. There was no sign of the dangerously ill and emaciated men who had actually built the railway, or of the graves of those who had died in doing so; the corpses of the thousands of Asian labourers who had perished were left to rot in the jungle. The Thai–Burma railway was indeed an extraordinary achievement in terms of engineering, but at a terrible cost.

With the two tracks joined – although there was still work to be done in levelling the track, building stations and other infrastructure – the Japanese were now willing to allow some of the more seriously ill prisoners to be sent south to the larger hospitals at the base camps. Peter remained at 226 Kilo until some time around Christmas 1943 when he was sent back to Chungkai, still sick, but alive.

The camp was now 10,000 strong and, as well as a hospital, a theatre had been built in which there were regular concerts. That Christmas a pantomime was put on at Chungkai, attended by prisoners and guards. For a few brief hours, the prisoners could forget the railway, the deaths of their friends, their aching bellies, and enjoy the performances. Some men took female parts, dressed in frocks and stockings made from mosquito nets. Among the prisoners were professional singers and actors, but the biggest applause came for the performance of a popular song, 'Oh! Oh! Antonio'.

By choosing an Italian song, the performer confirmed a rumour that had been circulating that the Allies had invaded Sicily earlier in the year. The Japanese in the audience were unaware of the significance. Had they known where the news had originated, there would have been serious trouble.

Early on during their captivity, several prisoners had managed to build wirelesses using smuggled crystals and batteries. Possession of one was punishable by execution but the brave men who operated the devices, hidden inside water-bottles, bamboo poles or even brooms, persisted, despite the regular searches.

Through them, the prisoners learned that not only were the Japanese suffering losses in the Pacific, but the Allies were making gains in Europe, too. The news had to be spread in whispers and eked out over weeks. One of the three wireless sets was found in a tin of peanuts and the two officers in charge of it were beaten to death. Nonetheless, others continued to risk their lives to receive and spread news. By the end of 1943 the Allies were in Italy, while the Americans were making gains in the Pacific. Such news brought hope, the most precious Christmas present of all.

Peter did not know that he had become an uncle again: in India, Tiggy and Edward were celebrating the birth of another son, Hamish, and in September, as Peter was shuffling bent-backed under heavy loads at Krian Krai, Bee had given birth in London to a baby girl. Mary Gaddis Plum's arrival was announced in *The Times* and copied to American newspapers so that Gaddis's friends and family at home would read the happy news.

As Peter was hovering between life and death in 226 Kilo camp, baby Mary was being wheeled in her pram around Cadogan Gardens, Knightsbridge, by Nurse Short, a uniformed nanny: Bee saw no need to be involved in the day-to-day business of child-rearing. 'So at least we are starting the nipper off in the genuine English fashion,' Gaddis wrote to his sister back in New Jersey.

Bee's privileged life could hardly have been more different from Peter's miserable existence. But there was a small glimmer of optimism in the skies above Thailand. While enemy bombers still flew over London – baby Mary apparently slept soundly through the noise of air-raid sirens and ack-ack guns – on the other side of the world, planes were flying above the Thai-Burma railway, identified as Allied aircraft, on their way to bomb Japanese installations in Bangkok. But, hopeful as this sign was, it made the Japanese jittery and watchful, which could only spell trouble.

II

'Never find yourself alone with him'

───◆───

IN HIS LETTERS home to his older sister, Sis (her actual name was Mary), Gaddis claimed that he did not find babies particularly interesting, adopting a studiedly casual air towards his daughter. But as he fondly describes baby Mary, rhapsodising about 'the nipper' for page after page, her fair hair, 'remarkably white skin, extremely long fingers, big feet, legs bent like a little frog, an engaging smile and a nose similar (so Bee says) to all babies', as well as her lusty pair of lungs, it is clear that, despite his protestations, Gaddis was completely smitten.

Mary only ever cried when it was time for her bottle - five days after the birth Bee had evidently stopped breastfeeding, if she had ever started - and Gaddis proudly reported that whenever Nurse Short took Mary out for a walk in her 'utility pram', a rather hideous contraption, like a box on wheels and almost impossible to steer, she was the object of many admiring looks.

Ruth was now back at St Thomas's, as was Harold. After the bombs that had nearly killed them in September 1940, the hospital had been hit again and again. One theory was that German bombers mistook it for the House of Commons, since it seemed to be targeted so relentlessly, suffering eight direct hits during the Blitz of 1940-41. The last major hit, in May 1941, had seen incendiaries set fire to the roof of one block, destroying an entire floor. Two members of the London Fire Brigade were killed, but after the night when Harold was injured, there were no more casualties among the hospital staff. As well as the direct hits, there were numerous near misses that shook the walls and blew out windows. When Ruth arrived back in September 1943, after two years at sector hospitals in Hampshire and Surrey, she found a hospital that, like much of London, was scarred and mutilated: windows yawned darkly without their glass, doctors and nurses picked their way gingerly along duckboards where floors had once been, heaps of rubble squatted sadly where buildings had once stood. Yet throughout that time the hospital had never closed its doors to patients.

Ruth was in the last stages of qualifying as a Nightingale nurse. She had passed her final exam in April 1943 and now had just four more months to go until she had 'completed her engagement' and was a fully-fledged Nightingale, eligible to wear the coveted badge. Harold had qualified the previous year and, after a stint in Godalming, had returned to the mother hospital as a senior casualty officer, dealing with the results of road accidents, factory injuries and, rather unglamorously, boils and whitlows, painful swellings caused by the herpes virus. He was already planning to specialise in obstetrics and gynaecology, inspired by the example of James Wyatt, his girlfriend Jill's uncle. He was playing cricket again, when time permitted, but Professor Elkington, with whom he had become good friends, had banned him from rugby. The St Thomas's side had to manage without him.

Ruth liked Jill, and was disappointed when her romance with Harold tailed off, for reasons she never discovered. As for romances of her own, she had neither the time nor the inclination.

As well as bumping into Harold, Ruth sometimes saw Bee, who was living with Gaddis in a flat in Dorchester Court, a mansion block on Sloane Street, not far from Harrods, with leafy garden squares nearby, ideal for giving the baby some air. With Nurse Short taking care of the more mundane aspects of motherhood, such as feeding and changing Mary, and a cook called Mrs Redmond in charge of the kitchen, Bee had more freedom than most young mothers. She had regained her slim figure rapidly, helped by the stringencies of rationing and her steely self-control. In a photograph of Mary's christening in November that year, Dorothea holds the baby while Bee looks stylish in a fur coat. Gaddis is in uniform, a study in paternal pride. Ruth and Harold came too. Although the two sisters still did not get on, Ruth took a close interest in Mary, who grew up to have more in common with her aunt than her mother: like Ruth she was a tomboy, who loved ponies and had no interest in fashion, the opposite of Bee.

Ruth told me that Bee would sometimes contact her at St Thomas's and, if she managed to get a message to her, would ask, 'Are you off duty? Can you take Mary for a walk?' If, by some chance, Ruth's free afternoon coincided with Nurse Short's day off, Ruth would walk the two and a half miles over to Sloane Street and wheel Mary around Hyde Park. Bee, she said, was not particularly maternal or affectionate and 'never looked after Mary'. Gaddis, however, described Bee as a capable and adoring mother.

Both were somewhat biased observers, so perhaps it would be fair to assume that, if Bee preferred to delegate some aspects of motherhood, this was hardly atypical of someone of her class, with the money to employ staff. And if she was not particularly demonstrative, it did not mean she did not love her daughter.

In the christening photograph, while everyone else is beaming delightedly at the baby, Ruth's gaze is elsewhere. She looks pensive and, although she may simply have been tired, or anxious to get back to St Thomas's for her next shift, it is tempting to wonder if her mind was somewhere else. Back in the summer, she had had a brief and unbearably poignant encounter at Waterloo station.

She had been returning from a visit to Weybridge to see her parents and was on her way back to St Thomas's when, passing through the station, she caught sight of a familiar back. Like St Thomas's, Waterloo had been hit during the Blitz but had gone quickly back to business, and that day the concourse was as crowded as ever, thronged with civilians and servicemen. But there was something about that particular serviceman, the way he stood, that caught her eye. Could it be him? He turned round. It was.

John Fisher was now Lieutenant Fisher, an officer in the Royal Army Service Corps. He had joined up after arriving back in England and had swiftly been commissioned, spending two months at Officer Training School in Southend. In June 1943 he was posted to County Antrim for weapons training, and after saying goodbye to Isabella and his mother, he was travelling to Northern Ireland via London.

It was there, while waiting for his train, that he and Ruth saw each other for the first time in six years. When I asked her what they had spoken about, Ruth could not recall the details of their conversation. There was so much to say that it was impossible to begin. His train was leaving in five minutes, so there was no time to discuss the future, or what John's marriage to Isabella meant. Soon John was striding towards his platform and Ruth was left wondering whether she would see him again.

The Blitz was over, but the bombers had not gone away for good. On 7 November 1943 there was another Luftwaffe attack on London, killing eighty-one mainly young people, when it hit the Black and White Milk Bar and the Cinderella Dance Club on Putney High Street, and injuring 248 others. But it was not until 22 January 1944 that the German bombers returned with a vengeance to take reprisals for the bombing of Germany, in what became known in Britain as 'the Little Blitz' or 'the Baby Blitz.' That first night, more than four hundred Luftwaffe bombers appeared over the London sky. This was Operation Steinbock, ordered by Hitler in revenge for the devastation wrought by Allied bombers. It lasted four months, targeting London and other cities such as Bristol, Portsmouth and Hull. Steinbock was a strategic failure as many bombs failed to hit their targets: Britain's defences, from Mosquito night fighters to radar-guided searchlights, were far more effective than they had been in 1940.

Of the 524 German aircraft involved 329 – 60 per cent – were lost, weakening the Luftwaffe so severely that when the Allied landings in Normandy began the Germans simply did not have the ability to strike back effectively.

This, however, was no consolation to those whose streets were hit by high-explosive or cluster bombs containing incendiaries. That first night nearly a hundred Londoners were killed or injured by bombs that were dropped across the city in two attacks, one at 8.40 p.m. and another just before dawn.

Londoners, who had become blasé about the minor raids, were once again subjected to terror from above, wondering whether they, or those they loved, would come safely through the night. Some were philosophical, greeting the Luftwaffe's return with a weary 'Here we go again,' as, once more, they got their blankets, gas masks and food supplies ready to troop down to the Underground stations and air-raid shelters. As Winston Churchill's daughter Mary later wrote, 'Londoners accepted this resumption of the air raids stolidly, but people were just that much wearier; three years of the sheer slog of wartime life since the first Blitz had inevitably taken their toll.' By the time Operation Steinbock was finally called off at the end of May it had caused the deaths of 1,500 people with another 3,000 seriously injured, a comparatively light toll compared with 43,500 civilians killed in the nine months of the Blitz that began in September 1940.

Harold had now begun his obstetrics training, which entailed going out into the community to deliver babies: although Bee had given birth to Mary in a clinic, most women still laboured and delivered their children at home. One evening he was in Battersea accompanying a midwife on her rounds when they were called to attend a woman in labour. Battersea was badly hit in the Little Blitz and when Harold got there an air raid was under way, so the delivery had to take place in an Anderson air-raid shelter in the woman's back garden. Anderson shelters, hump-backed corrugated-iron constructions six feet high and four feet six inches wide, were designed to shelter six people sitting or standing. Harold did not mention, in his article for the *St Thomas's Hospital Gazette* fifty years later, whether there were other family members or neighbours in the shelter as well as the three people at the centre of the drama. If so, it must have been very cramped and noisy, since the metal magnified any sounds from outside.

Despite this, the birth went smoothly and while the shelter reverberated to the sounds of destruction outside, inside Harold had the joyous task of placing the baby into his exhausted but happy mother's arms, a bizarre juxtaposition of life and death. However, Harold's work was not over. There was a complication. The baby had been safely delivered but the placenta had not. Normally the placenta is delivered within an hour of the baby's arrival, usually more quickly nowadays with the aid of an injection that speeds up the process. But in around two per cent of births it is 'retained' and must be removed by an obstetrician to prevent bleeding and potentially fatal haemorrhage. In such cases the woman is usually given an anaesthetic, but neither Harold nor the midwife had any to give her. If only she could get to hospital, not only would anaesthetic be available but so, too, would an experienced obstetrician. With the air raid on, and time of the essence, this was impossible. Harold would have to do his best. So, by torchlight, encouraged and advised by the midwife, Harold attempted the procedure. 'It was really,' he wrote, 'a "smash and grab" affair but the patient never turned a hair. The only complication was that the baby had one sticky eye later!'

Ruth was also at St Thomas's during those first weeks of the Little Blitz. She had several children under her care and when the drone of the bombers came closer they were frightened, asking her, 'Will we be all right?' This, she said, was one of the hardest questions she had to answer because she knew only too well that they might not be. There was no sense in worrying them further, so she just tried to keep them calm. This time, St Thomas's was spared, although the Houses of Parliament were bombed again. By the time the hospital was hit again, five months later, Ruth had gone to Hydestile hospital in Surrey. And the bomb that exploded next to St Thomas's on 4 July, damaging yet more of the beleaguered hospital's remaining buildings, was a new and terrible weapon.

In India, Walter had at last received the orders for which he had been waiting and hoping: he was going back to the war, to take the fight to the Japanese, to have a chance to avenge the defeats of 1942 and to test himself in battle against what he termed a 'first-class enemy'.

In September 1942, only four months after the retreat from Burma, the British had launched an offensive into the Arakan, a province in north-west Burma, now called Rakhine state.★ The first Arakan offensive had failed, and by May 1943 the British had had to abandon all the territory they had gained and retreat into India. But some gains came out of this disaster: the troops who had fought the Japanese in battle had seen that, although they were brave, they were not supermen and could be defeated. Slim had been sidelined in the Arakan, then fired by his immediate superior, the commander of the Eastern Army, but immediately reinstated when the commander was himself sacked.

In August 1943 Lord Louis Mountbatten, cousin of King George VI, was appointed Supreme Allied Commander, South East Asia, giving him control over all Allied land, sea and air operations in the region. Mountbatten is a controversial figure, but few dispute his energy and his willingness to move mountains to get things done. He took an immediate liking to Slim and asked if he would take command of a new army that would be formed for the reconquest of Burma. Slim was surprised but had no hesitation in accepting. The strength of the partnership between

---

★ Now infamous for the genocide carried out there against the Rohingya people

Slim and Mountbatten was to be a decisive factor in defeating the Japanese.

But, first, Slim needed to build his new army, which was named the Fourteenth Army, and to remedy some of the weaknesses he had identified on the retreat from Burma. The problem of logistics, keeping an army supplied hundreds of miles into enemy territory, had to be overcome, and for that air power would be vital. Combating disease, especially malaria, which had felled so many of the troops on the retreat, was imperative: there had to be greater prevention, as well as the means to treat sick or wounded men immediately, rather than ferrying them to hospitals in India, which kept them out of the battle for weeks or months. The inadequacies of soldiers' training had become painfully obvious in Burma and elsewhere: months of rigorous, comprehensive training were needed to remedy this. Once they were better trained they would feel more confident and their morale, at rock bottom after the defeats, would improve. They had to be motivated by a belief that they could and would succeed, and this sense of destiny had to filter down from the commanders to the lowliest private or rifleman.

But Slim did not just need a better army: he needed a bold plan to take back Burma, one that would play to his army's strengths and his enemy's weaknesses. The strategy he came up with was as risky as it was daring. He aimed to lure the Japanese across the border into Assam, in India. Here, separated from their supply lines, he would hold them, exhaust them and defeat them.

Over the winter Slim and his commanders trained and moulded the Fourteenth Army, practising patrols, jungle warfare, instilling in their troops the confidence that they could and would defeat the Japanese. Japanese tactics had been studied carefully and anticipated, and now the British had air power, meaning they could keep their forward troops supplied with everything from malaria pills to ammunition.

A second Arakan offensive was launched. To the surprise of the Japanese, the British did not retreat this time. They stood firm and fought back furiously, every man pressed into fighting, including clerks and muleteers – mules were the unsung heroes of the Fourteenth Army. The hardest-fought battle was that for the 'Administrative Box', an area 1,200 feet wide and a mile long where 7th Division had its main administration area. The fourth battalion of the 8th Gurkhas, a newly formed 'war-raised' battalion, was in the thick of this brutal nineteen-day battle, during which the field hospital was overrun and thirty-five patients and staff murdered.

The macabre spectacle of patients and doctors shot and bayoneted to death only served to stiffen the resolve of the defenders: each outpost, including one named Rorke's Drift, was doggedly defended until at last the Japanese, who were running short of ammunitions and food, were forced to abandon their attack. The battle of the Admin Box was a resounding victory for the Fourteenth Army.

But for the men of 4/8th Gurkhas there was a bitter postscript: just weeks later, their commanding officer was killed, along with his adjutant, when the vehicle they were travelling in hit a landmine. A new CO had to be appointed, Lieutenant Colonel N.D. Wingrove. Walter Walker, promoted to temporary major, was made his second in command. He said goodbye to Beryl and the twins in Quetta and once again journeyed across India to Calcutta, then flew into the Arakan, arriving on 4 April.

Within two weeks of his arrival the battalion was on the move again. Slim's design to lure the Japanese across the Burmese border was working. In fact the Japanese plans, though they did not know it, suited Slim's own strategy perfectly.

The Japanese counter-attack in the Arakan, named Operation HA-GO, had been a diversion, designed to distract from their real goal: the invasion of India. This was the brainchild of an ambitious general named Mutaguchi Renya, commander of the Japanese Fifteenth Army, who determined to capture the vast military supply bases on the Imphal Plain and cut the road linking the town of Imphal with Dimapur, a strategic railhead, vital for supplying the army.

Once the British were cut off in Assam they would retreat, as they had in Burma, or so Mutaguchi assumed. This new offensive, named U-GO, Mutaguchi vowed, would not only strangle at birth any British ambitions to retake Burma, but once his men had taken Dimapur it would open the gateway to India and all its riches. The people of India would then, it was imagined, rise up against the Raj and welcome the Japanese.

Furthermore, in taking Assam, the Japanese would neutralise its airfields from which aeroplanes flew supplies over the mountain range known as 'The Hump' to Chinese nationalist forces in China. So despite misgivings among Japanese high command about Mutaguchi's ambitious 'March on Delhi' as he termed it, and the risks of relying on a quick victory in Assam to secure supplies, U-GO was approved.

'The army has now reached the stage of invincibility, and the day when the Rising Sun will proclaim our definite victory in India is not far off,' announced Mutaguchi.

The truth was that the Japanese had overstretched themselves and, with their ships being sunk by Allied submarines, they were struggling to keep their extended empire supplied and wanted to inflict a defeat that would prevent the British from going on the offensive in Burma. Already the Chindits, a special long-range operations force, led by the maverick Brigadier Orde Wingate, had penetrated far into the north of Burma. The Japanese were rattled and saw a pre-emptive strike in India as the best means of defending Burma. They badly needed a victory at Imphal.

But Slim was equally determined to stop them and to deal their army a crippling blow in so doing. If he could tie up the Japanese for months in Assam, he would face a weakened foe when he took the fight back to them in Burma.

Although Slim had anticipated and hoped for the Japanese attack on Assam, he had not predicted quite how fast and furious it would be, or that so much of its weight would fall on the village of Kohima, which lay along the Imphal-Dimapur road. By early April, the garrisons at Kohima and Imphal were both surrounded and the Japanese had cut the road between the two. Kohima, garrisoned by a mere 2,500 men, many of whom were non-combatants, facing an enemy force of 15,000, saw some of the bitterest close-quarters fighting of the Second World War.

Its defenders hung grimly on, sometimes only yards apart from their attackers, while eighty miles to the south Imphal was being hammered from several different directions. Reinforcements were urgently needed and, flexing the muscles of his newly acquired air power, Slim arranged for an infantry division to be airlifted from the Arakan to Imphal. It was not enough. Further reinforcements were needed, and Walter's battalion, 4/8th Gurkhas, were among them. Hurriedly they packed up tents, mules and men, and travelled the six hundred miles by road, rail, barge and eventually air, arriving on 9 May.

Imphal lay on a plain surrounded by steep hills. Its loss would be catastrophic, and for two months the British-led defenders had been fending off repeated attacks. Now 4/8th launched into the fighting, tasked with attacking the enemy from behind in the hills north of Imphal. It was tricky terrain: the hills were covered with tall elephant grass that twisted around men's feet, tripping them. The monsoon broke as they arrived and heavy rain turned the steep hills into mudslides on which men and mules slithered and fell, while tanks had to be winched up with wires. It was exhausting just putting one foot in front of another in such conditions, let alone fighting.

The men of 4/8th had had little time to get to know their new CO or his second in command, Walter, before they were thrust back into battle at Sengmai, in the hills ten miles north of Imphal. Walter had turned up, fresh from enjoying peacetime life with his family in Quetta, while they had been sweating in the Admin Box. He wore immaculately pressed uniform, a stark contrast to his men's torn and sweat-stained jungle greens. Knowing nothing of his experiences on the Burma retreat of 1942, they eyed the dandyish newcomer warily.

As was their habit, the Japanese had dug deep bunkers and holes in the hillsides outside Imphal from which they could pour down a merciless fusillade on any advancing enemy. Pushing forward through mire and mortars, shouting the Gurkha battle-cry of '*Ayo Gurkhali!*' ('The Gurkhas are coming!'), 4/8th Gurkhas charged up the steep, slippery hillsides towards the Japanese bunkers, cutting the trip wires laid around them, and fell upon their inhabitants in ferocious hand-to-hand fighting with kukris and fists. It was a relentless, two-steps-forward-one-step-back slogging match of attack and counter-attack but, slowly, the Gurkhas edged forward, clearing one mist-shrouded hilltop after another, pushing the Japanese further back from Imphal.

Every unit kept a war diary, a brief, impersonal account of the movements, actions, casualties and enemy killed, typed up each day in terse, acronym-heavy military language. There are place names and map coordinates, but no sense of the battle's smells and sounds, no description of the horror of scaling a steep hill only to reach the summit and be met by a barrage of bullets and mortars from an enemy concealed on the reverse slope. The bare facts are noted: 'C Coy [company] reported 7 Pl [platoon] after having cut the wire reached objective killing 15 Japs in hand to hand fighting . . .'; '1045 No1 Pl [platoon] attack enemy

LMGs [light machine-guns] but driven back – 2 killed'; and another day, 'B Company was attacked strongly 3 times – all repulsed. Casualties 2 killed 3 wounded.' On 15th May D Company lost its commander and a week later another company commander was shot through both arms by a sniper.

On my grandparents' wall a picture hung that, as a child, both horrified and fascinated me. It was a print of a painting by the artist Terence Cuneo of the battle of Kohima. My grandmother, Beryl, banished it to the attic staircase because she disliked its gory detail, but after she died my grandfather brought it downstairs to hang proudly in the hall, an eloquent portrayal of the true nature of war.

The scene is a wasteland of shattered trees stripped of their branches, men rushing forward with their rifles, tank spewing flame from its gun, while further back a man falls, his arms in the air as he is hit. The ground is strewn with the twisted, mangled bodies of dead and dying men, Japanese, British and Indian. One man, still alive, lies clutching his stomach, his hands scarlet with blood pumping from a wound. Others sprawl dead, their bodies already bloating in the heat, pockmarked with shrapnel, their limbs a grotesque jumble among the other detritus of war, a discarded gun, an oil drum, a sheet of corrugated iron. You can almost hear the cacophony, the crunch of bayonets and kukris cutting through flesh and into bone, the groans of the wounded, whose blood seeps into the soil, the rattle of machine-guns and Bren guns, the whistle and crash of mortars, and smell the decaying bodies feasted on by flies, while smoke drifts over the battlefield towards the peaceful tree-clad hills in the distance. This was the reality of Walter's war.

Sometimes it was meltingly hot. Other days were rainy with swirling mists through which it was difficult to make out the landscape, let alone an enemy dug into the hillside, hidden by the elephant grass so that he was all but invisible until you were on top of him.

Tony Brand-Crombie, who, not long before, had been working in a bank and was now a captain with 4/8th, kept a diary during those weeks near Imphal. Intended for no one's eyes but his own, it now resides in the archive of the Gurkha Museum in Winchester and describes with painful honesty the misery of fighting on empty stomachs when poor weather made flying impossible – 'No air drop so we've definitely got nothing for tonight' – and scaling vertiginous hillsides while suffering from diarrhoea and exhaustion. On 26 June they climbed a long, steep path towards an airstrip: 'Jap bodies were lying on the side of the path and the stench was awful and some men were sick. In places it looked as though quite a number had been casualties and had been "finished off" to speed withdrawal.'

Moving behind the Japanese lines, 4/8th pushed, patrolling, probing, steadily, bloodily, dislodging the enemy trench by trench, bunker by bunker, hill by hill. In his memoir Walter did not write about this period in the war but it remained fresh in his mind. Just months before he died, in a letter to Angela (my mother-in-law), he wrote about an assault on three peaks near Imphal. Angela had written to him about an acquaintance's son who had suffered PTSD after serving with the army in Bosnia. Knowing his intolerance for modern sensitivities, I might have expected him to dismiss the diagnosis as modern namby-pambyism, but I could not have been more wrong.

In his reply, Walter described how the battalion had captured two hills after intense fighting, but had then been held up by the third. His senior officers were becoming impatient at the delay, so Walter left Battalion Headquarters and made his way forward to the rifle company that was supposed to be attacking, to find out what was happening.

It was, he wrote, 'a hazardous journey for the only way of reaching the troops who should have been carrying out the attack was along a ridge, which was covered by the Japanese with fire. I had to hang on to the reverse side of this ridge with my hands with a drop of several hundred feet below me until I reached the other side where my Gurkha soldiers were.'

There was no sign of the British officer commanding the company and the senior Gurkha officer, somewhat hesitantly, told Walter that the sahib was 'ill'. Walter eventually found him in a slit trench. This was a brave officer, who had fought with great courage in all the actions up until this point, but now he was exhausted and pushed beyond the limits of his endurance.

Walter left him in his trench while he briefed the Gurkha officer on how to carry out the attack, then called in an air strike and artillery on the Japanese positions. On a given signal, he instructed that the artillery should switch their explosives for solid shot to avoid blowing up the Gurkhas as they closed in on the bunkers. The only way to dislodge the

Japanese from bunkers dug twenty feet deep into the hill was by throwing in grenades, then going in with kukris. The attack went ahead according to Walter's plan and the hill was taken.

Meanwhile Walter took the officer back to Battalion Headquarters, explained to the medical officer what had happened and ordered him to get the man to the rear. Walter wrote a letter explaining why he had had to send the man back. 'About two months later, I received a letter from the Commander-in-Chief, India remonstrating and demanding why I had not court-martialled this officer . . .' He replied that the man had fought bravely in battles until that point and 'had simply had enough. In other words it was pure and simply a case of battle fatigue.' It is said that everyone has a well of courage and endurance but, if repeatedly drawn upon, the time may come when it will run dry. Walter recognised this and treated the officer with the compassion he deserved.

While 4/8th had been painstakingly removing the Japanese from the hills and ridges in their area, elsewhere on the Imphal perimeter the Japanese had been repulsed too, while at Kohima reinforcements had broken through the siege to come to the aid of the beleaguered British garrison. By mid-May the Japanese had begun to withdraw.

The Japanese had relied on supplying their army from the depots they would capture from the British when they took Imphal and Dimapur. As their offensive faltered and failed, Mutaguchi's men began to run out of food and other vital supplies. But, from his headquarters hundreds of miles away in Burma, the mulish general refused to accept the failure of his brilliant plan.

By 22 June the British had cleared the remaining Japanese roadblocks from the road between Kohima and Imphal. It was open again, although fighting continued in the surrounding hills to the east. Naga tribesmen from nearby villages began bringing in Japanese prisoners, who were too sick to escape, emaciated wrecks suffering from malaria and beriberi, their minds and bodies wasted as they raved and sobbed. Yet Mutaguchi still would not admit defeat. When his commanders begged to retreat to save his army from starvation he sacked them, still hoping to succeed. The village of Ukhrul to the north-east of Imphal became a rallying point for the tattered remnants of his army. Three brigades, including 89 Brigade, to which 4/8th Gurkhas belonged, were ordered to attack it.

On 2 July, after a thirty-five-mile march to get there, up and down steep climbs of 2,000 feet, they attacked the village with a burst of Tommy-gun fire that knocked two Japanese soldiers off the roof of the post office 'in the best Hollywood gangster tradition', as the scribe of the battalion newsletter put it. The Japanese had been taken by surprise but soon gathered themselves and mounted a fierce defence. The battle lasted six days as every attempt to dislodge the Japanese soldiers from their strong defensive positions was met with heavy fire, resulting in casualties. Only when the three brigades began to encircle the village did the remnants of the Japanese garrison give up their defence and break out. Ukhrul was taken.

Ukhrul was the last gasp of the U-GO offensive. By 13 July the newspapers in Britain were reporting the victory: 'Men of a battalion of the 8th Gurkha Rifles entered Ukhrul on Monday afternoon against opposition and are now mopping up the Japanese in the area which is encircled by 14th Army.' Of the 85,000 Japanese troops who had marched into India that March, around 53,000 were dead or missing. Many were found months later on the jungle paths leading back into Burma, their bones picked clean by maggots, arms still outstretched in appeal for food, water or pity. Meanwhile Slim's casualties were 12,500 at Imphal and 4,000 at Kohima: a terrible toll, but it was clear who the victors were.

The battle for Imphal and Kohima is now acknowledged as Britain's greatest victory of all time, although in truth it was not a 'British' victory since Fourteenth Army was a cosmopolitan force that included Gurkhas, Indians, Africans, Burmese and Nagas. For the Japanese it was among their greatest defeats. 'The March on Delhi' had turned into a rout.

Mutaguchi was recalled to Tokyo in disgrace, while General Slim and his two corps commanders were knighted on the Imphal Plain. Slim had got what he wanted: the Japanese had suffered catastrophic losses and the way was now open for the retaking of Burma. But not yet. 'Soldiers must be trained before they can fight, fed before they can march, and relieved before they are worn out,' was one of Slim's dictums. The Fourteenth Army had proved their mettle, but the fighting in Burma would be different and they would have to train hard for it. They were increasingly aware, too, of the triumphs and sacrifices beyond their own forces. News had reached them of the D-Day landings, the fighting in Normandy and of a new and terrifying kind of 'pilotless plane' that was now battering London: the V1.

The first V1s landed in London on 13 June 1944, one week after the D-Day landings. Having lost air superiority in Europe, Hitler retaliated with 'revenge weapons', *Vergeltungswaffen*. The aim was to undermine British morale by raining terror from the skies. The V1 - Revenge Weapon One - had a range of 150 miles and the government deliberated whether to call them pilotless planes or flying bombs, opting for the latter on the grounds that it was somehow less sinister. But for Londoners who had survived the Blitz, these new weapons, so swift, bringing death with almost no warning, seemed even more horrifying, more evil, than the bombers of the Blitz. The V1s, twenty-five feet long (about the length of a double-decker bus) and weighing two tons, one ton of which was explosive, made a whining, humming noise that rose to a loud rattling as it grew nearer.

When the engine cut out, the noise stopped and there was then an eerie silence before the bomb crashed to the ground. The destruction was horrifying. That first day, three V1s fell in Kent and Sussex, killing no one, but a fourth hit a railway bridge in Bethnal Green, east London, causing six deaths. It was three days before the government publicly acknowledged the new weapons, not wishing to give the Germans any indication that the V1s had hit their mark. The Allies had known about the long-range weapons for some time – back in February Churchill had warned in the House of Commons of possible attack 'either by pilotless aircraft, or possibly rockets, or both, on a considerable scale' - and Allied aircraft had been desperately trying to pinpoint and destroy the launch sites for six months. These operations now intensified as the ominous whine and rattle of the V1s were heard again and again over London.

A deadly armada of what looked from below like black crosses sped through the air and dropped on Kensington, Battersea, Wandsworth, Streatham and Putney. By the morning of 17 June, fourteen London boroughs had been hit, with eighteen people killed and many more injured. But the worst V1 incident of the war came the following day.

It was 11.11 a.m. on Sunday, 18 June when a V1 hit the Guards Chapel of Wellington Barracks on Birdcage Walk, near Buckingham Palace. The first lesson had just ended and the congregation had stood up to sing when there was a sudden blue flash, a tremendous crash, a shattering noise and the roof caved in. The V1 had exploded on it, bringing the walls tumbling down, burying people in rubble: 123 people were killed and another 141 seriously injured. It took until the Tuesday morning to dig out all of the living casualties. Stretchers ferried the injured into ambulances, which whisked them to hospitals around London, including St Thomas's. Some of those who were stable enough to be moved but still needed further treatment were taken to sector hospitals, such as Park Prewett, where the tall Guardsmen were too long for the hospital beds, and Hydestile where Ruth was working.

She was horrified by the 'slaughter', so many killed, so many left with life-changing injuries, but she got on with her job, cleaning and bandaging their wounds and preparing any that needed further surgery for theatre. The newspapers did not report the incident. By 29 June, just over two weeks since the first VI strike, 1,679 people had been killed and a further 5,000 seriously injured.

Since the end of the Blitz, children and families had been steadily streaming back to the cities from the countryside, but with this new, deadly menace that turned houses into matchsticks and busy shopping streets into bloodbaths, Londoners once again feared for their children. On 3 July, a second exodus began and by 3 August 225,000 mothers and children had left London. Those who remained in the city were once again living a partly subterranean existence, spending their nights in Underground stations or public air-raid shelters, their days alert for the sound of the deadly buzzing overhead.

In Knightsbridge, Bee and Gaddis were among the lucky Londoners who did not have to hurry to a public shelter: Dorchester Court had a basement. But with the VIs arriving by day as well as by night, even a stroll round the park with Nurse Short was not safe for baby Mary. Gaddis had to remain in London because of his role at the Air Ministry. Bee decided to stay with him, perhaps because she was still working there too. When she signed the marriage register at her wedding she left blank the space for 'Rank or Profession' but, then, so did most of the other women who signed it, not deeming their work professional or significant enough.

One family story seems to suggest that she was indeed still working at the Air Ministry when the VIs began to fall. She told her son that her closest call during the war was when she was running late for work one day and missed the bus. That bus, she said, was hit by a bomb, killing many of those on board.

On 30 June, a V1 rocket struck the Aldwych, in London WC2, a crescent-shaped street that was home to the Air Ministry's Adastral House and the BBC's Bush House. Five members of the Women's Auxiliary Air Force (WAAF) were among the forty-six people who lost their lives. It was 2.07 p.m. and the street was busy with office workers returning from their lunch break. Many were caught in the explosion and two double-decker buses were among the passing vehicles torn apart by the impact. It seems likely that this was Bee's brush with death, although as she left no records that confirm the anecdote, it is impossible to be sure. Perhaps she felt the need to have her own near-death story, like her siblings. But, then, almost every Londoner had a near miss. A detour to post a letter, or go back for something, stopping to talk to a neighbour, taking a different way to work: tiny, casual decisions often made the difference between life and death.

Bee and Gaddis decided that Mary would be safer outside London. Bee had friends, Austin and Joan Ferguson, who lived a short train ride out of London in a large house in Beaconsfield, with their three children and a Great Dane. It seemed the ideal solution: Mary and Nurse Short would live with them and Bee and Gaddis would visit whenever they could.

Gaddis must have struggled with the separation from his rosy-cheeked 'nipper'. But, as with other city parents, his child's safety had to come before his feelings so he agreed to the parting, certain that he and Bee were doing the right thing. Although it undoubtedly saved countless lives, some of those who were evacuated as small children have spoken of the lasting impact the separation from their parents had upon them. What's surprising is that even at the time many suspected it would do long-term damage. A study published in 1943 by the child psychologist Anna Freud, daughter of Sigmund, concluded that children who were sent away to safety in the countryside actually suffered worse mental trauma than those who remained in the city (at least, those who survived). For the under-twos, the damage was worst of all.

'The child feels suddenly deserted by all the known persons in its world to whom it has learned to attach importance . . .' she wrote. 'For several hours, or even for a day or two, this psychological craving of the child, the "hunger" for its mother, may over-ride all bodily sensations.'

It is unlikely that Bee or Gaddis knew of this research, and if they had, it would probably not have deterred them from doing what they felt necessary to keep Mary physically safe. But I wonder whether those months apart, even though Mary was too young to remember them, affected the mother–daughter relationship in years to come. Perhaps it was not simply a case of Bee being un-maternal but of the maternal bond having been severed too soon.

Bee and Gaddis visited their daughter at weekends, although perhaps not every weekend since Gaddis wrote that when they arrived at the Fergusons' house Mary 'looked at us without the least sign of recognition, but with Bee's handling the nipper soon knew her mother – as to "Dadie" he might have been "something that the cat brought in".' He consoled himself that the country air was doing her good.

As the months went by, each visit brought a new development, fondly relayed by Gaddis in his letters to Sis: 'We had tea in the nursery with the youngsters, the Austin Fergusons' two and our happy-go-lucky don't-care-a-damn galloper – she now crawls but it's much more like a slow motion, very slow gallop. I can see her in my mind's eye riding hell-for-leather across country with her old man . . .' Gaddis was right: Mary inherited his love of horses and was a fearless rider, never happier than when galloping across country or riding bareback on her favourite pony.

On Mary's first birthday, 17 September 1944, Bee and Gaddis went down to Beaconsfield to celebrate with her. Joan Ferguson had arranged a cake with icing and one candle but, wrote Gaddis, 'I fear that the nipper had no time for anything but the icing on her cake and even ignored the few presents that we were able to give her . . . I wait rather impatiently for the time when she can talk – I prefer a puppy dog to a baby that cannot express itself.'

He sent Sis several photographs of Mary, her cheerful, gregarious nature already evident as she strikes out across a sunlit lawn guided by Bee, whose reed-like legs (the 'Walker matchsticks' or 'bamboo shoots', as they were known in the family) and prominent cheekbones contrast with her daughter's sturdy toddler limbs and chubby cheeks.

Harold sometimes visited Bee at her flat and loved to annoy her by referring to the source of Gaddis's wealth: paper. He teased her that his fortune was founded on 'bog roll' and sometimes waved a piece at her, or pretended to find one on his foot. She seldom failed to rise to the bait.

Harold had left St Thomas's and was not there when the hospital suffered a direct hit: a V1 destroyed much of one block and damaged others, although once again there were, miraculously, no casualties. He had moved to Hammersmith Hospital, in west London, to continue his gynaecology and obstetrics training, when a V1 hit a nearby block of flats. Casualties were brought into the hospital, and for the next forty-eight hours Harold worked solidly treating them, knowing well that the skill of the surgeon and dedication of the nurses had saved his own life. Now he could do the same for these poor maimed and mutilated victims.

Ruth had been a St Thomas's nurse for five years now and she was becoming restless at Hydestile. Hitherto, her reports had been glowing, her record full of praise: 'Very conscientious. She is equable in temper and shows a great deal of common sense and is helpful to her colleagues and takes interest in her patients,' reads one such report. Elsewhere she is praised as 'quick and observant and has good technical and theoretical knowledge'. She was also, it was noted, 'not very tidy' and 'boisterous' – not a desirable quality in a young lady – but these minor quibbles were outweighed by her possessing 'the right spirit, character and instincts'.

But in 1944 there was an abrupt change of tone. Ruth, wrote Miss Hillyers, the matron, was 'not a happy influence whilst undertaking charge nurse's duties in the theatre'. Like her brother Walter, Ruth did not suffer fools gladly and always spoke her mind. If she felt that someone was not pulling their weight, or was being slow or clumsy, she would have said so. She was always frank and to the point, except when it came to talking about her emotions.

After more than four years of nursing air-raid victims, burned servicemen and traumatised children, of conforming to the strict rules of life as a Nightingale, of moving from one hospital to the next, battered St Thomas's, the huts of Hydestile and the former psychiatric hospitals of Park Prewett and Botleys Park in Surrey, Ruth wanted a more permanent change of scene. I suspect, too, that her heartbreak over John's marriage and the news that he and Isabella had had a son together in March 1944 might have contributed to her restlessness.

She decided to serve abroad with the Queen Alexandra's Imperial Military Nursing Service: some of her fellow St Thomas's nurses were already out in Normandy nursing the wounded in field hospitals. But by the time she applied there were no vacancies. Then, while visiting her parents in Weybridge one day, she met a friend of theirs who had worked for the British embassy in Cairo and told Ruth that the Anglo-American Hospital there was short of nurses. Normally they had twenty English sisters, but they were down to three. When the hospital authorities heard that Ruth was a Nightingale they offered her the job of theatre sister.

In October 1944 Ruth stepped aboard a ship bound for Ceylon via Port Said. The Mediterranean Sea was considered fairly safe now, with the Allied navies effectively in control, and although the passengers had to carry their lifejackets at all times and take part in regular lifeboat drills, on the ten-day voyage through the Mediterranean's smooth waters Ruth was able to relax for the first time in years. She was, she remembered, very tired. Cairo was a fresh start.

The Anglo-American Hospital was a private institution where the patients were a mix of wealthy civilians and officers. 'Other ranks' were not admitted. It was situated on Gezira Island in the Nile, in the centre of Cairo, and was connected to the rest of the city by several bridges, the newest and most elegant of which was the English Bridge.

It was the most sought-after residential area in Cairo, where English girls working for the embassy or Army Headquarters rented flats for exorbitant rents. Ruth was given her own room in the hospital, looking out on the Gezira Sporting Club, the oldest club in Egypt. Its sweeping lawns were immaculate, bordered by bougainvillaeas in every hue, jacaranda and acacia trees providing some shade while a panoply of tropical blooms burst forth from carefully tended flowerbeds.

There were two swimming pools, an eighteen-hole golf course, squash and tennis courts, cricket and polo grounds, a racetrack, a playground where wilting nannies pushed their young charges on swings, an elegant colonial clubhouse and a dining room, where home comforts such as steak and kidney pie and trifle were served. It was a little slice of England, an oasis from the squalid, dung-strewn streets where scrawny donkeys and once-fine horses dragging heavy carts were whipped to death, and where the raucous cries of street vendors and the pleas of beggars mingled with the incessant buzz of flies.

Again, social segregation was enforced: the club was open to Army officers only, not other ranks, smart expatriates and a few wealthy

Egyptians, although they were allowed only in certain areas. The club secretary, the steely-eyed, straight-backed Captain Pilley, patrolled the club on his bicycle throughout the day, barking reprimands at any who wandered beyond their allotted areas.

Ruth was given membership of the club as a perk of the job and spent all her spare hours on the golf course and tennis courts, or riding one of the club's horses around the racetrack in the morning before walking to the hospital to start her day's work.

One day she received a message at the hospital to see Captain Pilley. When Ruth entered his office his normally steely gaze softened. 'I've been watching you riding,' he told her. 'I've bought an ex-polo pony for my wife and she can't hold it. Would you like to exercise it every day for me?' So she did. Back in Tara days she had been a regular on the gymkhana circuit and now she began entering the gymkhanas held at the Gezira Club, winning rosettes and cups to decorate her room at the hospital.

There were two large army headquarters in Cairo and every afternoon the officers would break off work at 1 p.m. and not resume till the evening, leaving the afternoons free for relaxation or sport. As the historian Artemis Cooper describes, in *Cairo in the War*, 'Most English-speaking people in Cairo at this time were under thirty, and involved in the immensely significant task of winning the war. It gave their world a glamorous magazine feature quality; and within it, women were a privileged minority.'

Cairo can scarcely have been a better place for an exhausted young woman nursing a broken heart. Before the war it had been a cosmopolitan city of different creeds and races: Muslims, Jews, Copts and Christians, Egyptians, English, French, Maltese, Cypriots and Greeks. During the Desert War its streets had thronged with British and Australian troops, and although it was no longer the military nerve centre it had been back in the days of El Alamein, it retained its air of glamour and importance.

Compared with Britain, Egypt was a land of plenty. For someone who had spent the last four years eating powdered eggs and small portions of everything, to be able to go to the famous Italian bakery Groppi's and eat as many delicious cakes and pastries as she could consume felt fantastically decadent. If not quite paradise then Cairo, as far as Ruth was concerned, came pretty close.

Not everyone shared her view. The writer Lawrence Durrell, older brother of the animal-loving Gerald, arrived there in 1941, having escaped Greece as the Nazis invaded, and was revolted by the flies, cruelty, cripples and terrible disparities between the lives of the rich and the poor.

An Australian war artist, Harold B. Herbert, who had visited a few months earlier, complained that Cairo was so sweltering in midsummer that even the ice in the cocktails was hot, and if you drank too many and had to put a hand out to steady yourself on the iron knob of your bedpost, you almost burned it on the red-hot metal. But, he conceded, its sunshine was an antidote to London fogs and engendered a 'lazy, luxurious feeling'. Ruth did not have time to be lazy as she was the only theatre sister at the Anglo-American, but compared with the unrelenting hours at St Thomas's, life there was relaxed.

No more Matron castigating her for messy hair – the matron at the Anglo-American was much less strict than her St Thomas's counterpart and became a good friend. No more sterilising, scrubbing and dusting either: Egyptian orderlies took care of all that. And rather than thirty patients on a ward she had three under her care at a time. As well as officers, the hospital looked after the staff of the British embassy so Ruth met the cream of expatriate society.

The hospital's patients and their conditions varied hugely. With the Desert War long since over there was no stream of battle casualties or air-raid victims. But the army maintained a large presence in Cairo, so there was a steady arrival of officers suffering from dengue fever and other tropical diseases, and on the civilian side, there was everything from appendicitis to pregnancy.

The heat seemed to melt inhibitions even among the very upper echelons of English society in Cairo, as Ruth soon discovered. There was, she remembered, 'a lot of scandal'. One titled English lady came to give birth at the hospital and, between contractions, hissed that they must tell her husband the baby was premature or he would know that it was not his but his military assistant's. The medical staff did their best to be accommodating.

Ruth remembered another case where diplomacy was required. There were two prominent Jewish families in Cairo and the daughter of one was due to marry the son of the other. The bride-to-be came to the hospital one day and confided in Ruth: 'Can you help in any way, because I'm not a virgin, and I have to be?'

Ruth sympathised. If the bridegroom discovered on the wedding night that he had been 'cheated' by his supposedly virgin bride, the consequences for her would likely be terrible. 'I said I'd have a word with one of the doctors and he said, "Yes, we'll sew her up." So he sewed her up and she got married and went off on honeymoon and came back, and the husband came with her to see us, very pleased, and said, "Can you do anything? Unfortunately I haven't been able to consummate the marriage. Can you help?" So we said, "Oh, yes." We took the stitches out and all was well. She was delighted, she got away with it.' It is a grim thought that a young woman was driven to opt for genital mutilation to protect herself from a worse fate.

One day Ruth arrived in the operating theatre to assist at an emergency appendectomy to find that the surgeon who was due to perform it was blind drunk. Ruth was horrified but, with no other surgeon available and the risk that the appendix might burst, the operation had to go ahead. The surgeon's hand was shaking terribly as he made the first incision and Ruth was worried that he might cut a blood vessel, so she guided his hand throughout the operation.

'I'd seen so many appendixes taken out that I could say to him, "Not just there." Luckily it was straightforward and, with Ruth's help, the appendix was successfully removed. The following day, the surgeon thanked her profusely and apologised. Ruth told him in no uncertain terms that he must never drink again while he was on call.

She had frequently warned the matron that having just one theatre sister was not enough. 'What happens if I'm ill?' she asked. Her concern turned out to be prophetic. One day, while playing golf, she was seized with pain in her abdomen. As the hospital was just yards away she was able to see a surgeon immediately, who insisted that an operation was needed. But who would lay out the instruments and get patient and theatre ready for surgery? 'Well, I shall have to,' Ruth replied, and duly prepared everything before she was anaesthetised.

Had times been different, perhaps Ruth might have trained as a doctor or a surgeon, like her brother Harold. But, bright and capable though she was, it never occurred to her. Besides, she had gone into nursing to fill in the time before marrying and to help in the war effort, not to carve out a career in medicine.

Although Ruth's marriage plans had become a casualty of war, Cairo was full of opportunities for romance. The Gezira Club was awash with eligible young men, who were more than happy to escort her to a nightclub or for dinner. One man she and all other English girls in Cairo had been warned to steer clear of was King Farouk, Egypt's youthful playboy monarch, whose wandering eye and predilection for European women, especially blondes, was well known. 'Never find yourself alone with him,' was the stern advice.

She often saw him out on the town, sometimes at his favourite night-time haunt, the Auberge des Pyramides, which had opened a year earlier, a vast edifice in the desert, only a mile or so from the Pyramids, where belly dancers, who undulated to the best orchestra in Cairo, and dancing troupes performed spectacular shows on an open-air stage under a canopy of stars.

And then there was Shepheard's Hotel, the most opulent, most sought-after nightspot in Cairo. 'Anybody who has never sipped a drink on the terrace of Shepheard's really hasn't lived,' as the saying went. One evening Ruth was having dinner there with a friend, a pretty blonde. They were halfway through their meal when King Farouk arrived with a party to dine. Shortly after they had taken their seats a waiter glided over bearing a note on a silver tray. It was from the king, addressed to the blonde, requesting that she join him for dinner. She scribbled a reply: 'No, I'm having dinner with a friend, thank you very much.'

A few moments later the waiter returned. This time he handed over not a note, but a quantity of money. The blonde looked at it and picked up her pen to write another note. Before doing so, she asked Ruth, 'Are you ready to make a dash for it?' Ruth said that she was. The note was written and sent back to Farouk, with the money. The two girls got up from their table and ran out of Shepheard's. The note, admirably succinct, had read: 'If for dinner far too much. If for anything else far too little.' Farouk, used to getting his way where women were concerned, was doubtless not amused.

12

'A cool, ruthless type, like Montgomery, with a very good brain'

—•—

E DWARD'S EARLY ARMY career had been filled with promise and praise. He had done well enough to be sent to Staff College and had then been selected for staff jobs in Bareilly and Delhi. But he was impatient, as Walter had been, to go to war. He had been in the army since 1929: now he wanted to put into practice those fifteen years of training, the field exercises in Multan and Hong Kong, the drills and marches, the leadership techniques and battlefield tactics he had learned at Quetta, the knowledge he had absorbed at Army Headquarters in Delhi. It was all very well inhabiting the corridors of power, but men younger and less experienced than he were now being given command of battalions, leading men into battle. Edward did not want to be consigned to a desk job for ever. He wanted to fight, to lead, to triumph, to put his courage and military acumen to the test. With Walter now fighting the Japanese, and Peter their prisoner, Edward wanted a chance to strike back at Britain's enemies, whether in the east or the west.

It would mean separation from his family, but that would make little difference. He and Tiggy had seen little of each other in the last two and a half years, and while he was in Delhi, she had taken up residence in the hill station of Ootacamund where their second son, Hamish, had been born. During the war, many army wives with absent husbands left their army quarters for the hill stations, which soon became hotbeds of intrigue and scandal as bored and lonely women took refuge in the arms of other men. But if Edward had any concerns that Tiggy's flirtatiousness might tip over into infidelity, he had to cast aside his qualms when, in May 1944, he was at last posted out of India.

It was not the posting he might have hoped for: the battalion he was sent to join was doing nothing more exciting than guard duty in

Iraq, but at least the Middle East was nearer to the war in Europe. He reached Baghdad on 3 June, three days before D-Day, and spent the next months moving around Iraq and attending a course. Then, in September 1944, he received the longed-for news: he was promoted to (acting) lieutenant colonel and given command of a battalion, the 1st Jaipur Infantry. The regiment had been raised by the Maharajah of Jaipur himself, known as Jai, a polo-playing prince, a man very much after Edward's heart. Edward had met Jai in India, introduced by Tiggy, and the social connection might have helped to secure Edward's appoint-ment. The Jaipurs were as yet untested in battle, like their new CO, but they would soon have the chance to prove themselves. They were about to fight the Germans in Italy.

The Allies had landed in Italy the previous September, following their victory in North Africa and their successful invasion of Sicily in July 1943. Winston Churchill had hoped that Italy would be the 'soft under-belly' of Europe, through which the Allies would strike at Hitler. It had turned out to be anything but soft. Mussolini had been deposed, and on 8 September 1943, the Italians had surrendered to the Allies, and the British and American armies landed in southern Italy. But the Germans reacted swiftly and harshly, disarming their former Italian allies, and mounted fierce counter-attacks against the Allies. A bloody, slogging campaign followed, as the Allies tried to push north up through Italy, and the Germans fought doggedly to hold them back with a series of defensive lines that ran across the country from coast to coast. Despite fierce German resistance, the Allies eventually broke through one by one until, in August 1944, they had reached the Gothic Line, a swathe of defences stretching from west to east across the Apennine mountains.

The mountainous Italian terrain, a mass of ridges, rivers and ravines, favoured the German defenders, who could dig in on the high ground while attackers had to labour up precipitous slopes through their field of fire. The Allies had far superior air power, but the Germans had used slave labourers to construct fearsome defences of concrete and steel in the mountains until they bristled with thousands of machine-gun nests, bunkers blasted out of the rock, observation posts, booby traps, minefields and barbed wire everywhere.

The Allies, led by Field Marshal Sir Harold Alexander, Walter's old boss in Burma, hoped to break through the Gothic Line before winter and reach the Po Valley, over which tanks and other armoured vehicles could charge forward, rather than spending a miserable winter snowbound in the mountains.

By early September 1944, the Allies had punched several large holes in the Gothic Line. It seemed that they really would break through soon to the valley. But then the offensive stalled amid atrocious weather, and by the time 1st Jaipur arrived in the mountains to take up their position in the San Godenzo sector of the Gothic Line, it was becoming horribly apparent that they would be there for the winter.

When Edward took over command of 1st Jaipur Infantry he was the only British officer in the battalion of 865 men. He had a few short weeks to win their confidence and to train them for mountain warfare before they went into battle for the first time. But winning men's confidence, and giving them confidence in themselves, was Edward's forte. 'Popular with all ranks, British and Indian,' ran one of his confidential reports.

It is easy to be cynical about such descriptions. Did anyone ask the soldiers what they thought of Edward? And, if so, would they have felt able to say if they found him overbearing or unfair? But confidential reports were not generally whitewashes, and within a battalion it was usually obvious which officers were liked and respected, and which were not.

After taking command, Edward spent the first few weeks training his men, preparing them as best he could for what lay ahead. The first action came on 2 October when a patrol came into contact with the enemy and a short, sharp engagement ensued. The tempo soon increased. Over the coming weeks the Jaipurs pushed and probed, engaging the German defenders in a series of brisk but fierce engagements. Edward was an aggressive commander and the Jaipurs did well, inflicting more casualties than they received and inching gradually forward, each ridge and hilltop, each abandoned house or shepherd's hut bitterly contested. Even locating the enemy in the ruins of a building or dug into foxholes was no easy task amid persistent fog and smoke grenades.

After three weeks of intense fighting, the battalion was withdrawn from the front line for a brief respite. But Edward did not let them rest, taking the opportunity to train them further to ensure that they learned from their mistakes before they were sent back into battle. His battalion headquarters was almost constantly mortared and shelled - one night thirty shells dropped in the area around it, the shattering explosions breaking through the deadly rattle of the Spandaus (German machine-guns).

The brigadier dropped by to congratulate Edward and his men on their aggressive patrolling, but elsewhere on the Gothic Line the advance had stalled. Casualties on both sides were severe: the chances of survival for front-line troops on the Gothic Line were worse than those on the Western Front in 1914-18. In his headquarters Field Marshal Alexander was being forced to reshape his plans. Like Slim in Burma, he was suffering from his own theatre of war being the poor relation to the main offensive in northern Europe. Divisions, aeroplanes and supplies had all been diverted from Italy to France, reducing his strength and his ability to deal the Germans a killer blow that could have ended the Italian campaign by Christmas.

The rain and fog of October and November had now given way to freezing ice and snow, the harshest Italian winter in living memory. At the end of November the Jaipurs were given another rest, a chance to wash in a mobile bath, and to watch Indian films on a cinema screen rigged up in a nearby village.

1st Jaipur Infantry gets few mentions in histories of the Italian campaign: no war reporters visited to witness the patrols that could suddenly erupt into furious exchanges of machine-gun fire, or the long nights when the protective cloak of darkness was ripped away as one side or the other fired Very lights, flares that lit the sky like murderous fireworks, revealing their opponents' positions and enabling the silhouetted figures on opposing hillsides more accurately to rain shells down on the other.

However, 1st Jaipur's activities had not gone unnoticed by senior commanders, and in early December three members of the battalion were awarded medals, with the army's public-relations department on hand to photograph Edward awarding a Military Cross to the battalion's doctor. A couple of weeks later the PR men returned, this time with a film camera to record the Jaipurs going into action in the Apennines. The film reel is held in the deep recesses of the Imperial War Museum but it can be viewed on request so I took with me Edward's daughter-in-law, Maybe - his son Nick was unable to come - and together we watched the fifteen minutes or so of footage. I was hoping for a glimpse of Edward although, never having met him, I was not sure I would recognise him. But Maybe would.

The film begins with footage of a battery of mountain howitzers, manned by British gunners wearing what is described as 'windproof clothing'. The gun is loaded and fired across the snowy valley. The camera then moves on to an Indian Bren-gun team in a snowy foxhole. The Jaipur soldiers have no windproof clothing or greatcoats but appear to be wearing normal khaki battle dress in the sub-zero conditions. The camera crew becomes more intrepid, moving forward to where a section of infantry is climbing up a steep, snowy slope towards a stone building. A British officer spots them and gestures violently for the cameraman to get down. Still, he manages to capture them creeping past the building, along a section of broken wall. A Bren-gunner gives covering fire to the infantry.

All at once the bald notes of the war diary come alive. This is what it was like to huddle in the snow as a freezing wind whips the mountainside, slicing through thin uniforms. Then the order comes. That building over there, the one on the other side of the valley that may or may not be occupied by Germans and may be surrounded by mines ready to rip through flesh and bones if one man takes an unlucky step: you must attack it. Stealth is the word, creeping forward, but eventually you're going to have to get up close, close enough to throw a grenade. And then all hell might break loose. Despite the silence - these films have no sound - the tension is almost palpable.

Then, maddeningly, the camera cuts away - perhaps the film crew sensibly kept their heads down when the firefight broke out, or perhaps the building was empty after all and there was nothing to film. The last frames show a line of Indian soldiers walking on a narrow mountain path, wearing what appear to be rubber boots and tin helmets. The path is slushy and muddy but the men press on with their rifles and packs. In the middle of them marches a lone British officer wearing a beret rather than a helmet, a pistol at his hip. He looks up at the camera. I pause the reel, freezing the frame. Is it him? He's slightly blurred, but he seems to be the right height, with a moustache. He smiles. Maybe, watching with me, is confident: it *is* Edward.

He looks surprisingly cheerful for one who was about to spend Christmas Day far from his young family, attacking the village of Budrio, which they knew the Germans were occupying as they had seen mules bringing ammunition into the village at dawn. But he was fulfilling his life's ambition, commanding men in battle and doing it well. He was a good officer, considerate towards his soldiers but efficient, imaginative, zealous, working hard to outwit the enemy, to ensure that his men inflicted more losses than they took. He was a cog in a wheel – a small but vital one – that would eventually run over the German war machine and help bring Hitler to his knees.

Although he was nearly six thousand miles away, Walter's existence was similar. He, too, had been busy whipping his battalion into battle-readiness, not in snowy mountains but in the hills outside Kohima where 4/8th Gurkhas had come to rest after the battle of Imphal.

In September that year, as Edward was getting to know his battalion, Walter had taken over command of 4/8th. Not everyone was pleased with the appointment. The outgoing CO had not been popular and was not considered the right man to lead the battalion into the forthcoming battles in Burma, but Walter had hardly endeared himself to his officers either, having rubbed many of them up the wrong way with his forth-right style and intolerance for anything less than perfection.

Tony Brand-Crombie had taken an immediate dislike to Walter when he was still second in command, writing in his diary that Walter 'has it in for me – to think that in peace time I'd never even have spoken to his type let alone take orders from him – God forbid he should ever command this Battalion as I think most of the BOs [British officers] would walk out – in plain he's not liked or wanted !!!!'

I was a bit taken aback when I read this in the cool, polished surround-ings of the Gurkha Museum. Of course I was aware that the kindly, genial grandfather I knew, a generous host who charmed my friends with his courtly manners, impeccable attire and impish sense of humour, was a different person from the army commander with a fearsome repu-tation – even medal-festooned generals admitted to having been terrified of him as young officers. The address given at his memorial service at Sandhurst acknowledged that some had seen him as 'a tyrant and a bully – a cross between Beau Brummel and Captain Bligh.'

All the same it was a slight shock to read in that tiny pencil-written notebook quite what loathing he provoked in some quarters, at least at first.

Major Peter Myers, a company commander who had just been awarded an MC for going forward under heavy fire at Ukhrul to rescue a wounded man, was stunned to be bawled out by Walter, who was still second in command, over what seemed him to be a trivial matter, arriving minutes late to his company's physical training parade. Walter had summoned Myers to his tent, where 'the air turned blue' and Myers was threatened with being reduced in rank to captain if he offended again. Myers was so appalled at the way Walter had treated him that he seriously considered transferring to another battalion but a friend persuaded him to stay, a decision, he later wrote, that he never regretted.

Not everyone was so wary. Captain Scott Gilmore, an American publishing executive from Connecticut, who had joined the Gurkhas after two years as an ambulance driver with the American Field Service and was a similar age to Walter, wrote home to his family to tell them about his new CO: 'A cool, ruthless type, like Montgomery, with a very good brain.' He concluded that, despite being aloof, Walter was 'an outstanding commander'.

Walter had that relatively rare attribute of not needing to be liked: if his actions made him unpopular, then so be it. He would not be deflected from what he felt was right and he did not care who he offended as long as he got the results he wanted. In this respect he was much more his mother's son than his father's: Arthur was accommodating, while Dorothea did not try to avoid confrontation and never shrank from making her feelings plain.

Walter was worried about the state of his battalion. The men had fought gallantly, there was no question of that, but in ten months of almost solid action there had been no chance for training, for learning the lessons from what had gone wrong that would make the difference between life and death. They had become sloppy, careless, war-weary and, deep down, they knew it. Morale was at a low ebb. They were aware that, of all the battalions in 89th Indian Infantry Brigade, they were the least impressive.

The now-departed CO had allowed things to slide. Of course the men had needed to rest, to regain their strength and enjoy the tranquillity of the Kohima countryside, playing cards in the makeshift mess, watching pelicans paddle in the streams and the sun set over the blue-green hills, enjoying visits from the friendly Naga tribesmen, who came to trade their colourful beads for cigarettes – they bore no historical ill will towards the British for the war of 1880 in which Walter's grandfather had fought against them.

But now battle was looming again. The victories at Kohima and Imphal had paved the way back to Burma for Slim's Fourteenth Army to retake what had been lost, to inflict a decisive defeat on the Japanese. Slim's plan to lure Mutaguchi's army into India had worked brilliantly. But despite the decisive defeat on the Imphal Plain, they would still be facing a formidable foe in Burma. And Walter feared that, in its current state, his battalion was not ready to take it on. He had a few months to remedy this and he set about his task with determination.

He did not see the need to explain himself or justify his harsh approach. Neither did he mince his words nor shrink from punishing soldiers and officers alike if they fell short of his exacting standards. He stayed up late, sometimes all night, planning, devising new training drills, writing instructions and orders, studying accounts of ambushes that had gone wrong, working out why, refining the technique, then making his men practise it and practise it again until they were perfect, so that when they sprang a real ambush, not a single Japanese soldier would escape.

Walter had learned ambush techniques on the North West Frontier, where the smallest mistake could get you killed by an enemy as skilled as he was cruel. Now he was facing a foe of similar expertise and savagery: he had seen what the Japanese did to men they captured, hanging them, bayoneting them, even crucifying them. He did not want anyone under his command to suffer such a fate.

To succeed against this enemy was not simply about bravery: they would have to be meticulous, diligent, anticipating every possible move and forming a plan to counter each. They would have to be fit and healthy, too, for the kind of marches and battles that lay ahead.

No detail escaped Walter's attention. Latrines had to be exactly six feet deep; spoil from foxholes or bunkers had to be removed and taken to the rear rather than left in heaps. Some rules seemed petty and absurd but there were sound reasons behind them: if earth from bunkers was left in heaps it would be visible to the enemy, alerting them to the Gurkhas' positions. If latrines were not deep enough, disease would spread. If you fired when the enemy first approached your ambush, there was a good chance that many would escape. But lie still and silent, hold your fire until every man in the party is within range, and you might kill them all.

So, while men from other battalions were resting and socialising, Walter's were digging, drilling, bayoneting dummies, patrolling through the night, marching forty miles through thick bamboo jungle carrying 50-pound packs, charging up hillsides in simulated attacks – and doing it all again if it did not go precisely according to plan. If anyone raised doubts about whether or not something could be done, Walter would do it himself.

He held every officer responsible for his men's welfare, down to the tiniest detail: if a rifleman had not taken his anti-malarial mecaprine tablets, or was missing his hat, if a mosquito net was not properly tucked in, Walter would want to know why: he took his lead from Slim, who sacked officers who failed to ensure their men took their mepacrine.

There was inspection after inspection after inspection. The mules' harnesses, men's boots, the caps on water-bottles: all had to be in good condition for the months ahead in Burma, when getting a replacement bootlace or bridle would be difficult.

Some resented it, others grumbled or threatened to transfer to another battalion and a few did. None of the British officers in 4/8th were 'regulars', professional army officers. They had been civilians until recently and, for the most part, had not joined the army to make a career of it, simply to fight in the war. Little wonder that Walter's stern, authoritarian approach grated at first. Who was this martinet with his silk scarf and cigarette holder to treat them, the victors of the Arakan and Imphal, like schoolboys?

Walter's smart appearance certainly created a stir. Peter Myers recalled that during the fighting at Ukhrul Walter had suddenly appeared at his side. 'He was wearing the same uniform that we all wore, but that was the only similarity between his appearance and mine. I was scruffy and comfortably dirty, probably unshaven because we had limited water, while he was immaculately dressed in an ironed uniform, spotless and polished boots, stiffened and pressed Gurkha hat, and smoking a cigarette in one of those very slim "torpedo" Dunhill holders. I was certainly impressed, but also incredulous that any officer under those conditions could look like that and would also wish to.'

But the mutterings began to subside as it became clear what Walter was trying to achieve. 'They realised that I was trying to train them, like racehorses, and to ensure that when they went into battle they were not killed . . . to save lives,' he explained to Charles Allen.

He knew, of course, that deaths would be unavoidable in the forthcoming battles, but he did not want his men to die needlessly due to a 'friendly' bullet, an ill-sited trench, a sleepy sentry.

Patrick Davis joined the battalion in July 1944 as a nineteen-year-old lieutenant. The author of one of the most evocative and honest accounts of the Second World War, *A Child at Arms*,★ he was struck by the change in tempo when Walter took over, but saw the method behind the relentlessness of the new regime: 'I thought it right that he was tough and hard on us. We were not playing a game. There would be no umpire to rule the enemy offside. No one would bring back to life our dead.'

Another younger officer, Robert Findlay, thought that Walter had such magnetism that 'I would have done anything for him and believed his opinion could not be wrong. I was "his", hook, line and sinker, from the outset.'

Gradually a transformation came over the battalion. As they practised again and again, every man became an expert in his role. From making do, they now excelled. They knew they could march all day and all night if they had to. They knew the best method for crossing a river under fire, for laying an ambush, for making a flank attack, for patrolling, for digging bunkers at night, where to plant the panjis – sharpened sticks that were used in place of barbed wire and on which an enemy would be impaled as he tried to crawl or run towards a trench – and how many of them to carry. They were at a pitch of physical and mental toughness. They were battle-ready.

And, as his confidence grew in his men, Walter allowed himself to unbend a little. His officers saw his 'off-duty' character, relaxed, humorous and friendly. He was always polite, even when angry he never raised his voice, and he was as ready to praise as to punish. They could see that, although he pushed them hard, he pushed himself even harder. Perhaps his headmaster's advice all those years ago, about encouraging rather than

---

★ Fortunately for me, not one but three of Walter's officers wrote books about their experiences under his command: Patrick Davis, Scott Gilmore and Denis Sheil-Small (see bibliography)

alienating people, leading rather than driving, had hit home. By the end of 1944, even the sceptics had been won over.

Although Walter devoted much time and training to keeping his men alive, war, as he knew, was not primarily about preserving life but taking it. They were going back into battle against the Japanese not simply to wrest Burma back but to defeat them so comprehensively that the Nippon Empire would be dealt a mortal blow.

Beyond Burma lay Thailand. Walter was a professional soldier so emotion had no place in his planning, but having seen what the Japanese did to those they captured and knowing that his brother, if he was still alive, was their prisoner, must have sharpened his resolve.

Every night Walter would write orders for the next day's actions. With the practical details of who was to do what, where and how, he wrote a series of commands he called Golden Rules. Each night one would be printed and distributed around the camp and repeated by the Gurkhas. Some of the rules and slogans were practical; others were rousing, somewhat brutal, exhortations. 'Destroy the enemy. Do not allow him to retire,' was one. 'The only good Jap is a dead one,' announced another. 'Shoot to kill – kill to live'; 'Dig or die'; 'I prefer life to death, therefore I must never surrender'; 'In any situation the one unforgivable crime is inaction'; 'It should be the ambition of every man of the 8th Gurkhas to redden his kukri or bayonet in the enemy's blood.' The motto of the battalion was: 'LIVE HARD, FIGHT HARD and when necessary, DIE HARD.'

It is hard to imagine any British commander today giving such orders. Today the commands would be couched in more conciliatory language, urging magnanimity and preservation of life wherever possible. But this, as they all knew, was a fight to the death. Kill or be killed. Surrender was not an option: no one wanted to become the captive of an enemy who used prisoners for bayonet practice or burned them alive. The only way to end the war against the Japanese was to annihilate their army so thoroughly that they would have to surrender unconditionally. And, despite their defeats at Kohima and Imphal, and in the Arakan, the Japanese were still determined to hang on to their newly acquired empire at any cost. In October 1944, in the battle of the Leyte Gulf, the Japanese had deployed a new and desperate tactic, the kamikaze suicide bomber, flown by pilots who deliberately crashed their planes into American warships. In Burma, they would perfect another form of suicide attack:

they dug holes in ground over which tanks would pass. A soldier would then lie in the hole, clutching a bomb, which he would detonate when a tank passed over.

And in Burma they had the advantage of being the occupiers, knowing the ground and being able to prepare it. Thanks to the railway, they could move men and supplies there easily from elsewhere. While Walter had been fighting at Imphal, the railway on which Peter had toiled had brought nearly 50,000 tons of military supplies including fuel and oil, as well as a full division of troops, towards the front. When the fighting reached the central plain of Burma the railway would make it easy to resupply them, carrying more than 100,000 tons of ammunition, fuel and other goods to the front.

The orders to move into Burma came through just before Christmas. Like Edward, Walter would now lead his own battalion into battle. He knew that not all of them would survive. He himself might be among the casualties. He did not dwell on such possibilities when he addressed them on 20 December as they prepared to move out of the Kohima hills.

After praising them for their hard work over the previous months he warned them that the fighting ahead would be tough but assured them, 'I know we shall kill and utterly destroy the Japanese whenever and wherever we meet him . . . I pin my faith in you. You have character: you have grit and guts; you have supreme courage; you have high morale, you have discipline, you have pride in your race; and now that you have confidence as a result of our recent training, you are all going to be an everlasting credit to the cause, which roused the manhood of Nepal and the land which gave you birth.'

Many new recruits had joined the battalion since Imphal and about a third of the men, some barely out of their teens, had yet to experience battle. Until recently most fresh recruits had never travelled in a motor vehicle, worn boots or handled a firearm. But if any felt nerves they did not show them. Gurkhas were, and are, renowned all over the world for their courage, as well as an imperturbable cheerfulness under even the grimmest of conditions: 'Better to die than be a coward' is the Gurkha motto. Accompanying the battalion were around fifty non-combatants, mule-drivers, cooks, sweepers and water-carriers, the men who kept the battalion going.

Two days after Walter's rousing speech they said goodbye to Kohima, the glorious views and the nurses at the nearby hospital, with whom they had struck up friendships and, in at least one case, romance. They packed up their tents and piled into lorries for the first leg of their 450-mile journey into Burma.

At Kohima there is a memorial to those who died there, on which a bronze panel bears the inscription:

> When You Go Home,
> Tell them of Us and Say,
> For your Tomorrow,
> We Gave our Today.

There are perhaps no other words that so movingly and eloquently sum up the losses and sacrifices of war as the Kohima epitaph. That Walter and his men would soon experience those losses was brought home to them when they reached Tamu on Christmas Eve 1944, a town in which exhausted refugees had succumbed to death within sight of the border in 1942, and into which the starving, disease-riddled remnants of the Japanese Army had crawled from Imphal and Kohima two years later. The stench of death still hung in the air about the town but, fortunately, 4/8th camped just outside it.

The morning after their arrival a thick veil of mist gradually rose from the ground of the teak forest where they were, and huge drops of moisture, so heavy they sounded like hail, fell from the trees. It was Christmas Day.

It must have been a quiet Christmas in Weybridge for Arthur and Dorothea, with Ruth in Cairo, Edward in Italy, Walter in Burma and Peter, they hoped, still in Thailand. Only Bee and Harold remained on home shores. Arthur was feeling his age now and he wanted more than anything to have news of Peter, to know that he would see his son again before he died. Arthur's friend Colonel Grimston, Peter's godfather, had died the previous year and, since nothing had been heard from Peter for so long, had assumed that his godson was dead and written him out of his will. But Arthur had faith that somehow Peter would survive, that he would be reunited with his son.

After two weeks and yet more intensive training, Walter and his men

were on the move again. They now knew a little more of what lay
ahead. They were part of 89 Brigade, which was part of 7th Division,
which in turn belonged to 4 Corps and ultimately to the Fourteenth
Army, commanded by General Slim. While other elements of the
Fourteenth Army fought the Japanese around Mandalay and advanced
eastwards, the task of 7th Division – 'the Golden Arrow Division' – was
to strike south through Burma and cross the Irrawaddy River. They
would sweep across the plain of Central Burma and down through the
jungle to encircle and destroy the Japanese bases in that area, cutting off
any Japanese forces attempting to retreat south towards Rangoon and
Thailand.

In recognition of their transformation into a crack battalion, 4/8th
Gurkhas were given the honour of leading the brigade as it pushed
deeper into enemy territory. After the first 125 miles they said goodbye
to the trucks, keeping only a couple of jeeps and the steadfast mules,
which carried wireless sets, food, ammunition and other necessities.

The rest of the distance would be covered on foot. They would begin
each day at dawn, march for ten or fifteen miles, then find a spot suitable for an air-drop. Air supply was one of Slim's aces, enabling his
troops to be supplied many hundreds of miles from their bases. They
would not, like the Japanese, have to live off the land, stealing from
Burmese villages. They would receive food for men and mules, as well
as ammunition, spare wireless parts and other essentials, from parcels
dropped by Dakotas that came hurtling through the sky to land with a
resounding thump on the ground. Tragically, in one of the first deaths
4/8th suffered in Burma, a falling hay bale broke the neck of one man
who failed to get clear of the drop zone in time.

Once they had gathered in the supplies, the afternoons would be spent
digging foxholes, trenches and bunkers in case of a surprise attack. These
not only offered protection but would, if the worst happened, become
their graves. Meanwhile Walter pored over maps, planning the next day's
march, holding conferences with his company commanders and giving
them their orders, attending conferences at Brigade Headquarters, assessing
reports brought in by the Burmese intelligence officers attached to the
battalion, who would relay any information they had been able to extract
from the villagers. After nearly three years of Japanese occupation, the
Burmese had good cause to be wary of soldiers of any flag.

While the Japanese had left some areas of Burma relatively untouched during their occupation, elsewhere they had unleashed a reign of terror, seizing villagers' cattle and crops, raping women and girls. It was clear that their slogan of 'Asia for the Asians' and their promises of giving Burma its independence were empty. Anyone suspected of helping the British was treated mercilessly. Later on their journey the men of 4/8th were horrified to see the mutilated body of an Indian man, accused of collaboration, lying in a ditch.

The first part of the march was fairly pleasant, despite blisters. Burma then, as now, was a breathtakingly beautiful country. The tracks on which they marched passed through stubbled paddy-fields and past neat, orderly villages of wooden houses on stilts, monasteries and pagodas, their soft curves silhouetted against the sky and strung with silver bells that tinkled on the breeze.

According to what the villagers told them, the Japanese were with-drawing east: often they had been there a day, or two days, before the Gurkhas arrived. Walter sent out patrols into the countryside to search for any sign of them. One patrol, creeping through the jungle, was alarmed when the night erupted with a loud crashing coming towards them. They cocked their rifles but held fire as they had been trained until the enemy was upon them. But on this occasion they did not fire at all. The 'enemy' turned out to be a herd of elephants that charged right through their position without noticing them.

So far on their journey not a shot had been fired in anger. As they drew closer to the Irrawaddy the pace and air of anticipation increased. Morale was given a boost by a visit from none other than General Slim, who chatted to the men in fluent Gurkhali. Walter also did his best to keep spirits up, insisting that no officer could see to his own comforts until he had inspected his men's feet at the end of each day's march and sent their owners for medical attention if necessary. He remained immacu-lately turned out, even in the steaming jungle or on the burning plain, his trousers freshly pressed to a sharp crease – his mule carried a charcoal iron and starch – a green silk scarf at his throat. As Scott Gilmore shrewdly surmised in his memoir *A Connecticut Yankee in the 8th Gurkha Rifles*, his crisp appearance and air of nonchalance were designed to reassure: 'It said to the men, "Look how calm I am. Nothing to worry about!"'

On 1 February, after a night march of twenty-six miles in ten hours over hills and along dry riverbeds, with no moon and almost zero visibility, they finally reached their objective: the village of Myitche, near the banks of the Irrawaddy. Here, they would prepare for the river crossing. Would they be able to slip quietly across the river, unnoticed? Or would it be like the Normandy landings, as men struggled to get out of the boats without being mown down by guns on the cliffs above? And how easy would it be to get across that vast, silvery expanse, whose waters hid shifting sandbanks on which boats could easily be stranded? They waited in a lemon orchard for the order to begin the crossing.

4/8th Gurkhas would not be the first across. That dubious honour was awarded to the 2nd South Lancashire Regiment, who were given collapsible boats in which to make the mile-and-a-half crossing. On the night of 13 February the Gurkhas helped to unload the boats from lorries and carry them silently down to the river in the dark. Surprise was essential to success so it was vital that the Japanese should neither see nor hear the preparations for the river crossing. Wishing the Lancashires good luck, they crept back to their hiding places and waited for daybreak.

As the first light of dawn began filtering through the mist in the early hours of 14 February, the whine and crack of bullets signified that the battle had begun. If the element of surprise had been there, it had gone now. The men of 4/8th watched with horror as several of the collapsible boats became stuck on the sandbanks, caught in the whirling midstream currents, or became stranded when their engines failed, providing unmissable targets to Japanese machine-guns on the cliffs above.

Major Denis Sheil-Small, commander of Walter's B Company, felt 'a sense of horror . . . as those lads, with whom we had laughed and joked a few hours previously, continued to drop under the hail of bullets. The drifting craft, draped with the bodies of the dead, trailing their lifeless limbs in the fuming currents, presented an awesome sight as the cries of the wounded carried to our ears across the water,' he recalled in his memoir, *Green Shadows: A Gurkha Story*.

By the time 4/8th took to their boats, the Japanese machine-guns had been silenced with a barrage of artillery, tank gunfire and aerial bombing, and they crossed the river in a peaceful flotilla.

The Irrawaddy crossing was the longest opposed river crossing in the entire Second World War. Today the river is peaceful. Fishing boats and coal barges glide by as farmers take their water buffaloes for a cooling dip in the shallows. On its western bank, stately river-cruise boats anchor up beneath the cliffs where the landing craft beached in February 1945, and beyond, the town of Nyaung-U is now a mass of hotels and guest-houses. But in February 1945 it was a small village of pagodas and wooden houses on stilts. There was a chance that the houses were harbouring Japanese soldiers ready to ambush the troops who had just landed on the beaches below the cliff and stop them establishing a bridgehead, so Walter sent a patrol into the village to flush out any lurking enemy. So far, the battalion had 'failed to draw blood', as the aggrieved author of its monthly news chronicle noted. Was this about to change?

An army cameraman followed the Gurkhas as they headed towards the village and, again, I was able to view the film reel at the Imperial War Museum. There was no sign of Walter, but I watched the Gurkhas march cheerfully and briskly, one man leading a mule, bayonets on rifles, kukris gleaming on their belts beside their water-bottles. As they near the village their tread becomes visibly softer, slower, stealthier on the sandy soil. They fan out around the buildings. Two men approach a house on stilts, creeping towards it cautiously, then more confidently as it becomes obvious that it is empty and they can move on to their next objective.

The newsreel was an intriguing glimpse, bringing alive the bare facts of the war diary and the reminiscences of the diarists and memoirists. But it was just a few brief minutes, in black and white, over all too briefly. So I decided that I had to see for myself the country where Walter had fought the battles that had had such an impact on the rest of his life and on the lives of those around him. With my cousin Lucy I set out for Burma – now Myanmar – to follow in his footsteps as far as I could, armed with the 4/8th's war diary, his own memoir and those of other 4/8th officers who had fought under him. From Mandalay I took a boat down the Irrawaddy River to Nyaung-U, landing at roughly the spot where he had disembarked after crossing the river, and followed in his tracks as best I could.

Just a couple of miles from Nyaung-U lies one of the most astonishing sights in the world. The medieval city of Pagan (now Bagan) was the ancient capital of Burma where, a millennium ago, its kings built more than ten thousand temples and pagodas. Some fell victim to wars and earthquakes over the intervening years and the city was abandoned but around three thousand temples and pagodas remain, their curving bell-shaped stupas and tapering spires dotted across the plain as far as the eye can see, a fairytale city in the scrubby desert landscape.

But in 1945 there was no opportunity to explore. Pagan was a battle-ground as 1/11th Sikhs, who also belonged to 89 Brigade, fought to drive the Japanese out of the ancient city. Walter and his Gurkhas had to be content with seeing it from a distance. They continued south on their mission to meet 'the Jap' and utterly destroy him, while other elements of Fourteenth Army were embroiled in brutal fighting at Mandalay and nearby Meiktila.

Walter ordered one of his young officers to lead a night patrol into Kinka to see if any enemy were still lurking. Treading cautiously through the village in the moonlight, they came across a small party of Japanese and in a short, sharp fight killed eleven. It was a small victory, but a victory nonetheless. The battalion had had their first 'blood' of the campaign.

By 2 March they had reached the hamlet of Ywathit. According to information gleaned from local villagers, the Japanese had dug in at the next village along, Milaungbya. South of this village were the oilfields of Yenangyaung where, in April 1942, Walter had arrived in time to see their destruction. The Japanese had rapidly restored them to working order and were now determined to hold on to them.

The countryside here is parched and scrubby, small hills rising abruptly out of the plain, clusters of palms sprouting from the sandy soil. It is only a short drive from Bagan, but few tourists stop by so the villagers were surprised to see us when we turned up with a car and a guide-trans-lator. Armed with maps from memoirs, showing where the battalion's various companies had taken up position, and with copies of the war diary, we asked a few villagers if they knew where the fighting had taken place seventy-three years ago. Although we did not find anyone old enough to remember the war, one man's father had told him about it and he accompanied us on his motorbike down a dusty track off the main road and up a small hill to the village of Kya-O, a satellite of Milaungbya. This was where Walter had sited his headquarters, on a small hill topped by a pagoda, an intricately carved confection of icing-sugar white with a gold-leafed dome and tapering spire.

There were other buildings in the complex. Large cooking pots and baskets lay on the ground, a swing hung from a tree and a tan-coloured dog with a litter of plump puppies reclined in the shade of a well. It would be hard to find a more serene scene, yet this small hill became the crucible of battle in March 1945. Here, in the shadow of the pagoda, the Gurkhas dug out a bunker that became Walter's battalion headquarters for nearly a month. Looking down from the pagoda gives you an almost panoramic view of the surrounding countryside, making it the ideal spot for a commander. To the west, the land slopes towards fields, beyond which flows the Irrawaddy. To the east was the small hamlet of Ywathit and further south was Milaungbya itself, a sprawling village bisected by a road. Walter would have been amused to know that the hill has been known ever since as the General's Hill, although he was then a mere lieutenant colonel. Looking out over the peaceful, scrubby countryside, the village neatly laid out below us, I shuddered to imagine it transformed into a war-torn wasteland, leafy trees reduced to torn stumps, the wooden houses flattened like cardboard, families forced to flee into the countryside.

The battle began on 2 March when C Company attacked the enemy and succeeded in pushing them back, in the face of heavy grenade and machine-gun fire, into the southern end of Milaungbya. Eleven enemy dead were counted. But that was only the beginning.

Two days later, Walter summoned Denis Sheil-Small, commander of B Company, to a meeting at his pagoda headquarters. To the accompaniment of the tinkling bells strung from the spire, Walter gave him his orders. The Japanese might have been pushed back, but it was only a matter of time before they counter-attacked and Walter had identified the likely direction. Towards Ywathit and beyond, the terrain was softly undulating and criss-crossed with cactus hedges and knife-edge ridges, providing the perfect cover through which the Japanese could make a sweeping advance to attack the rest of the battalion in Milaungbya's north. They needed to be stopped. He told Denis to take up position along their likely path of advance, beyond Ywathit.

He set out with Denis and one platoon to select the best spot. A few hundred yards beyond Ywathit there was a *chaung*, a dry ditch, and beyond that a hill that rose from the dusty earth and dipped slightly in the middle, forming a natural fort. The villagers of Ywathit had already fled into the surrounding countryside. (By the time they returned some weeks later they found that every single house in the village had been flattened and the animals were all dead, except for a solitary horse. This was all too common: Burma suffered more damage in the war than any other country in Asia.)

Walter and Denis crept forward cautiously to inspect the position, which they named 'Fort'. The sandy ground made it impossible not to kick up clouds of dust that were an easy clue to their presence, but eventually they reached Fort and scanned the area with their binoculars. They could see no movement among the tall palm trees and stilted houses of Milaungbya, but Walter decided that B Company should dig in there as it was a good position. Just as he had returned to his headquarters, and before Denis's men had had a chance to dig so much as a single foxhole, the air erupted in a violent explosion. With ear-splitting bangs, grenades began smashing down among them and machine-gun bullets smacked into the soil, sending up geysers of dust, as three hundred Japanese soldiers emerged from the ditches where they had been hiding, screened by cactus bushes, and began rushing towards Fort. Denis's wireless was immediately smashed so he had no way of contacting Walter, or vice versa. All Walter could do was to listen to the sounds of battle, not knowing who was getting the better of it. Denis sent a runner to inform Walter of their predicament: they were outnumbered and badly exposed. A Japanese machine-gunner took up residence on a ridge overlooking Fort and began spewing a deadly fire onto the Gurkhas. Grenades arced and fell on Fort, although luckily many failed to explode. More parties of Japanese emerged from dead ground and ran towards them, yelling their blood-curdling war-cry: 'Banzai!'

They were held off for a while by the actions of a brave Gurkha, who stood on top of the ridge, firing his Bren gun in the direction of the closest Japanese machine-gun until he crumpled to the ground, his face a mask of blood. Denis managed to pull his body into a trench, where it transpired that he was still alive.

The Japanese were coming closer and their artillery continued to pulverise Fort with devastating accuracy. They could see more Japanese entering Ywathit. This was bad news as they would soon be in a position to attack the company from the rear, cut them off from the rest of the battalion and annihilate them.

Another breathless runner arrived at Walter's headquarters to explain their predicament. Walter now faced a terrible dilemma. The best way of halting the Japanese attack, or at least taking some of the heat out of it, would be to call artillery strikes down on the Japanese positions. But with no telephone or wireless contact, no artillery observer to co-ordinate the strikes and the situation so fluid, he could not be sure of the exact positions of Denis's men, so there was a grave risk of them being hit too. But if he did nothing, the whole company would be overrun and perhaps slaughtered.

He had repeatedly told his men that the only bad decision in battle is to take no decision. The decision was now his to take, his alone.

Over at Fort, Denis and B Company were holding their ground as machine-gun bullets and grenades ripped back and forth. Men crumpled and fell, their blood running into the soil. Despite their tenacity and bravery – Denis would later be awarded an MC, with one of his Gurkha platoon commanders – the Japanese were closing in on them fast. They were now only a few yards away so Denis and his men unsheathed their kukris, the Gurkhas shouting with excitement as they prepared for a hand-to-hand fight.

And then there came a roar, like an express train tearing through a station, and a series of loud thuds. It was shells, British shells from the artillery battery that supported 4/8th Gurkhas, and they were falling on the advancing Japanese. The yells of 'Banzai!' became screams of pain and the attack began to falter. But then, to Denis's horror, a shell fell on his rear position and suddenly it was his men who lay shouting and bleeding in agony. Two Gurkhas were killed, one instantly, and three others crawled towards shelter, badly wounded. All casualties are terrible, but those caused by your own fire somehow more so.

The explosions continued. The Japanese, pounded by shells that fell in front, behind and on top of them, surrounding them in smoke, killing and maiming, were trapped in a killing zone and had no choice but to stagger back towards the village to find shelter. Half an hour later they were seen retreating, carrying their dead and wounded. The attack had been repelled, the company saved and the battle won. Thirty-nine Japanese bodies were counted but many more had been killed and carried off.

Walter had made a difficult decision and it had paid off but not without cost. I do not think he was tormented by regret over it. He tended to look forward rather than back and, in any case, in his view, and that of Denis Sheil-Small, he had taken the only action possible in the circumstances and it had saved the day.

That night the attacks resumed but, with another company now joining the defenders at Fort, they held them off. When day broke Walter returned to check on their situation. He ordered a patrol to be sent into a nearby patch of long grass to flush out any enemy who might have infiltrated it. Almost immediately a rifle shot rang out, killing the leading rifleman, and two Japanese soldiers were seen fleeing back to the village. One was immediately brought down in a burst of Tommy-gun fire but the other figure continued running, twisting and turning, hurling himself from cover to cover as every man in the patrol fired upon him, joined by Denis and Walter, who grabbed rifles and also took aim, shooting frantically in what Denis later admitted frankly was a lust to kill. It might have been comic if it had not been murderous. Amazingly, every bullet missed and the Japanese soldier disappeared from view, apparently unhurt.

Throughout March the battalion remained at Milaungbya, mounting a series of attacks. The heat was stupefying, there was little shade and they were plagued by flies. 'Seldom have we been in quite such an uncomfortable place,' Scott Gilmore wrote home.

To the east, the battles for Mandalay and Meiktila continued. At Milaungbya, the task was not to gain or hold ground but to intercept and tie up Japanese troops who were heading north and to kill as many as possible. It was, as Walter described it, a 'rat hunt': the 4/8th had to lure the Japanese, trap them and kill them. For their part the 'rats' refused to be moved. They dug themselves into bunkers and trenches and laced the ground with mines. Shelling was relentless and Walter's headquarters were targeted, but although the next-door bunker was completely destroyed, his own was not hit.

On 8 March Walter launched another attack, accompanied by a squadron of tanks from the Gordon Highlanders. He had rehearsed it thoroughly with the officers involved, using a diagram in the sand, and the battle went according to plan, with large numbers of enemy killed. Afterwards Walter visited the battle scene. The once orderly village had been turned into a wasteland of spent cartridges, mess tins, bloody bandages, broken rifles, Japanese notebooks and diaries, all abandoned as they retreated. A few days later, the Japanese, seeing that the Gurkhas had not occupied their vacated positions, returned and took up residence again.

The heat grew intense as March wore on, 105 degrees in the shade. A water lorry trundled round the positions so that men could fill their bottles. Although most of the villagers had fled Milaungbya, the monks remained in the monastery.

Walter was under pressure from Brigade Headquarters to bring in a live Japanese prisoner for questioning, to try to elicit more information about Japanese positions and plans than could be gleaned from notebooks and diaries. But for the Japanese the shame of being taken prisoner meant that they preferred death to such dishonour. Or, at least, most did. At Milaungbya I heard a story that would have made Walter, had he been alive, erupt either with laughter or fury.

Several of the villagers told us that during the battle a frightened young Japanese officer had bolted, leaving his comrades to continue the fighting. He had fled to the monastery and been given refuge there. This was an unusual story: there are few accounts of Japanese soldiers, still less an officer, giving in to their fear and simply fleeing. It was unthinkable. I had to learn more, so we took a detour to the monastery. We were warmly welcomed by the monks, who bade us sit down, cross-legged, at a table and brought us tea, grapes and some odd but not unpleasant chicken-flavoured cupcakes. We drank and ate as they told us the story of the Japanese fugitive while two curious young novices peeped at us from behind a pillar.

The officer had apparently run away from his unit on the first day of battle, arrived at the monastery and begged for their protection. The monks, like most of their countrymen, had suffered at the hands of the Japanese occupiers: the abbot had relations who had been killed and raped, the villagers' crops had been ruined, their trees chopped down, their countryside despoiled. But, as they explained, Buddhists are obliged to save life if they can so they took in the frightened young man and gave him a robe. When Walter sent an officer to the monastery to ask them whether they had seen the Japanese, the officer had no idea that, hiding in plain sight among the other monks in saffron robes, their shaved heads bent over their bowls at lunchtime, was a Japanese officer who could have yielded a wealth of information. None the wiser, Walter's officer left the monastery, and Walter remained ignorant of the great prize under his nose for week after week.

The Japanese officer remained there for the rest of the war, only emerging at its end. But a few years afterwards the monks received a visitor. It was the Japanese officer, who had travelled from his home city of Kawaguchi to thank them for saving his life. After that he returned every year on the anniversary of the battle, bringing donations – clearly he came from a wealthy family – and the monks showed us pictures of his visits, at which he was treated as a VIP. When he died his family continued the tradition. We were shown a large new school that had recently been built in the monastery's grounds, funded by the family. I was intrigued to know what story the officer had told his comrades and his family to account for his whereabouts for five months of the war.

The family were due to visit the following week so I left a note for them at the monastery with our contact details, then emailed via the monks, but I never heard anything back. Perhaps they did not want to contact the family of 'the enemy' or perhaps they did not receive the message. In any case, it was refreshing to hear this story of survival and humanity that had had such a positive legacy, in contrast to the death and destruction of a battle that continued to cause suffering long afterwards.

The monks mentioned that some time after the war some small boys were playing near the monastery and found some shiny objects on the ground. Not knowing what they were, they banged them with a rock. The consequences were tragic. The bullets exploded, killing several children. For years afterwards, the villagers continued to find mines and other fatal detritus in the ground as they tried to rebuild their lives.

On 18 March Walter launched a large attack at Milaungbya, using tanks and artillery, to try to dislodge the Japanese from their positions in the north of the village where they were deeply dug into bunkers. It was a six-hour battle under burning sun, and before the infantry went in Walter and his officers watched as three Hurricane fighter planes swooped low, dropping high explosives. An RAF spotter plane circled overhead, finding targets for the artillery, and then the battle began. The Gordons' tanks clanked and lurched towards the Japanese positions as the Gurkha riflemen of A Company went forward under their unflappable commander, Mike Tidswell, a soft-spoken and unassuming but highly competent young man, popular with officers and men alike. Shouting their battle-cry of '*Ayo Gurkhali!*', they surged towards the bunkers and foxholes, but a concealed Japanese machine-gun wrought devastation on the Gurkhas until Walter, seeing what was going on, ordered a young signals officer to discover the gun's location. The man returned with a neat hole in his felt hat where a bullet had smacked into it and the gun's location was established.

For six hours they battled under the sun as the Japanese firmly refused to leave their bunkers. As these were often sited on the reverse side of slopes that tank fire could not reach, there was no alternative but to go in with bayonets and kukris. Only when they began to run out of ammunition and tank fuel did Walter call off the attack.

Then came the counting of the dead. Already in the searing heat the bodies were blackening and stinking. 4/8th had lost six men and counted 94 Japanese bodies, although the death toll was likely to be closer to 200: some bodies were buried in bunkers and others had been removed. This was a record 'bag', as it was called. It was not the last of the Milaungbya battles: there was one more to go, just two days later; but it quickly turned into a rout. As soon as the Japanese heard the tanks advancing they began to flee south. Walter's artillery caught them in the open and wreaked havoc, and the few men who did remain to stand and fight were killed. In all, 4/8th had accounted for 250 verified Japanese corpses at Milaungbya, with many others uncounted, removed or buried.

Throughout each battle Walter ricocheted between his command post and the forward companies, the men under fire. Somehow he was not hit, despite being a prime target in his jeep, followed by a telltale plume of dust as it whizzed over the sandy ground. He slept little, sometimes staying awake all night planning and strategising. The shelling went on day and night. When darkness fell the Japanese jitter parties would crawl towards the Gurkhas' bunkers, screaming to unnerve the occupants. Sometimes the screams would be of pain as one of the sharp panjis ripped open their stomachs.

Despite the heat, the thirst, the flies, the pounding from mortars and the casualties, the men's spirits remained high. Walter wrote of his pride in his men's achievements at Milaungbya. He recalled watching the enemy fleeing 'in utter disorder with my Gurkhas in hot pursuit with kukris drawn and [later] when they marched past me singing at the top of their voices they carried in their hands the heads of so many Japs . . . They were grinning and singing and gave me a tremendous cheer as they passed my TAC [tactical] headquarters.'

This 'somewhat crude celebration', as he described it, coincided with a signal from Headquarters querying the number of enemy casualties reported by some battalions and ordering that in future no casualties were to be claimed unless their bodies were counted. Since Walter's battalion had been one of those claiming a high body count, a senior officer was sent to discuss this with him. Walter was furious. He knew he had under- rather than over-estimated the counts, since so many bodies were removed or buried in their bunkers, and was determined to set the record straight, as forcefully as possible.

In advance of his visitor's arrival he washed, changed into a freshly pressed uniform and prepared to welcome him. He asked for two of the Japanese heads to be brought to his bunker and had them nailed to trees on either side of the entrance to his headquarters. The officer arrived to be greeted by the gory sight and was visibly appalled. 'Walker, must you do that?' he remonstrated.

'Must you send me silly signals?' Walter replied. 'If I say I have killed a Jap, I have killed a Jap.'

I have never known quite what to think about this story. When I was younger and read about it in his biography I was both shocked and thrilled by it. When I visited the pagoda at Kya-O, the thought of decapitated heads in this place of peace was horrifying. Patrick Davis, writing three decades afterwards, described how in battle soldiers instinctively suspend feeling for a corpse, friend or foe. 'A corpse is a corpse, impotent to help or hinder the living, and no deader for being decapitated.'

Taking heads was not uncommon in the Second World War: American troops in the Pacific adorned their jeeps with Japanese skulls or used them as candleholders. But the Gurkhas did not see the heads as souvenirs, simply as evidence of enemy dead, and it seems that Walter's intention in displaying them was not to gloat but to ram home to his visitor the brutal reality of war, and that he had no need to exaggerate kill counts. The heads were buried soon afterwards.

By the end of March they had been fighting for six weeks solidly and were pulled back from the front line. Although morale was high after their victories, they were exhausted, thin and in need of a rest and a bathe in the cooling waters of the Irrawaddy. There was no let-up from patrolling, however, as the quest for a live prisoner to interrogate continued.

Mandalay had at last fallen. So had Meiktila, the main Japanese supply centre and air base, a severe loss for them. Encouraged by Fourteenth

Army's successes, Burmese guerrillas now began attacking the Japanese. But just as things seemed to be going Slim's way, the Chinese nationalist forces and an American brigade that, as his allies, had been tying up large numbers of Japanese troops in the north of Burma were recalled to China. This freed large numbers of Japanese, while others were streaming from west to east, retreating from the Arakan. They would have to be cut off, fought and annihilated. Walter and his men were to be part of the action and they were ordered south, back across the Irrawaddy.

At home the newspapers were excitedly reporting on this drive south, Allied forces 'slashing forward through stubborn Jap resistance', and exulting in the victories that had so far killed more than a hundred thousand Japanese. Dorothea and Arthur would have followed such reports avidly, with those from Italy where Edward and the Jaipurs were still fighting hard. The enemy were fighting dirty there: the battalion diary records that on more than one occasion they raised a white flag. When Edward sent an officer forward to investigate, the Germans waited until he came closer, then lowered the flag and opened up with mortars and small-arms fire.

London was just starting to recover after the battering it had received from Hitler's revenge weapons. In September 1944 a monstrous new weapon had appeared in the skies: the V2. As tall as a four-storey building at 46 feet long, nearly twice the length of the V1s, these rockets travelled faster than the speed of sound and exploded with a deafening crash and blinding flash. Although in total they killed fewer people than the V1s, they had a shattering effect on morale as they could demolish entire streets. As they arrived with no warning there was no way of defending against them. Once again it was some weeks before the government would admit to their existence, referring instead to 'air-raid incidents' or claiming that gas mains had caused the explosions.

A V2 fell on Smithfield meat market on 8 March, killing 110 and injuring many more, and on 27 March another fell in Stepney, demolishing two five-storey blocks of flats and damaging a third, with the loss of 134 lives. Another, falling in Orpington later that day, killed one woman. No one knew it then, but that was the last of the V2 attacks on Britain.

But the Walker family had little to rejoice about. On 26 March, Gaddis Plum had left RAF Northolt in a plane bound for Canada as part of a delegation of VIPs taking part in a ceremony to mark the end

TRIUMPH AND LOSS

of the British Commonwealth Air Training Plan. Since October 1940, more than forty thousand RAF pilots, with many from other Commonwealth nations, had trained in Canada, its vast skies and aerodromes safe from enemy attack. One of those in charge of the scheme was Air Marshal Sir Peter Maxwell Drummond, an Australian flying ace for whom Gaddis worked as his personal assistant. Drummond was invited to attend the ceremony in Canada to mark the end of the scheme on 31 March 1945; Gaddis accompanied him, with the under secretary of state for air, Commander Rupert Brabner, himself a distinguished air ace, whose sister, a pioneering female surgeon, had been killed in a V1 attack some months earlier.

They were travelling in an aircraft named *Commando* that had previously been Winston Churchill's personal plane, flying the prime minister to North Africa in 1942. A very long-range Liberator, it had been modified to carry passengers in comfort on long flights. It was regularly maintained and had an experienced pilot, Wing Commander William Biddell DFC, at the controls for its lengthy journey to Ottawa, via the Azores to refuel.

Gaddis kissed Bee and Mary goodbye, promising to bring them presents from Canada. He sometimes asked Sis to send unattainable luxuries, such as nylon stockings, for Bee but this was a perfect chance to stock up.

The plane took off at 11 a.m. on Monday, 26 March. The crew checked in with its base at 5.22 a.m. the next morning, 27 March, as scheduled and made contact with RAF Transport Command at 7.16 a.m. The weather was clear and they were on schedule to touch down on the Azores at 8.10 a.m.

The plane never arrived.

Emergency radio calls failed to yield any response. The Royal Navy and the RAF both sent out searches but, on 28 March, Churchill had to announce the news to the House of Commons that the aeroplane had been lost with all fourteen passengers and crew. An RAF plane spotted some wreckage 150-200 miles north of the Azores: all that remained of *Commando* was some yellow dinghies, a few bits of detritus and an oil slick. A warship sent to search the area failed to find any trace of survivors and it was concluded that *Commando* had crashed into the sea.

The Walkers' luck, which had held so long, had run out. Bee was now a war widow.

13

'Annihilate them all'

———•———

I N THAILAND, PETER did not know that his sister had ever been married, let alone become a mother and a widow in short succession. He had spent the first half of 1944 becoming progressively sicker. He was admitted to the camp hospital at Chungkai on 9 February 1944 with amoebic dysentery and spent the next three months on the dysentery ward. In May 1944 he was still ill and was among a thousand patients selected for transfer to Nakom Pathom, a newly constructed hospital camp near Bangkok where, the Japanese promised, they would receive every medical attention. In fact the hospital had no equipment, no medicine, no dispensary: nothing, in fact, except the building itself.

Peter arrived on 19 May suffering a horrific roll call of conditions, as detailed in the admissions record: 'Amoebic and bacillary dysentery, dengue fever, anal fissure, jaundice, ulcers - posterior, haemorrhoids, scrotal dermatitis.' Patients could and did die from many of these conditions, but to have them all at once must have taxed the resilience of even the strongest body. There is no discharge date for Peter, so it is impossible to know how long it took for him to get back on his feet or whether he was still sick when he was discharged and sent back to work.

As news of Japanese defeats and Allied victories in Burma began to reach Thailand, the behaviour of the Japanese camp personnel towards the prisoners became markedly worse. In January 1945, while Walter was marching through northern Burma, an announcement was made to prisoners of war in Thailand. Officers and men would now be separated. Peter was on the move again.

The officers were taken to a large camp at Kanchanaburi, across the river from Chungkai and next to the railway. It was a shabby place where the three thousand prisoners were crammed into dilapidated bamboo huts and the whole camp was surrounded by a deep moat with a high bank and a ten-foot barbed-wire fence. At each corner of the perimeter sentries looked down on them from watchtowers. With the war going the Allies' way, the Japanese were taking no chances. Removing the officers from the men would, they thought, make it harder for them to organise into any kind of fighting force that might try to join up with Allied units in the area, or rise against the Japanese camp authorities. Any such uprising by the prisoners or any attempt by Allied forces to free them would be brutally crushed. The Korean guards told the prisoners that, in the event of a massacre, the moat would become their mass grave.

The camp commandant, Captain Noguchi, had a reputation he quickly confirmed as a sadist who delighted in inflicting numerous petty rules and punishments on the prisoners. The prisoners were sure that he was endeavouring to create an 'incident' that would give him an excuse to slaughter them all.

The railway that Peter had helped to build was now fuelling the Japanese in their fight against the Fourteenth Army. During the battle of Imphal the railway had transported an entire division of troops and 50,000 tons of military supplies into Burma. Now the trains, five or six a day, were still carrying fuel and food to the Japanese defenders of Burma, although they were not bringing fresh troops. Instead they were evacuating casualties.

An even more awful irony was that the Fourteenth Army's successes in Burma were making the position of prisoners such as Peter yet more precarious.

Because of its military role, the railway and its bridges were obvious targets for Allied planes. But as the prisoner-of-war camps were not marked as such and some were close to the railway, there were tragic incidents: in September 1944 ninety prisoners were killed at one camp, and nearly four hundred injured by Allied bombs, and in February 1945, at Tamarkan Camp, less than two miles from Kanchanaburi, several prisoners were killed in an air raid. Kanchanaburi Camp was just a hundred yards from the railway, and in a raid aimed at an engine, bombs killed three Dutch prisoners and injured several others.

Air raids were not the only danger. As the months went on and the tide of war turned further against the Japanese, the regime at Kanchanaburi became harsher still. The feared Kempeitai, secret police, arrived at the camp and began taking senior officers for torture and interrogation.

Their alleged crime? Buying newspapers and other items from outside the camp. It was from a Thai newspaper, wrapped around some violin strings delivered to the camp for the orchestra that Noguchi had grudgingly allowed, that the prisoners had learned of Germany's surrender. No one could rejoice as it would be dangerous to provoke Noguchi, who appeared increasingly psychotic. The camp leader, Lieutenant Colonel Philip Toosey, did his best to intercede on the prisoners' behalf, but it was often futile or even counter-productive. One officer was severely beaten by Noguchi and thrown into an underground dugout, where he was kept for seventy-seven days in the dark and starved nearly to death. Toosey's protests fell on deaf ears.*

Men were beaten for saluting incorrectly. All stools and chairs were taken away and burned. One officer was badly beaten and made to stand at attention for four days without food outside the guardhouse for looking through a hole in the camp fence; another had his arm broken and was thrown into a cell for a week without medical treatment simply for picking up a pamphlet dropped by an Allied plane. Some of the pamphlets dropped by the planes were written in Thai or Chinese, aimed at local people, but others were in English, bearing the message: 'It's in the bag!' The Allies were coming closer.

Cheering as this news was for the prisoners, the warnings of the Korean guards about plans for a massacre made them uneasy. They were right to be. Japanese high command had issued an order that prisoners of war should be killed if Allied forces landed nearby their camp, or on 28 August 1945, whichever came first.

A Japanese document, found after the war, regarding the 'final disposition' of prisoners of war stated: 'Whether they are destroyed individually or in groups, or however it is done, the mass bombing, poisonous smoke, poisons, drowning, decapitation, or what, dispose of them as the situation dictates.' And in case there was any doubt: '. . . it is the aim not to allow the escape of a single one, to annihilate them all, and not to leave any trace.'

The Japanese prison-camp authorities had already carried out this

---

* At Tamarkan, Toosey's leadership and courage in confronting the Japanese saved countless prisoners' lives, unlike the overly co-operative colonel in *The Bridge on the River Kwai*.

order elsewhere. In December 1944 at a camp at Palawan, in the Philippines, the presence of an American ship nearby had prompted the Japanese commandant to slaughter all the American prisoners of war. First, all 140 were herded into air-raid shelters. The Japanese guards then doused the wooden shelters with gasoline, set them alight and tossed grenades in. The guards laughed uproariously as the prisoners entombed in the shelters screamed as they burned alive, scrabbling desperately to escape. Those who managed to escape were machine-gunned or bayoneted. Only a handful survived to bear witness to this sickening atrocity.

Would a similar fate await Peter and his companions?

Ruth thought often of Peter, her favourite brother and the naughtiest of them all. She knew that Dorothea would contact her with news, good or bad, about her brothers so she prayed for their safe-keeping and kept abreast of the news. In the meantime she threw herself into all that Cairo had to offer, including romance.

She had met a young Shell Oil employee named Peter Cosserat while playing tennis at the Gezira and they became close. After a few months, Peter proposed and Ruth accepted. Instead of marrying John Fisher in Kuching Cathedral, she would marry Peter in Cairo's Anglican Cathedral. A date was set and she wrote home to tell her parents the news. Peter's mother, it turned out, lived near Weybridge so, naturally, Dorothea wrote and suggested a meeting. But Mrs Cosserat made excuses not to do so until after the wedding. Dorothea found this rather strange. Did she have something to hide?

Not long before the wedding, Peter came to see Ruth. Clearing his throat, he told her, 'I think I'd better mention to you before we get married, there's black blood in my family.' His previous fiancée had, he informed her, broken off their engagement for this reason.

When Ruth told me this I waited for her to tell me that she had dismissed his concerns and was not concerned about the colour of his or his ancestors' blood. But with her characteristic honesty Ruth told me she *was* deterred, so much so that she decided she could not marry him. 'I said, "I'm sorry, Peter, but I wouldn't have any children. I wouldn't take the risk."'

What risk? I asked her. Was it for her parents, rather than for herself, that she was concerned?

'No,' Ruth told me frankly. 'It was for myself. I think I wasn't prepared to take the risk . . . It was very different from these days. Nowadays you wouldn't think twice.'

I was shocked at first, but then I remembered reading her brothers' Sandhurst application forms, on which they were asked to confirm whether they were 'of pure European descent', the implication being that answering 'No' might lead to rejection. Mixed-race children would undoubtedly face a difficult life, beset by rejection, if their non-European heritage was apparent. And Ruth was from a deeply conservative family. The Walkers were Empire-builders, brought up with the prejudices and race barriers on which the whole edifice of Empire rested. So perhaps it is not surprising that she could not contemplate bringing mixed-race children home to Weybridge.

Or perhaps it was simpler. If it had not been that, she might have broken it off for another reason, she said. Her heart was not really set on marrying Peter, and his disclosure gave her the reason not to go ahead for which she had perhaps been searching. She had not forgotten John Fisher.

Meanwhile she continued to ride every day at the Gezira Club. More people had noticed her skill in the saddle and lent her horses to train and exercise. She alternated between a horse belonging to an Egyptian minister and one owned by a British officer, Major General Bernard Dixon, whose wife and schoolgirl daughter Eve were due to join him in Cairo. Eve, with whom Ruth remained friends until her death, remembered their days in Cairo fondly. Ruth, she recalled, was 'very attractive and very dynamic', with tremendous energy and a sense of fun. Eve fancied that her father was rather in love with Ruth as the two used to ride around the Gezira racecourse together most days. Ruth might have lacked Bee's film-star looks but she had a certain magnetism and *joie de vivre* that were irresistible, even in her nineties.

Although Cairo was no longer the epicentre of wartime intrigue and diplomacy that it had been earlier in the war, Winston Churchill stopped off there in February 1945 on his way back from the Yalta conference, at which he met with the American president Franklin D. Roosevelt and the Soviet leader Joseph Stalin and began to make plans for the post-war world, including the division of Germany. It was Churchill's fourth wartime foray to Cairo, and Ruth heard a story that was doing the rounds among the medical community about one of his earlier visits to the Middle East when he had become seriously ill.

The nurse assigned to him struck up a rapport with the convalescing prime minister. One day she had removed his bedpan to empty it and was walking away when the prime minister chuckled. She asked what was so funny. He replied, 'It's the first time I've seen one of my motions passed and carried' – a reference to the often stormy passage of legislation through the House of Commons.

In Italy, spring had dawned at last. The winter had been one of 'static warfare', a miserable endurance test of mortaring and shelling in which little ground was gained or lost, a stalemate in the snow reminiscent of the First World War, which allowed the Germans to strengthen their defences still further. But the grim winter had now given way to warmer, clearer weather: good news for Allied planes and tanks. The Allied army commanders in Italy were planning a new spring offensive to finish the Germans there once and for all.

'D-Day' is now synonymous with the Normandy beach landings on 6 June 1944, but as a military term it simply means the day that a planned operation or exercise is scheduled to commence. In Italy, the date chosen for the spring offensive against the German Tenth Army to begin was Monday, 9 April 1945. It would start with Operation Buckland, the crossing of the River Senio by the 2nd New Zealand Division and the 8th Indian Division to which 1st Jaipur Infantry belonged.

Monday, 9 April 1945 was a sunny day of cloudless skies, which meant that the Allies could at last unleash their air power. The operation began with what was euphemistically called a 'softening up' of the German defences, a honeycomb of tunnel and gun emplacements dug into the River Senio's high flood banks.

Early in the afternoon a low droning sound was heard, growing louder and louder as it approached the Senio. Wave after wave of bombers dropped their loads on the German positions. Fighter-bombers came next, swooping low as they machine-gunned German command posts, followed by the artillery, the heavy guns pounding away with a wall of solid sound that shook the ground.

Then came the weapons the Germans feared and hated most. Flame-throwing vehicles – Crocodile tanks and Wasp carriers – began spewing sheets of fire at the German positions. Their tunnels and holes were designed to protect them against shot and shell but they were no defence against fire, and when the flames reached them they became ovens in which men burned alive. Now, with the Germans disoriented and shaken, the air black with oil, the infantry seized their moment. At 7.20 p.m. the first troops began wading across the shallow river.

The Jaipurs were not in the spearhead of the attack and had a tense forty-minute wait as shells crashed and flames shot across the sky before, at 8.02 p.m., they were ordered to advance. By then the Germans had had a chance to organise their defence and the fighting was intense: the men still trying to cross the river were lashed by machine-gun bullets, while those who had made it faced a savage hand-to-hand fight on the bank.

The Jaipurs pressed on and the first men were soon on the far side of the river, coming under fire from enemy machine-gun posts. By 10 a.m. the next morning, Edward and all his men were across the river and beginning their advance on the small fortress town of Lugo, accompanied by a troop of tanks. They swept into it from several different directions, advancing on the main square. There were still snipers in the buildings but these were 'met and dealt with', in the words of the Jaipurs' war diary, and four German prisoners were taken. The mayor of Lugo emerged to greet Edward and his men, carrying a white flag in one hand and a bottle of wine in the other, while the townspeople, who had suffered badly under German occupation, rushed out weeping with joy and relief. Seventy-five years later, on 10 April 2015, another mayor of Lugo held a ceremony commemorating the town's liberation at the monument dedicated to the 1st Jaipur Infantry.

The Jaipurs could not stay to join in the celebrations in Lugo. Another regiment arrived to take their place while they withdrew outside the town to plan their next attack, scheduled for midnight. The countryside all around Lugo was heavily mined so every step into newly taken territory was fraught with risk. At 6.15 p.m. Edward went to consult with the commanding officer of the tank squadron, who would be supporting them, and the two discussed the attack, but then came news that it would have to be postponed. As Edward was walking back to his own headquarters he trod carefully, hoping to avoid any landmines that lay along the route, but in the darkness it was impossible to see where soil might have been disturbed, where a mine might lurk beneath the surface. There was nothing to be done but keep moving forward, keep hoping that his luck would hold. One wrong step would bring his war and perhaps his life to an abrupt end. Would he be lucky? He pressed forward and then, with a deafening, shattering noise, the world around him exploded.

When the smoke cleared, Edward began to pick himself up. It is not clear from the war diary exactly what happened, but it seems that he had not trodden on a mine but near enough one to cause it to explode. For some hours afterwards he remained stunned and disoriented but he was alive and unhurt, and for that he was profoundly thankful.

The following day they advanced across roads and junctions, often coming under heavy machine-gun fire, shells and mortars, towards the River Santerno, the next objective for 8th Indian Division, reaching its bank by 8 p.m.

Here they came under fire as soon as they began to cross the river and fought all night, a ferocious action of attack and counter-attack, bullets and mortars ripping through the darkness. At 5 a.m. the Jaipurs surged forward in a determined assault, and at last the exhausted Germans broke and ran, leaving fifty corpses in their wake. But they had not given up yet and began subjecting the Jaipurs to a lethal hail of shell, shot and mortar. Edward and his men held on as daylight dawned. By mid-afternoon the Germans were flagging and at last, shattered, they withdrew, having lost eighty men. It was another victory for the Jaipurs.

The army was now moving north towards the River Po, so long the Promised Land where their tanks would be able to annihilate the Germans on the flat river plain. But the German Tenth Army, or at least some elements of it, refused to concede that they were beaten. While some units continued to hurl everything they could at their pursuers, others, exhausted, demoralised and realising that defeat was inevitable, had no wish to lose their lives in the last days of a doomed campaign. These men huddled by the roadside, their faces blank with exhaustion and despair, and surrendered gladly to the first Allied forces to come along.

On 23 April, the Jaipurs took forty-six prisoners, and the following day, while on his way to the village of Mizzana near the ancient city of Ferrara, Edward found a party of Germans who had had enough. The war diary is frustratingly lacking detail, simply noting: 'CO takes 11 prisoners on way area Mizzana.' I wonder how Edward came upon them. Was he alone, as the diary implies, taking their surrender single-handedly? And who were these enemy? Perhaps they were men from 76 Panzer Corps, whom the Jaipurs had fought earlier that day, forcing them to retreat at Ferrara.

Despite their victories, the Jaipurs could not afford to feel complacent. There were more battles ahead. On 24 April, Edward fought one of his toughest actions at a canal near the River Po.

At 6.50 p.m., with some but not all of the battalion across the canal, half a dozen panzer tanks crawled out of some factory buildings on the far side and let loose a blistering fire on the Jaipurs. With his men pinned down and the situation deteriorating fast, Edward called for support. Before long the reassuring growl of Spitfires was heard in the sky, and a troop of their own tanks lumbered up to within range of the enemy. A tremendous battle ensued as British and German tanks pounded each other in the darkness. A panzer burst into flames, burning its occupants, then shells began falling with devastating accuracy among the German infantry. The survivors ran for their lives.

The following day, 25 April, Edward's headquarters came under sniper fire. They were not to know it, but it was their last day of fighting. On 29 April German commanders in Italy surrendered to the Allies and, although fighting continued in some areas, the surrender was made official on 2 May. The war in Italy was over at last.

In Germany, Hitler had committed suicide in his Berlin bunker on 30 April, and on 7 May the German commanders signed an unconditional surrender. The next day was VE Day, and among the general rejoicing, Edward received personal good news: his leadership of 1st Jaipurs had been recognised with the award of a DSO, Distinguished Service Order, for his 'untiring energy, gallantry and devotion to duty'. As well as performing the task of several officers, the citation noted, he had trained and built up his battalion to get it ready for action, transforming inexperienced troops into highly trained, battle-ready warriors, and it was owing to Edward's courage and 'aggressive initiative, that no German would venture forward of the Veno del Cesso escarpment in the Apennines'.

One of his friends from 1/8th Punjabs wrote to congratulate him. 'I could hardly be more pleased if I had won the DSO myself . . . you won it by sheer guts and determination of which you are brim full. I always knew you'd get a DSO or killed, I'm glad it was the former. I'm looking forward to the day when we wet it [drink to it].'

In England, Arthur and Dorothea could feel a measure of relief at the news of VE Day, or V-Day as it was called by most newspapers. Edward was safe – for the time being: there was a good chance that he would be sent east to fight the Japanese. Although the war in the east was going well for the Allies, there was no expectation that it would end soon. Everyone knew that Japan would fight until the bitter end and, with Walter in the thick of it, Peter's fate unknown and Edward soon perhaps to join in, the sight of bunting being strung from bedroom windows around Weybridge and 'welcome home' flags being unfurled was bittersweet for those, like Dorothea and Arthur, whose boys would not be coming home yet.

In Burma the news of VE Day reached the 4/8th Gurkhas in the surreal surroundings of Yenanma, a village to the west of the Irrawaddy. The last five weeks had been a mixture of fighting and marching. From Milaungbya they had marched south to a town called Singu, which they captured after fierce fighting in blazing heat. Here, or somewhere around here, an army psychiatrist arrived to check on the morale of men in the front line. It was the night before they were due to launch an attack so Walter invited him to join it in the morning. The man bravely agreed, and at dawn he was with Walter in his slit trench while shells crashed down around them and the Gurkhas charged into battle with kukris drawn. The psychiatrist could report that there was clearly nothing amiss with morale in 4/8th Gurkhas although, after several hours in the trench, his own morale was less certain.

They had re-crossed the Irrawaddy and moved away from metalled roads, the flat green paddy-fields and swamps, through which they waded thigh-deep and emerged festooned with leeches. Now they were in terrain creased by forested ridges and valleys where it would be harder for air supplies to reach them and impossible for tanks.

The air hung heavy with humidity as the monsoon waited to burst through the suffocating, energy-sapping heat, and the enemy were always nearby. As they marched south and west, Walter sent patrols to seek out the Japanese. Sometimes they made contact and there were short, fierce firefights, but other days were spent in a frustrating game of hide-and-seek through the jungle. Sometimes the Japanese were only yards away from their camps, watching them through the jungle, waiting to ambush them. One misstep, a wrong turn into the dark, and a man could stumble into enemy concealed in the undergrowth yards from the camp perimeter. This happened to one Gurkha officer who was bayoneted but managed to stumble back to camp, bleeding heavily. He was evacuated the next morning but later died.

Other divisions were advancing on Rangoon, and on 3 May the capital was taken. It was a symbolic victory, one that made front-page news around the world. It must have seemed to those reading it that the war for Burma had been won. But it was not over yet, and for 4/8th Gurkhas more hard fighting lay ahead. The Japanese were on the back foot but they were a long way from beaten: they still had seventy thousand men in Burma. They might easily head east towards Thailand and regroup, ready to fight again, and prolong the war for months or more. It was vital that they be caught as they headed east and destroyed.

Many of the Japanese forces in Burma were weary, battered by defeat after defeat. But those that Walter and his men were about to face were of a different calibre from those they had fought further north: Japanese 54th Division were tough fighters, some of the best shock troops remaining to the Japanese, troops led by one of the finest and boldest of the Japanese commanders, Lieutenant General Shigesaburo Miyazaki. He was determined to get his men over the Irrawaddy and into the hills to its east. Slim was equally determined that they must be stopped by an 'extermination battle'. 4/8th would play a leading role in it.

Walter was told to take his men south from Yenanma to the village of Shandatgyi. To the west lay a ridge of thickly forested hills and beyond them the village of Taungdaw through which ran a stream and a track that allowed for motor vehicles. It was thought that the Japanese rearguard would try to sidestep their pursuers by heading down the valley, and Walter's orders were to block the track and stop them at Taungdaw. There was no time to lose: the Japanese could be there within hours.

It would be quicker for one company to cover the twelve miles in a rapid forced march than the whole battalion, and it was vital they reach it before the Japanese did. Walter ordered Denis Sheil-Small to take B Company immediately and cut the road at Taungdaw by occupying it. He and the rest of the battalion would follow as quickly as they could as far as the village of Yebok, which lay just over a sharp, hilly ridge from Taungdaw and where there were reports of other Japanese.

Walter was taking a gamble by sending just one company, which could be overwhelmed by a far larger force, but he felt he had no choice. If he did not get at least some men occupying Taungdaw before the Japanese arrived, the enemy could cruise through it unopposed and escape from the trap.

After a breathless march up and down hills, Denis and his men arrived at Taungdaw at midday on 11 May. The village lay at the bottom of a valley of staggering beauty. At either side, steep, tree-clad ridges rose abruptly a thousand feet or so from the flat floodplain. Fields spread across it, punctuated by clumps of lofty palms, while the village was tucked at the foot of the eastern ridge. This peaceful Shangri-La was about to be plunged into war. The villagers of Taungdaw had already left but the monks remained in their small monastery beside a stream.

To cover the twelve miles to Taungdaw quickly, Denis and his men had travelled light, taking the bare minimum of ammunition and rations. He rapidly assessed his surroundings to work out the likely direction the enemy would take and decided that the best place to cut them off was where the track met the stream on the floor of the valley. On flat ground, overlooked by the tree-covered west ridge, it was badly exposed but it would have to do. Only minutes later, the first shots rang out. The Japanese had arrived. Denis saw the monks gather up their saffron robes and flee from their monastery. Japanese machine-guns crackled; the Gurkhas answered with bursts of Bren-gun fire. Those not firing were digging for all they were worth.

Walter remained at Shandatgyi, twelve miles away. It was frustratingly far from the action but he had to establish whether other Japanese parties were in the area and deal with them, before bringing the rest of the battalion towards Taungdaw. For now, he must rely on wireless reports from Denis. To his consternation, Denis told him that the Japanese force now approaching them was about fifteen hundred to two thousand strong. They were outnumbered ten to one, as well as outgunned. As the rifle shots rang out, followed by the chatter of Japanese machine-guns, Denis ordered his men to dig. Foxholes would give some protection but not much.

He explained to Walter that although they were blocking the track, preventing the Japanese from moving through the valley, they were in a tricky position, surrounded by bushes and trees that provided excellent cover for an approaching enemy, overlooked by a high ridge and highly vulnerable to being encircled.

Walter decided to send C Company, commanded by the experienced Major Peter Myers, to their aid. If they moved fast they might just get there before the Japanese launched a full attack. Myers and his men marched with astonishing swiftness, arriving just as the light was starting to fade. He and Denis conferred: tempting as it was to join forces on the valley floor for safety in numbers, they decided that Myers and his company would be of more help if they could scramble up the side of the ridge and seize this commanding position of the valley. After a breathless, sweaty climb through the thick trees and thorny bushes, they arrived at the top of the ridge just in time to see a party of forty Japanese forming up, ready to attack Denis and B Company.

And then they charged. Down on the valley floor, Denis and his men waited, kukris at the ready, rifles at their shoulders, grenades placed near the lip of their trench, ready to hurl. The Japanese were closer now, moving fast and screaming their war-cries, but still the Gurkhas held their fire. Not until the enemy were nearly at point-blank range did they unleash volley after volley. The attack faltered and stopped. But there was not much respite. From his vantage point on the ridge, Peter Myers saw the enemy gathering in the evening light for another attack. He immediately sent a shower of mortars down onto the massed Japanese. The effect was devastating but it saved Denis and his men. Twice more the enemy began to charge, yelling and screaming, but each time their attacks were broken up.

As darkness fell, both sides settled down to a tense night. Japanese jitter parties crept up to the perimeters of both companies, shouting, shrieking and firing shots, hoping to provoke the Gurkhas into shooting back and giving away their position, but discipline held firm. Not a man fired back.

Walter was also spending a sleepless night. The hills and ridges interfered with the wireless, making it hard to keep in contact with Denis and Peter. He was champing to move closer to Taungdaw but he still had to find out more about the Japanese forces in the area. Were more on their way to Taungdaw? When day broke, he sent out the intelligence officer, Douglas Farnbank, who had joined the battalion only days earlier, on a jeep patrol with five soldiers. He gave him strict instructions not to do any shooting but simply to trawl the area for any signs of Japanese and report back: this was purely reconnaissance, not a fighting patrol.

But Farnbank, coming round a corner to find a party of thirty Japanese bathing in a stream, instinctively leaped from his jeep and began charging at them. The Japanese had, wisely, posted sentries and a fierce exchange ensued in which a burst of machine-gun fire cut through Farnbank's legs. The patrol scattered into the jungle, Farnbank carried by one of his men, who hid him in the undergrowth.

When the first man arrived back at Shandatgyi and relayed the news that four of his men were missing, including the wounded Farnbank, Walter was both furious that his orders had been disobeyed and desperately anxious. He sent the rest of the battalion forward to Yebok but felt unable to head there until Farnbank had been found: he could not leave him, badly wounded, to be discovered by the Japanese.

It was not until the following day that Farnbank was brought in by stretcher and Walter felt able to jump into his jeep and head for Yebok. Now, at last, he could conduct the battle from close at hand, although two miles and a sharp ridge lay between him and Taungdaw and there was a Japanese roadblock on the road between the two villages.

In the early hours of 13 May, two hundred Japanese had unleashed a furious assault on Peter Myers and his company. The men in the forward trenches bore its brunt but hung on grimly as determined Japanese soldiers rushed at them, shot and shell pounding down upon them. A young rifleman, Lacchiman Gurung, only four foot eleven inches tall, was in a forward trench that held the key to the whole position of the company. Wave upon wave of enemy charged towards it through the darkness, screaming, yelling and hurling grenades. One landed on the lip of the trench. The quick-thinking Lacchiman grabbed it and hurled it back at the enemy. Another fell inside the trench and again he seized it and threw it back. A third grenade landed just in front of the trench. Lacchiman tried to seize this one too and fling it back but it exploded in his hand, blowing off his fingers, shattering his right arm and severely wounding him in the face, body and right leg. Two comrades beside him were also badly wounded.

Sensing victory, the enemy began to rush the position, charging towards the injured men. But Lacchiman took up his rifle with his left hand, his right now hanging useless and bleeding, and kept up a steady rate of fire on the advancing enemy, firing and loading one-handed. When morning came, at least eighty-seven enemy dead lay on the ground in front of C Company, thirty-one of them in front of Lacchiman's section. By holding his position, Lacchiman had saved C *and* B Company as they would have been next.

They had held them off, but at a heavy price. Men lay with stomachs torn open and limbs blown off. Nothing could be done for them except to lay field dressings on the wounds, which quickly became soaked with blood. A gunner officer, whose job was to direct the artillery onto the Japanese positions, lay beside Peter Myers in the trench in terrible pain from where a sniper's bullet had ripped into his torso. Walter knew of their plight but could do nothing to help them. There was no way of evacuating them while they were still all but surrounded by the enemy. There were Japanese to their north, to their south, where they were now occupying the village of Taungdaw, and to the east on the ridge and the road between Taungdaw and Yebok.

All that day, 13 May, the Japanese kept up their attacks on the ridge. The battle now hung in the balance. Walter needed to turn the tide not only to save his men but to stop a flood of Japanese pouring through the valley and heading east. They were the cork in the bottle: if they gave way the consequences could be devastating.

He requested an air strike on Taungdaw village. It was risky: the village was only 150 yards from B Company's position in the valley, but the Hurribombers (Hawker Hurricanes) screamed over and dropped their bombs with superb accuracy, not only wreaking havoc among the Japanese but giving the whole battalion a morale boost, the knowledge that they were not alone.

Walter tried sending reinforcements over the ridge from Yebok to help relieve the men in the valley but they could not get through. He tried sending D Company from the north but they, too, met fierce opposition. This was grave and deeply frustrating: he could not see what was going on as the ridge between Yebok and Taungdaw obstructed his view, but with the road still blocked and the ridge still occupied it was too dangerous to go forward into Taungdaw and see the situation for himself. The battalion could not afford to lose its leader at this crucial juncture.

237

One of his officers, Robert Findlay, who observed him that day at his headquarters, marvelled at how calm he appeared. 'Hollywood might portray the situation with ragged, slept-in clothes and an unshaven chin. But no. I remember being impressed with the green silk scarf at his throat . . . a cigarette in a longish holder, and clean, pressed bushshirt and trousers. He knew that everyone in the battalion depended on him, a wellspring from which to refresh their own taxed reserves of courage. This was how he showed himself when in such a corner.'

But behind the calm façade Walter's anxiety was mounting. That evening he went forward a little way from Yebok village to a patch of jungle from which, concealed, or so he thought, by the trees, he spoke to his brigadier on a wireless strapped to a mule. He finished talking and replaced the headset, then jumped over a small ditch onto a lower piece of ground. As he landed, a mortar bomb burst on the mule, tearing it apart, killing its driver and the wireless operator, and injuring several men nearby. It was the closest of calls. Had he leaped seconds later, Walter would have been lying disembowelled and dead on the hillside. So much for being concealed.

All that night, mortars fell around Walter's position and a party of ten Japanese launched a suicidal attack on Yebok. It was beaten off and all ten of the attackers killed. For Walter it was, he later wrote, 'probably the most anxious and sleepless night of the war'.

At first light the next morning Walter went around the perimeter at Yebok talking to each man, checking on their physical and mental condition. Morale seemed reassuringly high, and their wounds were being treated. At one point he came across a havildar (sergeant) with a small pile of gold. Walter asked where it had come from and was told that it had been extracted from the teeth of dead Japanese.

Walter considered how to break the deadlock. It was vital to open up the route between Yebok and Taungdaw, to allow ammunition, rations and relief to reach the men now under siege. On the spine of the ridge between the two villages there was a saddle, a slight depression, and above it on both sides higher ground on which the Japanese were concentrated. If they could be driven off, the way to Taungdaw would be opened. But it would be a difficult task and men would certainly die as they advanced up the steep slope into a barrage of enemy guns.

One company was at Yebok and had not yet joined the battle. Its commander was Mike Tidswell. Walter regarded him highly and had recently promoted him to major. It was to Mike and A Company that Walter gave the task of taking this crucial feature, the saddle, and the hill above it, regardless of casualties. The next morning, Mike was to take his company and attack the Japanese on the hill above the saddle. He should remain behind his leading men as he would be a target and, as he was fair-skinned and tall, he would be easily visible among the diminutive Gurkhas. Walter could see that Mike was in no doubt of the desperately dangerous nature of his task, attacking uphill, against an enemy who would be well concealed and dug in, but the younger man did not question the order. He calmly accepted it and went away to prepare.

At 5.30 a.m., following an air strike on the enemy positions, the attack began. A Company fought its way up the hillside, through bamboo thickets and trees, the perfect cover for enemy snipers. Bullets cracked and whined around them from the invisible enemy, machine-guns hammered out their death-rattle, sweat poured down their faces and streamed into their eyes. Their own artillery boomed and crashed, but many of the shells fell short or went over the crest, missing the Japanese altogether. As they progressed up the slope the trees became thicker, making progress harder still. It was difficult to see the enemy and to tell from which direction the bullets were coming.

By 9 a.m. the platoon leading the attack was pinned down under heavy fire. The advance had stalled. The situation was critical, and Mike Tidswell, knowing how crucial it was to maintain the momentum of the attack, went forward to encourage them onwards. Almost immediately a bullet smacked into his neck and he fell to the ground. His orderly immediately ran forward and killed the sniper, who was tied into the branches of the tree. Scott Gilmore took over as company commander in place of his friend.

Mike was carried by stretcher back to Yebok where Walter saw him, still alive but paralysed. 'Poor Mike, my most promising officer. I am so sorry,' he told him. Mike opened his eyes for a flicker of a moment. Walter looked at the medical officer with him, who gave him the thumbs-down signal. Walter had to hide his distress as he saw Mike into a jeep. He died on the way to the advanced dressing station. He was twenty-three. Only days before, Mike and Scott Gilmore had chatted about life after the war, their plans for the future and Mike's rather endearing concern that, after a British public-school upbringing, he lacked the social skills to talk easily with women. Now for Mike there was no future.

When darkness fell, A Company's position was still precarious. They had secured the southern part of the ridge and twenty enemy lay dead on the ochre soil, but the Japanese still clung to the vital pass and the heights above it. The men were exhausted and hungry, two were dead and eleven wounded. Nothing could be done for them. A mule party bringing rations under cover of darkness missed the track and stumbled into the enemy, with the loss of one man and two more wounded.

Walter had another sleepless night, as did the men in the valley: they were attacked throughout it. Rain added to the misery, the heat causing the vegetation to steam 'as though we were in some monstrous Turkish bath', recalled Patrick Davis. The next morning, 15 May, Scott and his men began their attack again, but once more encountered fierce resistance. In Taungdaw, Peter Myers could still not evacuate his wounded and five of them had died.

Walter knew that it was now or never. Everything depended on taking the saddle on the west ridge. He got onto the wireless to Scott Gilmore. 'Take that hill, Scottie, and I'll make you a captain on the spot,' he promised him. He ordered D Company to attack from the other direction. Then he asked for another air strike from the Hurribombers. After some resistance, permission was granted and he spoke on the wireless to the squadron leader, promising to present him with a Japanese sword if the hill was captured as a result of his air strikes. The officer said he would do his best.

Walter had now played all his cards: it would either be victory or disaster. As the Gurkhas waited to attack they heard the throaty growl of Hurribombers approaching. Down came the silvery bombs, tumbling through the sky. With incredible precision they fell, just yards from the Gurkhas' positions, on the Japanese dug in on the hill and on those now in the village. With the explosions of the bombs still ringing in their ears, the Gurkhas advanced once more, dashing up the slope shouting, '*Ayo Gurkhali!*'

At first the attack stalled. At his headquarters Walter watched the faces of his officers fall as they listened to the gloomy reports but steeled himself to appear outwardly confident. And then, gradually, the tide began to turn. When D Company reached the saddle at 10 a.m. the Japanese were already retreating south. By the time D and A Company met on the ridge, they had melted away.

On the valley floor Denis Sheil-Small and his company had at last been able to emerge from their trenches as the Japanese had abandoned their attack on them. The valley seemed to be emptying. Patrols of Gurkhas crept through the village of Taungdaw, cautiously at first, among the shattered huts, splintered trees and bomb craters, then more boldly as they realised that the only Japanese remaining in the village were twisted, torn bodies.

In their trenches, the remaining men of B Company noted with alarm a large force of men moving towards them. They held their fire as they had been trained to do until the men came close and then, with relief, lowered their weapons. The approaching soldiers were not Japanese but Sikhs, from their own brigade, and they had come to their aid by attacking the Japanese to their north.

The battle was over. Walter jumped in his jeep to join A and D Company on the ridge and congratulate them on their victory. Then, suffused with relief that it had not all been in vain, he drove down the steep track to the valley floor to greet the men of C and B Company. A scene of utter jubilation ensued. This, not VE Day, was their day of victory. The exhaustion of the last five days erupted in elation, edged with sadness at the loss of the men they must now bury. The wounded, too, could finally be evacuated, although it was too late for some. The young artillery officer who had hung on for so long, so bravely, with a gaping stomach wound died on his way to the casualty station.

'Next to a battle lost, the greatest misery is a battle gained,' the Duke of Wellington famously reflected, after Waterloo. For Walter, the most melancholy task came that evening when he sat down to write to Mike Tidswell's mother. She would, he acknowledged, have been justified in accusing him of sending her son to his death, and it was with a heavy heart that he explained what he had asked of Mike and how he had done his duty unquestioningly and bravely. Some weeks later he received a gracious letter from her expressing her understanding and her pride that he had fought and died for his country.

I do not know if Walter wrote to the families of the ten Gurkha soldiers killed at Taungdaw. I think it unlikely as most of them would have been unable to read. But the news would have reached them some weeks later, delivered to their hilltop villages, devastating parents, who had hoped their son would one day take over their farm, and wives, who had longed for their husbands' return. They had lost them to a war that was far removed from their lives in the Himalayas. Their loss must have been hard to bear indeed.

And so, after they had buried their dead and those of the enemy, 4/8th Gurkhas left Taungdaw. They counted 218 corpses but reckoned that the true number was far higher: many of the enemy wounded had crawled away to die in the jungle where, uncounted and unburied, their bones would eventually sink into the soil. An even more critical loss for the Japanese was the seventy-five lorries, artillery guns and other supplies they had had to abandon as they fled from Taungdaw, losses they would feel sorely when they next went into battle.

Less than a year before he died, Walter wrote about Taungdaw in an article for a Gurkha journal. He had been asked for his memories of the battle, and the account he wrote was accurate in detail and heartfelt, admitting to emotions he was unable to show at the time. 'My heart had been in my mouth on many occasions,' he wrote, but he had maintained an outward aura of calmness and confidence to cloak his anxiety.

Patrick Davis observed Walter after the battle of Taungdaw. 'He was an extraordinary man, and I use the word "extraordinary" with care. He was extra ordinary. I knew how I longed for sleep, how my own nerves were worn thin, like an overused truck tyre, how almost everybody was, to a greater or lesser extent, suffering in the same way. I also knew that Walter Walker took less sleep than any of us, could never relax, was for all of every day and much of most nights thinking, planning, encouraging, prodding, looking ahead both in time and space, whether on the move or chained to his command post, never inactive. Yet now . . . he seemed much the same as ever. The shadows about his eyes were perhaps deeper, the bones of his face a little more prominent, He was certainly living on his nerves, he must have been, but it hardly showed.'

Walter spent several days and nights writing citations for medals for the men who had showed such outstanding bravery at Taungdaw, including a bar to the Military Cross (MC) for Peter Myers and an MC for the Gurkha who had commanded the platoon on which the main Japanese attack fell on the night of 12 May. He also wrote the citation for Lacchiman Gurung, the young rifleman who had fought back so tenaciously while so terribly wounded, whom Myers had recommended for a Victoria Cross. Lacchiman had volunteered for the army on a whim, having popped out of his hut in the Himalayan foothills in Nepal to buy some cigarettes for his father. He returned six years later.

At Taukkyan on the outskirts of Rangoon – now Yangon – is the Commonwealth War Graves cemetery where the remains of 6,374 Commonwealth servicemen are interred. Burma was the bloodiest theatre of war for Britain and her imperial allies; yet, those who fought there were aware that public attention back at home was often focused elsewhere. They called themselves the Forgotten Army. But here, they are remembered. Many of those who died in Burma were buried where they fell, in unknown graves on remote hillsides or hidden valleys such as Taungdaw. The names of these 27,000 are carved into the stone of the Rangoon Memorial in the centre of this immaculate cemetery, Mike Tidswell's among them with those of other men from the battalion. So many names: so many young lives brought to a shattering end. Flowers grow between the slate-grey gravestones in bursts of glorious tropical colour, life amid death, hope amid the sorrow.

14

'Release Peter'

—•—

IN JULY 1945 the first general election in ten years was held, resulting in a landslide victory for Labour. Winston Churchill, whose campaign had rested on his credentials as a war leader, emphasising the need to finish the war against Japan, had failed to appeal to a war-weary nation.

The unity that had held Britain together for so long had now collapsed and the euphoria of VE Day had evaporated: housewives still had to queue for food, servicemen still had to wait to be demobbed, and families like the Walkers were still waiting for news of their boys.

For Edward, the end of the war in Europe brought mixed blessings. He was no longer in command of the Jaipurs, having handed over his battalion to a new CO, although he stayed around for a week of celebratory dinners. They had now left Italy and were stationed on Rhodes and it was there that the Maharajah of Jaipur visited the battalion to congratulate the men on their recent feats, throwing a feast for the soldiers and a separate dinner at a hotel for the officers.

In July Edward wrote to his mother and father to tell them of the maharajah's visit and the congratulations that had been showered upon him, by both Jai and a visiting general, who let slip that he was to be awarded a further decoration in the form of a bar to his DSO although, as he warned his parents, 'Sometimes these things get turned down at the War Office so am NOT expecting it until it arrives.' He did well to be cautious since it never did.

As for what was in store for him next, they asked him to take command of another Jaipur regiment, the Jaipur Guards, established by Jai himself. The regiment was, wrote Edward, the 'apple of the Rajah's eye'. All the soldiers had to be six foot and over, and the officers were Jai's relations, but their role had always been ceremonial. 'I protested,' he told his parents, 'and said I was a fighting soldier and therefore could not command a non-active battalion.' But they promised him that the Jaipur Guards would soon be going into battle, and he would be allowed to appoint some British officers, so he accepted. 'So,' he concluded jubilantly, 'no more restlessness - back to fight - grand. Release Peter and avenge the 1/8th Punjab Regiment.' Although, he added, 'When I shall ever see the UK again I don't know.'

Walter had written home of his own battles in Burma, and Dorothea sent his letter on to Edward, who remarked that it made 'very good reading', adding, 'My own unit has had more MCs and MMs [Military Medals] as well as thirty or more men mentioned in dispatches.' It is hard not to detect a note of sibling rivalry alongside Edward's evident pride in his men and desire for his parents' approval: he signed it 'your ever loving, devoted and adoring eldest son'.

Edward would have to return to India to take command of the Jaipur Guards and train them up before they could fight the Japanese and, as he hoped, help liberate the prisoner-of-war camps. The maharajah was also returning to India and invited Edward to travel with him via Cairo. Edward jumped at the chance to see Ruth and to visit a city that was renowned for its exciting nightlife, romance and intrigue, in the company of Jai.

Jai and Edward arrived in Cairo at the end of the month. Ruth remembered meeting Edward for supper there one night, catching up on the eight years since they had last seen each other when he had introduced Tiggy to his family on his visit home in 1937.

So much had happened in the intervening years: Ruth had been engaged twice, Bee had wed and been widowed, and all six siblings had narrowly escaped death, Harold, Ruth and Bee in the Blitz and V-weapons attacks, Walter and Edward by mortars, shells and bullets. As for Peter, had the Walker luck kept him alive? They both prayed so. And what about Edward's marriage? Would it have survived his year-long absence?

While Edward was in Europe, Tiggy had met an army psychiatrist who had been in Burma but was back in India on leave. It is not quite certain how the affair began - perhaps she met him through her voluntary work as a VAD nurse, or perhaps he offered a sympathetic ear to a lonely and grief-stricken woman: not only was Edward absent, but her sister Prudie had died in Trinidad in 1944 in what was reported as an accident but might have been suicide. Or perhaps it was simply in Tiggy's nature to stray. She was vivacious and flirtatious, 'quite a popular lady', in the words of one of her sons, 'quite a wild woman' in her daughter's.

If he harboured any doubts they can hardly have been allayed by a letter from an old army friend, who asked him to 'Give Tiggie [*sic*] our love, and say we hope she has been behaving herself in Ootacamund – many separated wives in Quetta seem to be no better than they should be.' If this was a dark hint, Edward must have decided to ignore it. In a picture of them from this time, lunching al fresco with friends, Tiggy is svelte and glamorous in a midriff-skimming halterneck, rather racy for 1945 and a daring choice if she was under a cloud of suspicion as a *femme fatale*.

Just as Edward was returning home, John Fisher, Ruth's erstwhile fiancé, was going to war for the first time since being shot down in 1942. This was a different kind of warfare from that of the Walker brothers, his Blundell's schoolmates. He was to be dropped behind enemy lines in Borneo as part of a guerrilla war against the Japanese in preparation for an Allied landing there. In France, operatives from the Special Operations Executive (SOE) had waged a campaign of sabotage against the Germans, following Winston Churchill's remit to 'set Europe ablaze'. Now in Borneo a handful of carefully selected men would be inserted covertly into the countryside. There they would link up with local people to wage a campaign of disruption and confusion against the Japanese, undermining their morale and diverting their resources in preparation for Allied landings.

Since joining the Royal Army Service Corps on his return to Britain, John had taken part in various training exercises. Then, in February 1944, he had received a curious summons. SOE's Australian equivalent, Special Operations Australia (SOA), was looking for men who would be willing and able to take part in operations in Sarawak and north Borneo, men who knew the country, its languages and its people. Someone at the Borneo Office in London had recommended John.

John's SOE personnel file, held at the National Archives in Kew, documents his recruitment and training by SOE. After his name was put forward in January 1944, MI5 ran a check on him and, finding nothing amiss, summoned him to a shabby hotel in London's West End where he was interviewed, briefed about SOE's activities and asked to sign the Official Secrets Act. Today the work of SOE is well known, and the names of agents, such as Violette Szabo and Odette Sansom, are famous, but in 1944 only a tiny handful of people knew that it existed and SOE preferred that it remain that way.

On 25 March 1944, John Fisher became a member of SOE. Officially he was appointed as a planning officer to MO1, ostensibly the 'military preparations' branch of the War Office, but this was a cover for SOE. In reality, he was being sent to train in the arts of secret warfare. On his personnel record he recorded his fluency in Sea Dayak and Malay, his next of kin and his appearance: six foot three and a half inches tall, dark brown hair, blue eyes, fair complexion, and under 'Distinguishing Marks', the tattoo of a fish.

As the agents would be dropped into Borneo by parachute, an essential part of his training would be learning how to jump out of an aeroplane, an unappealing prospect for John, who had had a horror of flying since he was shot down in 1942. Nonetheless on 16 April 1944, he presented himself at specialist training school STS 51a in Cheshire, ready for his parachute course at the nearby RAF Ringway. It must have come as a huge relief when the doctor who examined him there concluded that both of his knees were in such poor shape that parachuting was out of the question.

Prospective agents who were deemed unsuitable for deployment, but knew too much about SOE's work to be allowed back into society at large, were relegated to a highland camp, known as 'the cooler'. Mostly this was because they were judged to lack the physical or mental toughness to survive in the field but one poor man was consigned to the cooler simply for being 'outstandingly ugly'. His trainers concluded, 'He'd be recognised anywhere. Once seen never forgotten. He had no teeth at all except two gold tusks and two incisors.'

John's failure to gain his parachute wings was a minor setback rather than a cooler-worthy disaster. There were other means of inserting agents into enemy territory. Far more important was his knowledge of Sarawak, its people and their languages. His training continued. His next stop was a two-week course at SOE's 'finishing school' at Beaulieu Manor in the New Forest. At the end the instructors gave their views on each student's skills and suitability for the task ahead. In John's case they were frank.

He is of average intelligence, quite practical but lacking in imagination. Although he has plenty of initiative, his manner is lackadaisical and he did not create the impression of being particularly keen. In character he seems honest and straightforward but he is not very forceful. He is easy-going, pleasant and socially popular. He has not, however, any particular powers of leadership.

Despite these reservations, he was sent on to the next step, paramilitary training school at Arisaig in Scotland, to learn the art of what Churchill termed 'ungentlemanly warfare'. Tom Harrisson, a maverick anthropologist who was recruited at the same time as John for the Sarawak operation, described the kind of skills that were imparted during the training: 'Coding, disguise, hiding, searching, tailing, burglaring, stealing trains, blowing up railway bridges, hamming deafness, passing on syphilis, resisting pain, firing from the hip, forgery and the interception of mail . . . None of them would be of much use in the east. But the acquisition of so much criminal and lethal knowledge gave a kick of self-confidence.'

At Arisaig, John impressed the instructors with his ability in fieldcraft and close combat, and was deemed 'a good average shot with Sten and Pistol [and] his handling is fair'. His explosives handling improved as the course went on and he proved able enough at navigating, writing reports and making sketch maps.

But it was his personality rather than his tactical abilities that impressed his instructors: 'A raconteur by nature, he has been largely responsible for the ever present cheerfulness during the course. In spite of some illness he appears to be well suited to the work generally although at times is a little apprehensive.'

In Sarawak they would be working in small teams deep in the jungle, with limited wireless contact with the outside world. In such difficult circumstances John's amiability and humour would be a vital asset.

He was passed fit for deployment and flown to Australia for further training. The British SOE operatives would be joined in Sarawak by Australian soldiers from a secret Australian Army unit, Z Special Unit. One of these men, Sergeant Keith Barrie, who would work closely with John in Sarawak and came to admire him greatly, described his first meeting with him. '"Fish" was on the surface the quintessential P. G.

Wodehouse foppish character. That was just a typical Englishman's "act",' he wrote, in an unpublished account of his time in Borneo, *Borneo Story*, which has been digitised and can now be read on the Australian War Memorial website.

In March 1945 the first of the Sarawak teams, led by Tom Harrisson and codenamed Semut - Malay for 'ant' - parachuted into Borneo, deep in the interior and far from the nearest Japanese forces, who mainly stayed near the coast. The Semuts' role was, initially, to gather intelligence about Japanese forces in Sarawak in advance of the landings planned by regular Australian forces, to whom the task of liberating Borneo fell. For this, they would depend on the help of local people. But would it be forthcoming, or would they find a hostile reception that would result in their heads decorating a longhouse?

To their relief, they were welcomed by the Dayak tribes, who had suffered badly under three years of Japanese occupation and were desperate to rid the country of their hated oppressors. Very soon they had hundreds, then thousands of volunteers. Not only were the Dayak tribes willing to supply intelligence, they wanted to fight. When they learned that headhunting, for so long outlawed, was permitted once more, so long as the heads were Japanese, and that a bounty of five Dutch guilders would be paid for each one, their enthusiasm soared. The Semuts divided into three groups, Semuts I, II and III, each with their own area and army of local recruits.

Semut III operated in the south-west of the country, covering a vast expanse of territory. Key to its success would be the support of the Sea Dayaks, now known as Ibans, who dominated the area but had a reputation for being more volatile and less trustworthy than other tribes.

Bill Sochon, a former Sarawak prison official, was given command of Semut III, and Keith Barrie also joined the team. John Fisher did not parachute in with the others but followed later, landing on the Rejang River in a seaplane on 25 July 1945, five weeks after 25,000 Australian regular forces had landed on the Borneo coast and begun pushing the Japanese further inland. Semut III had now turned from intelligence-gathering to fighting an offensive campaign, ambushing Japanese patrols and taking territory.

According to Keith Barrie and Tom Harrisson, Semut III owed a large part of its success to John's genial presence and his restraining influence over the Dayaks, who were delighted to see him again. To them he was known as Tuan (Mr) Pisser, not a reference to his *borak* (rice wine)-quaffing prowess but because they found it difficult to pronounce the letter F.

Although the Semut teams had distributed some firearms among the Dayak tribes, in Semut III's area the weapon of choice was not the rifle but the traditional Dayak hunting weapon, the *sumpit*, a blowpipe. One shot from a gun would alert every Japanese soldier in the area but a poisoned dart from a blowpipe killed silently, albeit with excruciating agony.

Bill Sochon, in an unpublished account written long after the war, described how the Dayaks would hide just off the trail, silent and invisible as a Japanese patrol passed within feet. Then, at a distance of 20 yards or so, they would pick off the last man in the line. 'The blowpipe dart would fly silently on its way, burying itself in the rearguard's back. Happily chattering to his comrade, the man in front of the target would continue his conversation for some time until he realised he was receiving no reply. Looking back he would find his friend missing and, reporting this to his commander, would run back to find him in his final death throes.'

The patrol would continue, badly shaken. A little further along the next man would disappear and eventually an entire patrol would be picked off one by one. The effect was utterly terrifying and demoralising. A patrol sent to find out what had happened to them would receive the same treatment. Soon smoked Japanese heads were adorning the rafters of Sarawak's longhouses, and the Semut operatives found themselves the reluctant guests of honour at head-smoking ceremonies. Human heads roasting over a slow fire produced a sickening stench, while the ritual of carrying the smoked head around the longhouse, then feeding it delicacies as a sign of respect, took some getting used to.

The Dayaks had ingenious methods of luring the Japanese to their deaths. Bill Sochon described one technique, which was to welcome a Japanese patrol into a longhouse for a feast. After the soldiers had eaten and were both full and pleasantly inebriated on rice wine, the warriors of the longhouse would fall on them and very soon a fresh bunch of heads would be dangling 'like oversized rotten grapes from the rafters'.

All the tribes fighting for Semut had been instructed that the only heads they were sanctioned to take were Japanese. But there were suspicions that some of the heads they presented, already smoked and shrunken, were those not of enemy soldiers but of Chinese civilians. Among the Semut operatives, John was the only one able to discern the difference between a smoked Chinese head and a smoked Japanese head, to the irritation of Dayaks trying to claim a reward. Instead, he ensured that the heads of Chinese taken by Dayaks were returned to the families and prevented further headhunting of Chinese along the Rejang River.

As John travelled between longhouses he was often accompanied by a much-revered Dayak leader, Temenggong Koh. He later recounted how, on one of their journeys, Temenggong spotted a Japanese officer on the veranda of a building. Silently Temenggong put his blowpipe to his lips and, within seconds, the officer had fallen to the floor. Temenggong duly removed the officer's sword and his head, presenting John with the latter. It proved to be a somewhat costly gift since, from then on, every feast day John would receive an invitation to the longhouse to honour 'his' head, which meant footing the bill for the *borak* and food consumed at each ceremony. Eventually they swapped: Temenggong took back the head and gave John the sword instead, an arrangement that suited them both.

Although John arrived in Sarawak shortly before Japan's official surrender on 15 August, it was not until more than a month later that the Japanese were finally persuaded to lay down their arms, with some units still holding out in the jungle beyond that. John's task then became one of restoring order in the aftermath of the fighting.

Compared with the many books (and films) about Special Operations work in Europe, little has been written about their operations in the Far East, particularly Borneo. The achievements of the Semut teams and their allies were barely acknowledged after the war, and because they had signed the Official Secrets Act, they were unable to speak about their work and the heavy losses they inflicted on the Japanese. Semut III alone killed more than 265 Japanese and took some 25,000 square miles of territory, at the loss of not a single Semut operative.

Only recently has this secret, utterly unorthodox war begun to receive the public acknowledgement it deserves. Anthropologist and Borneo expert Professor Christine Helliwell is writing a book on 'Operation Ant', and in 2018 she co-curated an exhibition by the Australian War Memorial that paid long overdue tribute to this guerrilla army, which included New Zealanders, Canadians, Australians, British, Dayaks and Chinese, and the brutal but brave campaign they fought in the jungle shadows.

While the Semut operations were wreaking havoc in Sarawak, the fighting in Burma continued. The night after the victory at Taungdaw in May 1945, 4/8th Gurkhas continued to advance east but were then given a brief respite, resting at a town on the Irrawaddy before the next major battle began: the Japanese were not beaten yet.

But when they next went into action it was without Walter. He had been appointed to another staff job, a more senior one this time, as general staff officer (grade one) to the commander of 7th Division, Major General Geoffrey Evans. He protested that he wanted to stay with his men and that, with more fighting to come, now was not the time to change command, but Evans brushed aside his objections, telling him to take a week's leave first as he was looking drawn and underweight.

In the middle of June 1945, Walter arrived unannounced at the family home in Quetta – his signal to Beryl warning of his arrival had failed to arrive – and was bemused to find her holding a baby about whose existence he knew nothing, as well as an enormous Great Dane that began barking. After a rapturous reunion he ventured the question: 'Where on earth did we get these?' Beryl burst into laughter and gave the innocent explanation. The baby and the dog belonged to a neighbour, who had gone away for the weekend with her husband.

After an all-too-brief week together, Walter returned to Burma to take up his new post. To his dismay he found his old battalion in disarray. Not long after he had left them they had suffered heavy casualties at a battle on the Sittang River when the regimental aid post was hit by shells, killing and wounding all those in it.

It was a bitter blow and morale, so high after Taungdaw, now slumped. Some felt that the commanding officer had been at fault for having planned the battle poorly. Walter Walker, they muttered, would never have taken them into battle with a half-baked plan. Such was the lack of confidence in the new commanding officer that, rather than send the men back into battle under a leader they did not trust, Walter was authorised to take over the battalion again, alongside his staff job. He was greeted with joy and relief, not least by some of those who had loathed and resented him a year earlier. A further fillip to morale came with the news that the two Military Crosses and the Victoria Cross for Lacchiman Gurung had been approved and awarded. It was a proud and joyful moment for the whole battalion. Lacchiman returned to his village an invalid but a hero.

When the Japanese fled Rangoon in May they had left the prisoners of war in Rangoon jail to liberate themselves, but elsewhere in Thailand and in southern Burma they were still being beaten, starved and humiliated, and their lives were hanging in the balance. Only when the Japanese were finally defeated would they be liberated. There was still no news of Peter. Would Walter reach Thailand only to find that his brother had been dead for two years?

In Kanchanaburi camp the prisoners remained subject to Noguchi's reign of terror. Peter kept his head down. No one wanted to incur the wrath of the guards, or of Noguchi, when liberty seemed to be on the horizon. The Korean guards had already told the prisoners that the Japanese were planning to kill them. Then in mid-June Noguchi announced that they would soon be moving to a 'better camp', which the Koreans helpfully informed them was actually 'an officer bumping-off camp'. But if it *was* an extermination camp, there was little they could do about it. They could hardly refuse to go.

The new camp was at Nakhon Nayok, east of their current position and further away from advancing Allied forces, which would be likely to invade from Burma in the west. The prisoners were divided into eight parties of 400 men and the first party, made up of volunteers headed by Philip Toosey, left Kanchanaburi on 28 June, with other parties following at intervals.

Peter was in one of the later parties, which left Kanchanaburi early in August, arriving at Nakhon Nayok on 7 August 1945. The journey was, he later said, one of the lowest points of his captivity. The prisoners travelled by railway at first in open luggage trucks in the monsoon rain. Many railway bridges had been damaged or destroyed by Allied air raids, so they had to get off the train and clamber over precarious footbridges.

For the next stage of the journey they were crammed into the holds of rickety barges, into which the Japanese herded them by beating them with bamboo sticks, cramming so many into such a tiny space that the prisoners feared the overloaded barges would sink, drowning them all. Perhaps this was how their captors planned to dispose of them. But somehow the barges stayed afloat.

They slept in warehouses for the night, and in the morning they were told to start marching. They were tired and unfit after months of enforced inactivity at Kanchanaburi, but the guards urged them on, prodding them with bayonets and hitting them with rifle butts. Hour after hour they stumbled forwards, long after night had fallen. If they collapsed they were kicked and beaten. A Korean guard urinated on the face of one fallen prisoner.

Peter described this journey as a 'death march': he felt sure that, even if he survived it, he was simply marching to his execution. Although none of them knew that the date of 28 August had been fixed for their death, they feared that it was imminent. Rumours had already reached them about the massacre in the Philippines, and at Nakhon Nayok Philip Toosey had even begun making what preparations he could to try to avert a mass execution.

According to another prisoner of war, Toosey plotted with a Korean guard, who promised to hand over all the weapons in the guardroom as soon as the order for the massacre was given. The best shots among the prisoners would each be given a rifle to try to hold off the attack while the others fled into the jungle. Toosey ordered the prisoners to sharpen bamboo sticks to use as spears and hide them in the roofs of their huts.

But in the end it did not come down to spears against machine-guns. On 6 August, as Peter was still marching towards Nakhon Nayok, the USAAF B-29 bomber *Enola Gay*, commanded by Colonel Paul Tibbets, flew over the Japanese city of Hiroshima. Opening its bomb bays, it dropped a single bomb nicknamed 'Little Boy'. It was the first atomic bomb used in war and the devastation caused by its explosion was unprecedented. Some 80,000 men, women and children were killed within seconds. A further 37,000 were severely injured, their skin hanging in shreds, leaving red raw flesh. Survivors saw horrendous sights: a woman whose intestines had burst from her body and lay strewn around her, another whose eyeball had popped out; 10,000 people were reported missing. The final death toll was estimated at around 146,000 but may have been higher still.

Most of Japan's major cities had already been levelled to the ground by conventional bombs the USAAF had dropped. The firebombing of Tokyo on the night of 9 March had killed between 80,000 and 130,000 civilians. But this new weapon was something different, something even more horrific.

Events now unfurled at a rapid pace. At 11 p.m. on 8 August the Soviet government told the Japanese they were revoking the neutrality pact that had existed between them since 1941, with a declaration of war effective on 9 August. Sixty-one minutes later, at a minute past midnight, Soviet troops invaded Manchuria, the Japanese colony in north-east China that they had seized in 1932. The Japanese were now fighting two major powers, the Americans and the Soviets.

Then at 11.02 a.m., local time, on 9 August, another atomic bomb was dropped. 'Fat Man' fell on the port of Nagasaki, incinerating the city and its inhabitants, killing between 35,000 and 80,000, with another 5,000 reported missing.

On 14 August Emperor Hirohito overruled his military leaders, who were still insisting that Japan could and must fight on, and recorded a speech announcing Japanese capitulation on the Allies' terms: unconditional surrender. At midnight the news was announced in London and simultaneously in Washington and Moscow.

'End of the World War,' declared *The Times* on 15 August, reporting Prime Minister Clement Attlee's words: 'The last of our enemies is laid low.' Ships on the Thames blasted their horns in celebration, hundreds of bonfires were lit and trains sounded the Morse victory sign on their whistles.

But in Nakhon Nayok camp, life continued as normal. The clandestine wireless from Kanchanaburi had been smuggled to Nakhon Nayok and arrived there on 14 August, its constituent parts audaciously hidden within the wireless belonging to Noguchi, who arrived to take over Nakhon Nayok. But they still had no batteries and no means of getting any, so on 15 August they were completely cut off from any news.

Meanwhile Noguchi gave no indication that anything had changed, continuing to behave with his usual imperious cruelty towards the prisoners and crowing that the war would end by Christmas, when Britain surrendered. Only on 16 August did the operators manage to get the wireless working with a battery from Noguchi's own car and heard a report from India: 'General MacArthur has flown to Tokyo to take control.'

It was the news for which they had hoped and prayed for three and a half long years. It was almost impossible to take in and, in any case, they did not dare rejoice as there was every chance the Japanese would turn on them and kill them all in an act of awful retribution. It was not until the following day that Philip Toosey was summoned by Lieutenant Tagasaki, Noguchi's underling, and told that Japan had been forced to surrender because a weapon of terrible magnitude had been used against it.

'Now we are friends, we can shake hands,' he offered. But Toosey refused: Tagasaki had ordered the execution of six prisoners who had escaped from Tamarkan camp two years earlier.

When Toosey announced the glorious news to the prisoners they broke into song: 'Land of Hope and Glory', 'God Save the King' and 'Jerusalem', which would have stirred memories of home for Peter, who had sung them often in the Blundell's chapel and at church in Tiverton. He did not know that Tara was no longer the family home or that Arthur, whom he had last seen six years earlier when he was still playing a mean game of tennis, was now an elderly man, whose main pleasure in life was tending his roses in his Weybridge garden.

Letters that had sat in Japanese guardrooms for years were now distributed, bringing news of home, not all of it good. Some men, who had been kept alive by the thought of their longed-for reunion with wives or sweethearts, were bitterly crushed to find that their devotion had been in vain when they received letters informing them that their wives had left them or their sweethearts had grown tired of waiting and married other men.

Freedom was not easy. Some wandered around the camp in a daze, unable to believe that their nightmare was finally over. Medical officers warned the newly liberated men not to overeat as it could be fatal. In some camps the guards vanished overnight, in others they remained. Incredibly, their former prisoners refrained from exacting revenge or reprisals. The time for reckoning would come: British intelligence officers toured the camps, questioning the prisoners about their treatment, gathering evidence for war-crimes trials. This evidence eventually secured the conviction of several Japanese camp officials under whom Peter had suffered.

Captain Noguchi, the sadist of Kanchanaburi camp, was hanged, as was Kokubo Nagataro, the drunken bully of Thakilen. Fumimoto

Tetsuichi, the Korean at Krian Krai, who had forced sick prisoners to work, was sentenced to death but this was commuted to ten years' imprisonment.

The sickest prisoners were given priority when it came to repatriation. Planeloads of liberated men were flown from Bangkok to Rangoon to travel home by ship. But there were storms that September and, tragically, a Dakota carrying newly liberated prisoners of war from Bangkok to Rangoon vanished in an electric storm. Walter was flying through the same storm in a Dakota heading in the opposite direction: 7th Division had been given the task of occupying Thailand and he had been given responsibility for the negotiations for the formal surrender of the Japanese. He and his staff took off from Rangoon in a cloud-blackened sky and within minutes were being thrown around so violently he felt sure that, having survived so many battles, he was about to meet his death. Somehow they landed safely in Bangkok.

Walter still had not discovered Peter's fate. Knowing that his parents would be frantic with worry, he sent his adjutant Peter Wickham to Rangoon to see if he could get any news of his brother. Wickham visited the hospital ships in the harbour to ask if Lieutenant Peter Walker was on board. Each time the passenger list was checked and there was a regretful shake of a head. 'Sorry, sir, not here, not this ship.'

After he had visited five hospital ships in the harbour to no avail, Wickham faced the prospect of having to break the news to Walter that his brother had not survived. There was just one ship left to visit, SS *Versova,* and it was here, at last, he found Peter. He was able to report back to Walter that his brother was alive, but only just. Peter said that his weight had fallen to five stone at one point during his captivity. He may have regained some by the time Wickham saw him but he was still painfully thin and ill. The repeated bouts of dysentery had taken their toll, along with hookworms and other parasites that had taken up residence in his intestines and liver.

In Weybridge the local papers were full of news of sons and husbands who had been held in Japanese captivity. Some families, like the Walkers, had not seen their boys for six years or more and had heard nothing of them for three. Now they were at last learning their fates in telephone calls or telegrams from Thailand, Rangoon, India and even Australia, where some had been repatriated. To have hoped and prayed all that time, only to receive the news they most dreaded, as the rest of the country were picking themselves up after the war and looking to the future, must have been bitter beyond belief. As they waited for word from Walter, Arthur and Dorothea must have been filled with dread. Their other children had each missed death by the narrowest of margins. Had Peter been lucky too?

On Saturday, 15 September, the *Surrey Advertiser* carried a report on 'Far East Captives Freed'. The Surrey men liberated from Japanese captivity included one whose brother, taken prisoner with him, had died of malnutrition in another camp, and another pair of brothers who had both survived.

Among the relieved and happy families were 'Captain and Mrs A. C. Walker of Brandon, Portmore Park Road, Weybridge [who] have . . . received notification that their son, Peter Walker, of the 1/8th Punjab Regiment, has also arrived in India after liberation.' Walter's news had reached them.

Peter disembarked at Calcutta on 20 September and, after a brief stop in a prisoner-of-war camp outside the city, was sent on to Lahore, 8th Punjab's regimental centre, arriving six days later. Edward was still at Ootacamund, with Tiggy and their two boys. He had heard that Peter had survived and was heading for India so had asked a friend in Madras to look out for him among the arrivals there, not realising he would be arriving in Calcutta. To his disappointment, Peter declined his invitation to stay with him and Tiggy after learning that they had other house guests, Douglas Finlayson and another officer from 1/8th Punjab. 'I gather from Peter's letters that he did not get on with these two,' wrote Edward to his parents. Peter evidently believed that they had somehow let him down in Malaya.

'The annoying thing is to have missed Peter - both Wally [Walter] and I have missed him,' Edward continued, with characteristically British understatement, adding, 'Longing to hear news of Peter's arrival [in Britain]. Have heard about his time in Siam [Thailand] from various chaps. I hope he is out of his flat spin and has been able to settle things.' He wrote proudly of his son Hamish, aged eighteen months and already 'very tough . . . and very quick to pick things up'. He concluded, 'Well, drink a nice long drink on my behalf for Peter's health and I hope he has a bloody good 3 months [army leave] . . . Tons of love, Your ever loving, devoted and adoring eldest son, Edward.'

In Bangkok, Walter began the process of disarming the Japanese, ensuring that their weapons and ammunition were handed over, their planes grounded and that they were not allowed to board their ships. 7th Division was also responsible for the recovery of Allied prisoners of war, and through this work Walter encountered the liberated prisoners who had volunteered to remain behind to help identify the war criminals among the Japanese and Korean personnel who had run the camps. From those survivors he learned something of the cruelty and humiliation that the prisoners, Peter among them, had suffered for the past three and a half years.

Appalled and angry, he compiled a dossier on the crimes, which he submitted further up the army chain. He had it translated into Japanese and forced the Japanese liaison officer, a lieutenant colonel assigned to him to help manage the surrender and disarmament of Japanese troops, to read and digest it. 'I then went through it with him line by line during several sessions. Having done so I then rubbed more salt into the wound by making him learn it off by heart and repeat it to me,' he recalled, in his memoir. It is hardly surprising that he felt the Japanese needed to acknowledge their crimes. Many of the troops in Thailand, who had not been involved in the fighting in Burma and had not been defeated on the battlefield, found it hard to accept that they now belonged to a vanquished army, a surrendered nation, and continued to act as occupiers and overlords.

Walter complained that their arrogance and pride remained intact: their convoys tried to force British vehicles off the road and, as the minutes of his meeting with the local Japanese commanders reveal, failed to comply with orders, such as handing over their armaments and vehicles to Allied forces. They simply would not obey any order that did not come from a Japanese officer. Walter would not tolerate this and, as he wrote, 'Within a comparatively short time every surrendered Japanese officer and soldier had been brought to heel.'

Peace, as the rest of the Walker family would soon discover, was not without its complications.

On 20 October Peter arrived in Britain. A photograph of him taken shortly afterwards shows a man who looks tanned and surprisingly fit, with a fine military moustache, but a decade older than his thirty-one years. His hair has receded so that he is almost bald and his uniform looks too bulky for his frame. Although he is smiling, it is a slightly diffident smile, a long way from the cheerful, ebullient grin of pre-war photographs.

Arthur had always refused to listen when well-meaning friends tried to prepare him for the worst, holding to the belief that he would one day be reunited with Peter. Now his refusal to give up hope was vindicated. 'I can die now,' he said.

He had remained friendly with Alexander Ross Wallace, the former Blundell's headmaster who was now head of Sherborne School in Dorset, and the two had corresponded regularly over the course of the war. 'My Dear Old Pal,' he wrote to Arthur, in November 1945, thanking him for a card depicting the Tara clan, each sibling represented in caricature. 'It embodies . . . all the characteristics and services of what I believe is one of the finest families in England,' wrote Wallace. 'I only wish to Goodness there were more like it both in quality and quantity. That's the sort of thing that is really the backbone of the Empire.'

There were, of course, many other families who had made similar or even greater sacrifices, and who had not been as fortunate as the Walkers in seeing their sons and daughters return alive. But Wallace's tribute was kindly meant and would certainly have been warmly received. 'It is lovely to hear of old Peter being back among his clan again,' he continued. 'It reminds me of the story of the prodigal son. I hope you killed the fatted calf for him. I bet you did.'

But with rationing still in force – it would be another nine years before meat rationing ended – corned beef would have to substitute for fatted calf and there would be no gathering of the clan to welcome Peter home. Walter was still in Thailand, Edward was about to be sent east to Hong Kong, while Ruth remained in Cairo, where she had recently been presented with a gold watch by King Farouk for winning the ladies' events at a gymkhana. Only Bee and Harold remained in London, and Bee was about to leave for New York, where she was taking two-year-old Mary to meet Gaddis's family.

It would be years before the Walkers were together again, and even then things were not as they had been in pre-war days. The war that had kept them apart for so long had changed them all. The life they had known before 1939 had altered in ways they could not have anticipated and some would struggle to adapt to this new world. The Empire that Edward, Walter and Peter had fought to defend was on borrowed time, the home in which they had grown up was no longer theirs, and although war had brought terrible suffering and hardship, there had been simplicity and a sense of purpose: to serve, to survive, to triumph.

Post-war life would be less straightforward.

PART FIVE

After the War

15

'Bloody well stay in England till I get there'

———

THROUGHOUT THE WAR the Walkers had been scattered across the globe. Sometimes their lives had intersected and they had tried to help each other when they could - Harold pulling Ruth from the rubble, she refusing to give up on him when he was pronounced 'a vegetable', Edward pledging to avenge Peter, and Walter searching for him at the war's end.

But aside from Harold and Ruth they had seen little of each other since 1939, and the war had brought them very mixed fortunes.

Dorothea approached the advent of peace with the same robust practicality that she had always brought to family life, advising, directing, and intervening when she saw fit. Three years after she had nursed Harold back to health, it was Peter who most needed help and she set about his rehabilitation with her usual energy and forcefulness. But Peter's injuries, both physical and mental, would take longer to heal than Harold's. Like many returning Far East prisoners of war, he struggled for years with disabilities and other repercussions from the camps that went unrecognised and untreated.

The liberated prisoners were ordered not to talk to their families about their experiences in the camps. A leaflet entitled 'Guard Your Tongue' was circulated on board ship to those being repatriated, warning them that it would do neither them nor their families any good to dwell on what had happened to them. They should not speak of their experiences in public or to the press. 'If you had not been lucky enough to have survived and had died an unpleasant death at the hands of the Japanese, you would not have wished your family and friends to have been harrowed by lurid details of your death. That is just what will happen to the families of your comrades who did die in that way if you start talking too freely about your experience.' They were ordered not to say anything at all until they had told their stories to 'interrogating officers'.

Instead they were encouraged to pick up the reins of family life, get a job, forget the past and look to the future. Their families were given the same instructions: do not ask questions about their imprisonment or war, do not talk about it. As a result, many released prisoners felt that their friends and families did not care about what they had been through. Peter certainly felt that no one understood what he and his companions had suffered.

While Dorothea fed Peter with nourishing food, she set about making plans for his future. What he needed, she felt, was stability, a family of his own to provide for and inspire him to get on. And she happened to know just the girl.

Kathleen - Kay - Price was an attractive young woman from a 'good' family who had been to Benenden School in Kent, a debutante breeding ground, and had worked as an ambulance driver during the war. Peter, encouraged by his mother, became engaged to her within months of returning home. They were married in Chelsea early in 1946. Peter had been back in England only a few months, and in the wedding photographs he still looks thin, the trousers of his morning suit, clearly borrowed for the occasion, hanging baggily.

That May, he boarded a ship bound for India, with Kay following later. He was looking forward to taking up where he had left off, planting tea, playing polo, socialising at the club, and now with a wife waiting for him when he returned to the bungalow of an evening. Another man had been given his old job on the Sealkotee estate but he managed to find a new post at a different Assam tea garden. He would once more be a sahib, not a slave. It would be a fresh start and a comfortingly familiar existence.

At first, all went well. Although Kay found the life of a tea-planter's wife isolated and monotonous, Peter was in his element. But he was not as strong as he had been before the camps: the beatings he had suffered caused him pain in his leg and back, and his eyesight had been ruined by being made to stare at the sun as a punishment. He could cope with grey British skies but the tropical sunlight was too much. After little more than a year, he was forced to come home. He and Kay settled first in Kensington and then in Chertsey in Surrey, not far from Arthur and Dorothea.

Peter had spent almost none of his adult life in Britain. He had never had an office job or worn a city suit, but now he was expected to get a brolly, a bowler hat and a job in London that would support the kind of middle-class life Kay envisaged. His dream of returning to Assam had sustained him in the camps but had been wrecked, his godfather's legacy lost, and now he was forced to commute to London to a job he loathed. Kay thrived on company but Peter hated parties and either refused to go or complained that everyone was 'awful'. They were hopelessly ill-matched.

They had two sons, Richard and Michael, who remember these years as filled with arguments and slamming doors. Peter later said that he wished his mother had stepped back and let him arrange his own life, rather than acting as a 'Miss Fixit' by steering him into marriage when he was still reeling from his imprisonment.

Dorothea's interference was undoubtedly well meant. She had always done her best to equip her children for the world. Arthur might have taught the boys to 'look after themselves' by teaching them to box but it was Dorothea, herself brought up by a strong, determined mother, who bequeathed to her children emotional resilience, and she who felt compelled to keep her hand firmly on the tiller of the family ship.

Understandably, Peter felt resentful not only at his mother's interference but at the contrast between his own fortunes and those of his brothers. While he had lost his health and his job, and had had the ill-luck to have fought in a campaign that ended in surrender, Edward, Walter and Harold had had good wars. It had not been easy – each had come close to death, each had been tested to the utmost – but they had survived and now, unlike him, they were thriving.

Like Edward, Walter had been awarded a DSO after the war in recognition of his undaunted leadership of his battalion. He had more than fulfilled his boyhood dream of fighting with the Gurkhas and leading them to victory as his grandfather had done. The war had been his finest hour – so far. There would be others to come. His confidential army report marked him out as a highly capable officer, destined to rise high.

So, his future was set fair when, in 1946, he got his first home leave in a decade and arrived in Weybridge to introduce Beryl and their twins, Anthony and Nigel, to his parents. He just missed Peter, who had left for India before he arrived, so it was not until some time later that he heard Peter's own account of his time in the camps and was horrified by what he had endured.

In later years, Walter would do what he could to help Peter, recognising how badly the dice had rolled for his brother. Had the Burma retreat ended differently, had Burcorps not been commanded by a man of Slim's calibre, Walter, too, might have spent his war in a prison camp. He and Edward returned home as heroes, having fought in victorious campaigns. By contrast men like Peter, who returned from Japanese captivity, felt, as one put it, that they were 'remnants and survivors of a defeated army. Apart from our nearest and dearest, nobody wanted to know . . .'

Despite Dorothea's attempts to thwart Walter and Beryl's marriage, when she finally met Beryl the two of them got on warmly, all Dorothea's former frostiness forgotten. Arthur, however, found the presence of two lively four-year-old boys something of a strain. When he reprimanded him they called him an 'old fool' in Urdu, not realising that their grandfather would understand perfectly. The pre-war Arthur might have chuckled and called them chips off the old block, but age and the years of anxiety and strain had taken their toll on him. He was far from amused.

Worse still, both boys had been given Gurkha kukris as presents and, naturally, wanted to test the sharpness of the blades. Unfortunately they chose to do this in the rose garden that was Arthur's pride and joy, and in their enthusiasm lopped the head off every last rose. When Arthur discovered their crime he exploded, 'I never want to see those boys again.'

As Fate would have it, he never did. Walter returned to India and was then sent to Malaya, once again as CO of 4/8th Gurkhas and then as a staff officer to South East Asia Land Forces. Beryl and the children – the twins and a new baby, my mother Venetia – joined him there after a terrifying journey across a newly independent India engulfed in sectarian violence and mass killings. It was while in Malaya that he was called upon to witness the hangings at Pudu jail, Kuala Lumpur, of some of the Japanese soldiers and officers who had been found guilty of war crimes and sentenced to death. He told me it gave him a certain satisfaction, in the knowledge of what they had done, although many escaped justice.

In November 1947, Arthur died. His sons and daughters would miss his genial guidance as they navigated the choppy waters of the post-war world in which the old certainties had vanished. Peter, in particular, was devastated. His father had been the centre of his world: he had followed in his footsteps as a tea-planter; Arthur had been more sympathetic and approachable than Dorothea, whose response to problems was to try to fix them rather than to listen. Now he was gone and Peter, already struggling to adapt to life after liberation, was without his closest confidant and friend.

The British Empire was now being dismantled. The map of the world Arthur's sons had studied at Blundell's, on which the Empire's extensive possessions were coloured red, was out of date. The red was receding rapidly. Peter found this hard to comprehend: he had believed passionately in the Empire and suffered terribly in its cause, only to be told that it was dying anyway.

Walter transferred from the Indian Army to the British Army – the Gurkha regiments were divided between the two – but for Edward things would not be so simple, either in his professional or his personal life. He remained in the army at first, but post-war life did not provide the same sense of fulfilment and purpose that he had found in battle. Something about the proximity of death made some people feel intensely alive, pushing other concerns and complications below the surface. Peace brought them bobbing up.

After the war, Tiggy travelled back to England with the boys while Edward was posted to Hong Kong as CO of the Jaipur Guards. His star seemed to be in the ascendant – Lord Mountbatten and the Maharajah of Jaipur heaped praise on him for his exemplary command of the Jaipur Guards and he was promoted to brigadier. But then he met the woman whom he later came to see as his nemesis, Linda Morse. Linda, who already had two marriages behind her, was no beauty but she was erudite, well connected – she had worked for SOE in Cairo during the war – witty, charismatic and extremely tenacious. What Linda wanted, Linda usually got, and what she wanted then was Edward: charming, handsome, a decorated war hero and a newly promoted brigadier. He seemed to be friends with the right people, too, such as the maharajah.

So brave and decisive in war, Edward was far less resolute when it came to women. According to his own account, which he wrote years later in an attempt to make sense of it all, Linda pursued him relentlessly, writing him adoring love letters when they were apart. He wavered: he had a wife in England and two small sons. Yet here was Linda, eager and apparently adoring. He was flattered and succumbed to temptation: an affair began.

In June 1946 he finally returned home on leave to see his parents for the first time in nine years and to be reunited with Tiggy and his boys. But their reunion did not go as he expected. Tiggy told him she wanted a divorce. Her affair with the army psychiatrist had resumed, if it had ever ended, and they wanted to get married.

It seems that Edward did not admit to his own infidelity, but agreed to a divorce and returned to India. There, against his better judgement, he took up again with Linda, who had followed him, and married her in Madras in 1947. 'She had become a habit,' he wrote ruefully. 'My decision to marry was more convenience than love.'

It was Linda, he said, who pressed him to retire from the army and return to England, where he fought Tiggy for custody of his sons and won. This seems to have been motivated less by paternal devotion than a desire to punish Tiggy for her infidelity, even though he, too, had had an affair. Tiggy was devastated, the guilt she had felt over her affair compounded by having her sons taken from her. Only later did she learn that Edward had also strayed, yet she was the one who was punished.

Her second marriage fell apart even before their child was born, and after the birth she developed post-natal depression that left her unable to look after her daughter. Barred from seeing her boys – even the cards and letters she wrote were kept from them – and unable to care for her daughter, Tiggy broke down completely, suffering from bouts of manic depression so severe that she spent several years in and out of psychiatric hospitals, receiving treatment such as ECT (electroconvulsive therapy) for her depression.

Edward soon realised that leaving the military and marrying Linda had been terrible mistakes. He struggled with civilian life, working in London briefly before moving to Ireland to try his hand at chicken farming, but the business failed and he returned to the military, joining the RAF Regiment. Once again, he was in his element. He was promoted and posted to Germany, Suez and Iraq, but his success was marred by the running sore of his unhappy marriage to Linda, who was high-spending, demanding and brazenly unfaithful. Both he and she had believed they were marrying into money, and both were disappointed to discover, too late, that they were wrong.

Linda effectively ended his military career, by demanding that he return from Iraq or she would abandon his children. Their arguments were terrible, with Linda calling him a 'DSO coward', while Edward was consumed by disappointment that his military career had never reached the heights for which it seemed destined, for which he blamed Linda.

To Hamish, Linda was 'a rascal' but great company, and an entertaining step-grandmother to his children. But to Nick, she was the archetypal wicked stepmother, frequently banishing him to stay with Dorothea, who would confide in him her concerns about her children. Edward, she told him, was 'weak' when it came to women. Dorothea still banged the Tara gong for meals even when Nick was next to her.

Edward, who had been so solicitous and caring towards his men during the war, was far less attentive towards his sons. Soldiers obey orders, battalions are run on rules and structures, but family life is far more complicated and does not always conform to plan. Edward had been a fine soldier, but as a father he was difficult and distant. He had fought for custody of his children but he showed no great interest in them.

The disappointments of post-war life were bitter indeed, particularly as he watched Walter climbing ever higher up the military ladder, being decorated and lauded. He could not help but feel aggrieved at how the cards had fallen for him.

Much, much later, long after Edward had divorced Linda, he and Tiggy became friendly again, often meeting at their son Nick's house. One day, sitting together on the sofa, they held hands and reminisced about their life in India before the war. 'We were so happy then, weren't we?' Tiggy asked Edward. Yes, he agreed, perhaps forgetting the rows, they were. If it had not been for the war and the separations it had entailed, they would have stayed together. Their marriage, they concluded, had been yet another casualty of war.

As a young war widow, Bee, too, had to forge a new life when the war ended. In November 1945 she had travelled to America to introduce

Mary, now two, to Gaddis's family. She sailed with her little daughter and a new nanny, Margaret Brown, known always as 'Nan', who would remain with the family for decades. They arrived in New York to stay with Gaddis's brother, Matt Plum, in the Plums' house on East 80th Street, just around the corner from Park Avenue.

Matt's son, Matt Plum Junior, a schoolboy at the time, remembered Bee as 'pretty, quite thin, quick to laugh and game to participate'. Gaddis's death had left her bereft but not broken. The Plums were a warm, loving family, and the kindly welcome they gave her, the elegant opulence of their New York house, with its small army of servants and the lively bustle of Manhattan outside the front door, must have been balm to Bee's soul after war-shattered London. The Plums assured Bee that she and Mary would be well provided-for and they were as good as their word, making over Gaddis's share of the family fortune to her in trust. Bee returned to Britain a wealthy woman.

Back in London she became a merry widow, appearing in *Tatler*'s society pages, attending glamorous parties and nightclubs, and, once again, Dorothea began to worry about Bee's racy London life. She was heartily relieved when Bee met Roland 'Roy' Hudson, who, like Gaddis, was half a generation older than her, had served in both wars and seemed a steadying influence.

For all her flightiness, Bee showed shrewd judgement when she chose Roy, a steady country gentleman from Norfolk, rather than any of the gold-diggers that inevitably circled round a wealthy young widow. They married in 1949, with Mary, who adored Roy from the outset, as a bridesmaid, and had a son together, Peter. Thanks to Gaddis's legacy, Bee was able to live in some style in London and their country house in Sussex, employing a full-time cook in both houses as well as a nanny, butler and other staff. Like her mother had before her, it was Bee who controlled the household finances, although her idea of economising was to instruct the butler to serve margarine instead of butter.

It was a true *Upstairs, Downstairs* household, at least at weekends when Roy returned from spending the week in London. He was a stickler for formality, insisting on all the children changing into suits and dresses for formal dinners, which the butler served. During the week, when Bee was in charge, things were more relaxed. In the afternoons, she liked to watch the horse-racing on the television with the cook in her tiny sitting room: like Edward, Peter, Ruth and Harold, she had inherited her father's love of the turf and bought a couple of racehorses and a livery stables where the children rode their ponies every day. She liked to watch the polo at Cowdray Park, where she would sometimes run into Jai, Edward's old friend, the Maharajah of Jaipur.

Although she created an idyllic Enid Blyton-esque environment for her children, like many wealthy upper-class parents in the 1950s Bee left the daily business of child-rearing to the devoted Nan, while she busied herself with her social life and attending fashion shows. She remained disciplined about her diet – 'Play play, darling, play play,' she would say, while pushing her food around her plate, restricting her intake largely to coffee and cigarettes – and fitted into mannequin's sizes all her life.

Harold, too, prospered, turning his misfortune to his advantage, working hard and ending the war far ahead of most of his medical-school contemporaries, who were serving in the military, as he would have done had it not been for his injury. He passed his exams to become a consultant and, still only thirty, began lecturing at Hammersmith Hospital. Here he met a pretty young nurse, Nancy Hughes. Although she had a boyfriend, a medical student, she was swept off her feet by Harold's charm. He took her to West End shows and dancing in nightclubs, driving her around London in his open-top car. For a girl from a small village in mid-Wales, it was intoxicating and romantic.

Despite his love of a good time, Harold remained driven by the urge to make a difference and put his miraculously spared life to good use. In 1948 he went abroad for the first time, travelling to Nigeria, then still a British colony, to establish a medical school as its professor. He worked long hours teaching and operating on women who had suffered terrible damage due to difficult childbirths, saving them from pain, disability or death. But in a climate of post-war austerity, the Colonial Office failed to provide adequate funding for the medical school. Harold resigned in protest and returned to Britain.

He and Nancy had married in Nigeria, ignoring the misgivings of Dorothea, who, never short of an opinion about her children's romantic choices, thought that Nancy's background was insufficiently smart. She was once again proved wrong as Harold and Nancy had a long and happy marriage. They had two daughters, Pamela and Penelope, and Harold became a consultant at St Mary's Hospital in Manchester, where he was described as 'a pink-faced, prosperous-looking practitioner with a suave manner and an eye for organisational detail'.

Like Walter, Harold was an innovator and was not content to accept established practices if he could find a way of improving them. He was instrumental in developing the amniocentesis test to diagnose and treat rhesus haemolytic disease, in which antibodies in the mother's blood react against the baby's red blood cells, causing complications and even stillbirth, and became known as 'The Rhesus King' of Manchester. Although private work gave him a comfortable living - he drove a Rolls-Royce - he continued to work for the NHS too. He took a keen interest in horse-racing, placing bets on the horses and ringing up Bee's son, Peter, a racehorse trainer, for tips.

For Ruth, the end of the war brought a chance to take stock. She was keen to see more of the world and secured a job at a nursing home in South Africa. She was preparing to travel there in 1946 when she received the worrying news from home that Arthur was seriously ill: she should return as soon as she could. She got the next ship home, to spend what remaining time there was with Arthur, although in fact he lived for another year.

So, Ruth never went to South Africa but took up private nursing in England instead. She did not have a serious boyfriend - there was still no one who matched up to John Fisher - and the prospect of marriage seemed a long way off, so she decided to throw herself into her career. In March 1948 she began training as a midwife at Hammersmith Hospital.

John Fisher had returned to Britain at the end of 1945 after being invalided out of Sarawak: he had become seriously ill in the jungle with amoebic dysentery. Recuperating in Tiverton, he was reunited with Isabella. But while war had torn some couples asunder, for others the peace proved a greater strain. John and Isabella had spent most of their four-year marriage apart and now, to their distress, they discovered they were unable to live together. They tried to save their marriage for the sake of the three boys, John's two stepsons and two year-old Michael, but to no avail and they separated, Isabella eventually returning to Holland and John to Sarawak.

In 1948 John was given leave to come home again from Sarawak. Travelling by boat, he stopped off in Malaya, where Walter and Beryl were now living. John learned that Ruth was back in Britain and unmarried. Although he had fallen in love with Isabella, John had been unable to put Ruth out of his mind and never stopped loving the girl he had fallen for more than a decade earlier back in Tiverton. He discovered her address and sent her a postcard from Port Swettenham before he boarded his ship: 'Bloody well stay in England till I get there. John.'

Ruth met him on Waterloo station where they had last seen each other four years earlier. Within weeks their engagement was reinstated and Ruth prepared for a new life in Sarawak, praying that nothing would derail it this time. John obtained a divorce from Isabella, and, on 30 December 1948 at Chelsea Register Office, he and Ruth were married at last. As it was John's second marriage it was a quiet wedding: no church, no bridal gown and just a handful of friends, as well as Dorothea and Edward. The reception was held at the Special Forces Club in Knightsbridge, to which John, as an SOE man, belonged. In the photographs taken on the steps outside the register office, John stands a step below Ruth so they are able to link arms despite the discrepancy in their heights. Both look suffused with joy, John dapper and proud, Ruth petite and pretty in a floral dress, her hair beautifully coiffed. Her St Thomas's matrons would have been impressed.

It had been a long and winding path to the altar for Ruth and John, but nearly twelve years after John had proposed at Tara they had their hard-won happy ending. When, after a brief honeymoon, they sailed for Sarawak, they were accompanied by Jonathan, the dachshund John had given Ruth all those years ago as an engagement present.

They began their married life at Limbang, deep in the Sarawak jungle and five days' travel by boat up the river. There was no electricity, no telephone, and while Ruth could go for weeks without seeing another European, she did not mind this in the slightest. She enjoyed travelling around the jungle by river, visiting longhouses with John and meeting some of his Dayak comrades from the war.

Their house was run by Malay servants, who included Udin, John's houseboy from before the war, who had joined him on Semut operations, and was now married to Ooni, John's former 'sleeping dictionary'. Ruth bore no historical jealousy towards Ooni or vice versa, apparently. When her sons David and Jonathan were born – Jonathan the dog had died and been replaced by another dachshund – she employed her as their amah (nanny).

LATER YEARS

THERE WERE, OVER the years, several family reunions in Weybridge, although with Edward intermittently abroad and Walter and Ruth in the Far East, it was not easy to assemble the whole clan with their spouses and children for a family photograph.

Like most parents, Dorothea wanted her children to find happiness and stability, but for both Peter and Edward these were to remain elusive in the post-war years. Peter's health continued to trouble him. As well as a painful leg and back, the parasites in his intestines and liver would remain there for decades, giving him severe digestive problems and making mealtimes such an ordeal that he ate separately from his family, a limited diet of vegetables and rice.

He received a negligible disability pension, for which he had to be regularly examined by a military panel. Only when he eventually came up before a panel that included a doctor he had known in one of the camps was his pension increased dramatically. He was awarded three medals for his war service but he never wore them.

Even more debilitating than the constant physical pain were the nightmares. He would return frequently to the camps in his sleep, reliving the torments and terrors so vividly that he would shout and throw up his arms in an effort to defend himself from another beating, and awake screaming and flailing in terror. But there was no recognition or treatment then for such mental scars. Post-traumatic stress disorder (PTSD) became an officially recognised condition in 1992, too late for many.

He gave up his job in London to become a market gardener, but although that suited his temperament better it was comparatively poorly paid, which put a strain on the family finances and stability. The comfortable house in Chertsey had to go and the family had to move every time Peter changed job, which was often since his outbursts of temper became more frequent, caused by the physical and mental pain that wore away at him. The boys could not understand why their father was often so angry. No one spoke about the war, about what had made him that way.

At one point the family had to live in a caravan for six months; at another they moved in with Dorothea in Weybridge. This was misery for Kay as Dorothea invariably took Peter's side in any argument so she often escaped to London, leaving the children with their tyrannical grandmother.

In the late 1950s, at one of the plant nurseries where he worked, Peter met a young botanist named Jennifer. She was in her early twenties, more than two decades his junior. Instinctively drawn to people who needed help, who were damaged in some way, she had always regarded prisoners of war as heroes. She idolised Peter, although initially she did not see him as a romantic prospect and used to tell him her dating troubles. One day as they were digging side by side in a flowerbed and she was wondering aloud which of her two boyfriends she should marry, he turned to her and said, 'I wish to God you'd marry me and settle down.'

It was not, of course, as simple as that and, as with Edward, it was the children who suffered most from the fallout. After he and Kay divorced, Peter vanished from their lives. Kay struggled to support herself and her boys, who were bewildered at being seemingly abandoned by their father. It took many years for them to understand that his behaviour was caused by what he had suffered in the camps, that they, too, were victims of those years of brutality.

Dorothea tried hard to dissuade Jennifer from marrying Peter, warning her, 'You're going to have an old crock on your hands.' But Jennifer was undeterred and they married in 1962.

On the first night of their honeymoon in the Scilly Isles, Peter struck out in his sleep, dreaming that he was thrusting a knife at one of the guards who tormented him. He cracked Jennifer so hard across the temple that she had to go to hospital. Peter was mortified when he realised what he had done but for Jennifer it was further evidence of his heroism and suffering. 'I thought it was wonderful! I was such a Florence Nightingale. Although after that, we slept in separate beds, then in separate rooms and then on separate floors as his nightmares were so bad.'

Despite the continuing nightmares, Peter found a measure of peace and contentment. Jennifer did not expect him to socialise and she shared his passion for gardening, working side by side with him when they set up their own gardening business. Times were sometimes tough financially, and Walter tried to help, calling upon his military contacts to find Peter work with the Red Cross.

Jennifer observed the family with the objectivity of a newcomer. After Dorothea's initial hostility melted, she was kind to her, while Bee was warm and welcoming. Ruth, by contrast, was forthright in her disapproval at first, although they later became friends. Ruth shared with Walter a black-and-white view of the world and both spoke their minds forcefully. What all four brothers had in common was, she said, tremendous charm, a twinkle in their eye, a joke always at the ready. One of the few people to whom Peter would talk about his time in the camps was John Fisher. John knew what life was like in the jungle and he had a unique capacity to listen without judging, to know exactly what to say.

Peter and Jennifer had two sons, Adam and Matthew. Although he remained prone to occasional rages, these became vanishingly rare and for much of the time Peter was the easygoing, kind character he had been before the war, with a mischievous sense of humour. Uncle Peter was a great favourite with his nieces and nephews, who remember him as sweet, calm and patient, with a gentle magnetism. To his younger sons, he was a devoted father, who loved playing with them, teasing and joking, helping them with their schoolwork, telling them not to worry about small problems and setbacks, they simply did not matter. He was, quite simply, their hero.

He and Jennifer eventually moved to Tiverton, a short walk from Tara and the garden where he and his brothers had played cricket and fired rubber-tipped arrows at Ruth.

He never forgave the Japanese for what had been done to him. He would not let any of his family buy Japanese-made goods and after his nephew, Jonathan Fisher, once came to visit him riding a Suzuki motorbike, Peter sent him a cheque, with generosity he could ill afford, 'to buy yourself a (British-made) Triumph instead'. He avoided Remembrance Day and even Fireworks Night, and abhorred anything he saw as warmongering, saying, 'These people would run a mile in a real war.'

He credited Jennifer with his survival when so many of those who had lived through the camps died long before their time, from illness or, tragically, suicide. When Edward was ill, and at a low ebb, Peter wrote a letter, commiserating: 'It can make one very depressed and made me feel like ending it all. Jennifer has been my support and saving grace as I am sure without her I would have packed up long ago.'

Jennifer never regretted defying Dorothea's attempt to warn her off

Peter: 'Dear, brave Peter, he never said "Poor me." He had tremendous spirit. What an example he was. Nobody will ever come close to him. That's why I've never remarried.' It was his compassion that she admired the most. 'He was so nice to everybody, even when he was ill. He was calm, dignified, quiet, helpful, sweet and kind and wise . . . such an inspiration.' With her, she said, he was infinitely patient, forgiving her youthful naivety, never judging her mistakes.

Along with other survivors of the Japanese camps, Peter became a regular patient at Queen Mary's military hospital in Roehampton and found some solace in speaking to other former prisoners of war there. Sometimes he would spend four or five weeks as an inpatient while tests were carried out, tenderly cared for by the motherly Sister 'Scarlett' O'Hara of the FEPOW (Far East Prisoners of War) ward, who would cluck with fond exasperation at 'naughty' Peter's habit of wandering around the ward, sitting on the beds of other patients, helping them write letters about their disability pension and other matters. Sometimes he would be absent altogether, and would be discovered on the disabled children's ward, visiting the young victims of the thalidomide scandal, who had been left with missing limbs by the drug taken in pregnancy to counteract sickness.

Peter felt tremendous sympathy for them and did whatever he could to help and cheer them. Perhaps they reminded him of the amputees in the camps: had it not been for good luck and the doctors' dedication, he could easily have lost his leg to tropical ulcers. He counted his blessings often, frequently telling Jennifer how lucky they were to have healthy children. Having suffered such ill fortune, he treasured any good luck that came his way, while shrugging off setbacks with a 'Nil desperandum.'

Despite his brothers' outward success, Peter carried with him a sense of quiet triumph and confidence: he had seen and suffered things that they could not even imagine, had defied the odds and survived. It left him not with a sense of moral superiority, but a deep inner strength that belied his outward frailty.

As with many large families, friendships among the siblings shifted with time and geography. Bee saw little of Edward, to whom she had once been so close, even though their London flats were only a few streets apart, and did not even visit him at the end of his life. She and Ruth continued to keep each other at arm's length. Ruth described Bee as 'tough as boots', but to others, Bee was the most bountiful of aunts, kind, generous and funny.

It was Bee who regularly invited Peter's older two boys to stay after Peter had left, showering them with presents and kindness when their world had been turned upside down. And it was Bee who gave Walter's three children a home in the school holidays when they were unable to join their parents abroad. The army was not, in those days, generous with schoolchildren's airfares, and private air travel remained the preserve of the wealthy, so Anthony, Nigel and Venetia spent many of their school holidays staying at Bee's rambling Sussex house, joining Mary and Peter at the stables every day. My mother, Venetia, remembers Bee as warm, loving and funny, although she was perhaps easier to have as an aunt than a mother: the relationship did not come with the weight of expect-ation that motherhood can bring.

In contrast to Ruth, who did not 'do' emotion, having learned early on to keep a tight rein on her feelings, Bee wore her heart on her sleeve, while Roy was also quick to anger. It was a combustible combination. While the household was relaxed and harmonious during the week, when Roy returned from London at weekends the atmosphere would change. Bee was modern, sociable and informal, while Roy wanted to lead the life of a country gentleman, a throwback to the Edwardian times in which he had grown up. Their different outlooks led to furious, bitter rows. But for the children there was always the reassuring presence of Nan in the sanctuary of the nursery. When Nan finally retired, Bee bought her a flat in Chelsea and looked after her financially until her death.

For Walter the war did not end so much as pause. He did not just have 'a good war', he had three good wars. Within a year of his arrival in Malaya he was fighting again in what became the twelve-year-long Malayan Emergency, and called upon many of the tactics he had honed in Burma to fight Communist insurgents in the jungle. Once again he led from the front, pushing himself as hard as his men, securing his own reputation, and that of the Gurkhas, as the finest of jungle warriors. His success in Malaya earned two more mentions in dispatches, an OBE, a bar to his DSO and promotion to brigadier.

By 1960 he was a major general, and when war unexpectedly broke out in Borneo in 1962, he was appointed director of operations. Here, he deployed innovative tactics to defend a 1,200-mile border against Indonesian invaders, using Gurkhas, SAS and Commonwealth troops, helicopters, marines and some of the same Dayak hunters who had helped the British twenty years earlier. Once again it was John Fisher, now Walter's brother-in-law, who enlisted the help of the Dayaks in Sarawak, calling them to arms in the traditional way by sending a red feather up the river. Walter found himself working closely with John, for whom he had 'fagged' all those years ago at Blundell's.

Borneo was a highly successful war and, although little reported at home, Walter's leadership earned him a place among the military greats of the post-war era. It should automatically have earned him a knighthood, too, but he had made enemies in Whitehall through his habit of speaking his mind, particularly in his defence of the Gurkhas against efforts to cut their numbers drastically. He had to make do with a third bar to his DSO and later a CB (Commander of the Bath). The knighthood did not come until 1968 and he ended his career in a senior NATO role, as a full general and Commander-in-Chief Allied Forces Northern Europe.

Dorothea was not alive to see her son knighted. She had died in 1964 while staying with Bee in Sussex. Ten years later, Edward died from cancer. In his final weeks he was nursed devotedly by Peter, who travelled from Devon to London to be at his brother's bedside.

Bee died in 1988, leaving a third husband, whom she had married after Roy died. Even in her seventies, Bee had remained the epitome of glamour, still slender as a willow, witty and gregarious.

Despite the terrible price that the war had exacted on his health, Peter survived into old age. He had been reunited with his older sons after Richard, encouraged by Kay, reached out to the father he had not seen for eleven years. He had become, in Richard's words, 'A very nice, gentle old man, not the angry person we knew as children. Everyone liked him . . . He'd made peace with what had happened to him.' They were able to build a relationship with him and learned something of what he had been through, which had made him behave as he had, and to come to terms with it.

The brutality of men such as Noguchi and Kokubo damaged not only the prisoners of war but continued to affect their families, too, for years after the war. They lived with husbands and fathers who were terrorised by nightmares, who plunged into black moods. Some took to drink or, tragically, took their lives, while others died early from heart disease and other physical conditions resulting from the years of malnutrition and abuse. For those men, the end of the war did not bring peace but an ongoing battle against suffering.

Peter lived long enough to see his younger two sons, Adam and Matthew, grow up and to meet his first grandchildren, Michael's eldest two. He died on Remembrance Day in 1989. He had been to the Tiverton bookmaker earlier in the morning, just as Arthur used to do, and he was in a cheerful mood when he placed his daily bet on a horse race. He was alone in the house when he began having a heart attack. Realising what was happening, he wrote a note to his family, then got into bed and died at, it was thought, around 11 a.m., the hour of remembrance. His doctor had always said that he would die when he was ready to, at a time of his choosing. On his coffin his family placed a wreath of poppies and the Union flag. Peter remained fiercely patriotic to the end.

Harold and Walter died within months of each other in 2001. Harold had endured failing health and the loss of his eyesight with characteristic stoicism and absence of self-pity. His had been a life well lived and he could take comfort in the knowledge that he had indeed made a difference.

Walter was also afflicted by disability in old age due to a hip replacement operation that went badly wrong and left him in constant pain. His beloved Beryl died in 1990, leaving him bereft. After he retired from the army, they had settled in the West Country, where Walter fought battles of a different kind. Having been out of the country for the best part of forty years, he was aghast at the state in which he found it in the 1970s, beset by strikes and chaos, 'the sick man of Europe'.

With other ex-military men, he set up an organisation, Civil Assistance, to help run essential services if public order broke down, which seemed all too likely. It was viewed with suspicion in some quarters as a 'private army', although he was adamant that it was neither paramilitary nor extremist. It was in any case short-lived but he remained closely interested in politics, the army and society all his life, writing trenchant letters to the *Daily Telegraph* expressing his deeply conservative opinions - all four brothers held extremely right-wing political views - and seldom entertaining the notion that there might be alternatives.

But right-wing views did not preclude private philanthropy and compassion. Walter kept up friendships with many of the men who had fought with him in Burma, and when an officer from Burma days wrote that he was struggling to obtain the disability pension he was owed as a result of being wounded in Burma, Walter swung into action and ensured that it was awarded. In the 1990s he learned that Lacchiman Gurung, the VC hero of Taungdaw, was crippled as a result of his war wounds and living in poverty, unable to access medical care from his remote Himalayan village, Walter went into battle again, waging a highly successful campaign to raise money for a new house for Lacchiman, suitable for his disability and near a clinic.

Walter and Ruth lived within a mile of each other in their final years and saw each other often. Despite his physical disability, Walter's mind remained agile to the end. He was always immaculate - he looked dapper even in a dressing-gown - and sociable, still combative and enquiring, enjoying a joke and gentle teasing. As a father he was stern, but as a grandfather he was jovial, kind and never, ever dull.

He died in August 2001, mourned not only by his family but by all those who had fought with him, in Burma, Malaya and Borneo, and particularly within the Gurkha community. The tributes paid to him in print spoke of his brilliant wartime leadership, his sense of humour, fairness, patience and loyalty. 'We have all lost a good friend and a great soldier,' wrote an old comrade.

I was saddened by his loss, of course, but he was eighty-eight and, despite the agony of his last years, his life had been a rich one. It was when I began writing this book that I wished, inevitably, that I had talked more with him about the war, about those nerve-stretching moments at Milaungbya and Taungdaw, about how it had felt as a thirty-two-year-old commanding officer to have to send men he liked and admired to their deaths.

A few months before he died, Walter had written a long account of Taungdaw for a Gurkha magazine, reliving the battle hour by hour. He sent me a copy of the article and I read it with interest, although I found it hard to envisage what he described. So, seventeen years on from his death, I decided I had to see the place that had meant so much to him.

After our encounter with the monks at Milaungbya, we journeyed south and west, past the Yenangyaung oilfields, across the Irrawaddy and into the lush green hills and valleys just east of Rakhine state. The light was already fading when we neared Taungdaw and were directed by some road workers to a rocky track leading off the tarmac road, which led us eventually to Yebok. This was the village where Walter had paced anxiously, waiting for the wireless to crackle with news, craning his neck to see the Hurribombers bringing deliverance and death. Over the next ridge lay Taungdaw but the track there was vertiginously steep, a mass of rocks, bumps and potholes with the occasional sheer drop. It was clear that our saloon car would not make it, and it was too far to walk before the sun set. Then some villagers, hearing of our plight, offered us a lift on the back of their motorbikes. Off we set, clinging on tightly, bouncing briskly down the hillside as the riders skilfully evaded potholes and boulders.

This was, I realised, probably the very track down which Walter had sped in his jeep on the morning of 15 May 1945 to see for himself whether victory was really in his grasp.

And there, silhouetted by the setting sun, was the pass itself and the saddle that dipped in the middle of the ridge, with a bristle of trees on the crest either side of it where Mike Tidswell had been killed. Beyond it lay the far ridge, where Peter Myers had held on with his company, and the wounded Lacchiman had flung grenades with his left hand. And then there we were, in Taungdaw, which, in May 1945, had been left shattered and splintered, filled with bloated, bloody corpses.

We began walking through the village, guided by our escorts. The houses were on stilts and were made of bamboo and thatch, although a few had tin roofs and there were one or two solar panels. Cows were being led on ropes to their night-time quarters underneath the houses. Wooden bullock carts stood laden with fodder. It was the most tranquil, beautiful corner of the world I have ever visited. A hidden valley where life seemed to meander along at much the same pace as it had seventy or so years ago.

Intrigued as to what two Westerners were doing in their midst – we were, apparently, the first tourists to visit – villagers came over to talk to us, through our interpreter-guide, to find out why we had come. No one remembered the war, but they knew that a battle had been fought there, that the British and Gurkhas had beaten the Japanese, and that many bodies had been buried. It was a poignant moment. I was glad to have seen Taungdaw, restored and peaceful once more, silently to pay my respects and remember the Kohima epitaph: 'When you go home, tell them of us and say, "For your tomorrow, we gave our today."'

Walter never went back but he did not need to. Taungdaw, and the men who had fought there, remained with him all his life.

Walter's death left Ruth as the last of the Tara Walkers. She endured a long widowhood. John and she had led an idyllic existence in Sarawak, living on the edge of the jungle for years, with a resident python in the attic, orangutans and hornbills in the nearby trees. They hosted a continual stream of guests, from Dayaks to Prince Philip. John's bonhomie and generosity with the pink gin was legendary, though few would guess that this lanky, languid *bon viveur* had once fought a clandestine war as a guerrilla. Later he became mayor of Kuching, Sarawak's capital, and he and Ruth exchanged the jungle for a social whirl of cocktail parties, tennis and drinks at the club.

In 1965, when Sarawak became part of the newly formed Malaysia, John retired from the Sarawak service. He and Ruth returned to Britain with their sons, David and Jonathan, and settled in Dorset in a house they named Tara. Jennifer and Peter, the brother to whom she had always been closest, were living nearby so they saw much of each other.

Tragically, Ruth and John did not have long to enjoy their retirement as John became seriously ill with cancer. Ruth nursed him devotedly but there was little to be done. His death in 1968 was devastating for her and their children and left a gaping hole in the wider Walker family. John had been part of the Walkers' lives for so long, a fifth brother at Tara, a friend and confidant to his nieces and nephews, a port in a storm for anyone feeling troubled or in need of a good listener, and an irrepressible practical joker. When a notoriously parsimonious neighbour bragged constantly about the fuel economy of his car John, although seriously ill by then, had sneaked out in the darkness, accompanied by his sons, and drained petrol from the tank, leaving the neighbour scratching his head about why his previously efficient car had become so costly. Forty years later, his grandchildren visited Sarawak and found longhouses where John Fisher's name still evoked memories, tales of the war and enduring affection.

Ruth was distraught. After waiting a decade for her happy ending, twenty years together was too short a reward. But she was never a lonely widow. She had her children, to whom she was an affectionate, fun-loving mother, who preferred to encourage rather than intervene as her own mother had done. She had a long-term male companion, and friendships that had endured from St Thomas's, Cairo and Sarawak. She took a close interest in horse-racing and became a skilled angler. The dynamism and energy that had impressed her matrons at St Thomas's never left her: she played regular bridge and walked briskly around town doing her errands until her late nineties. Even her hair remained naturally dark – her buoyant dark curls became flecked with grey only three years before she died. The two great sorrows of her life were losing John and then, years later, her elder son David to cancer.

She died aged ninety-eight, by then a grandmother and great-grandmother. Although few of her contemporaries were alive, friends, acquaintances and relations spanning several generations filled the church. Until her last months Ruth's memory remained sharp and she would fondly recall those days at St Thomas's, and her childhood at Tara with her brothers and her white knight, John.

On a sunny spring morning in 2018, six months after Ruth died, her family gathered in a pretty churchyard in Dorset, a few miles from Tara, where Ruth and John had lived until his death. There was a brief but moving service over the grave where John had been buried fifty years before and Ruth's ashes were interred beside him, uniting them once more. Their son Jonathan laid a plaque on which their names were inscribed, with the lines: 'They loved each other and taught us the true purpose of life is to love.'

Epilogue

———⊷———

THE WALKERS WERE a fortunate family indeed. It was, as Ruth often said, nothing short of amazing that the whole family came through the war unscathed – or, at least, alive. She knew of parents who had lost their only son and others who had lost all their children. In the Blitz, entire families were wiped out by a single bomb. One family with four boys who joined the RAF lost them all. The Brabner family, whose son was in the same missing plane as Gaddis Plum, also lost their daughter to a VI. Compared with such losses the survival of all the Walkers was indeed miraculous.

Through their letters, interviews, army files, and the words of those who knew them, who saw them in their finest hours and at their lowest ebb, I have got to know Arthur, Dorothea, Edward, Bee, Peter and Harold posthumously, and discovered more about Walter and Ruth than I learned when they were alive.

At times I have felt like a spy, peeping through the curtains at Tara, riffling through school reports, army appraisals, nursing records, letters and newspaper reports, things they would never have imagined being read by a relative several lifetimes later.

I have warmed to them all in their different ways: Arthur, genial and improvident, deferring to Dorothea, the formidable matriarch; Edward, the handsome playboy for whom peace was harder than war; Bee, spiky but spirited, who found love after a few turbulent years, only to have it wrenched from her abruptly; Walter, no longer simply 'Grandpa' or 'the General' but a headstrong schoolboy, a love-struck subaltern and young commanding officer, trying to remain outwardly calm as a battle hung in the balance; Peter, who was nearly broken by the war but triumphed spiritually, later in life; Harold, the sunny youngest son, who owed his life to his friends and never forgot his good fortune; and Ruth, ever brave and stoic, who dealt with burned skin more readily than emotion, but whose wartime heartbreak ended in happiness.

The war changed all their lives. Without it, Ruth might simply have graduated from schoolgirl to housewife without embarking on a nursing career. Bee would not have met her husband, but neither would she have lost him. Harold's career would almost certainly have prospered but perhaps less rapidly. Walter would probably have confined his fighting to the North West Frontier and climbed more steadily up the military ladder. Edward would likely have shuttled from one posting to the next, playing polo, working his way slowly up the hierarchy, perhaps remaining married to Tiggy. And Peter might have carried on contentedly in the tea garden for some years, his future certain rather than hanging by a thread, his health intact.

Would their personalities have been different had their early adult years been shaped by peace, not war, had they not all - perhaps bar Bee - come within inches of death? It is a question that one could ask of any of that resilient generation, who fought and lived through those seismic years, soldier or civilian, in the factory or on the frontline.

Certainly Harold felt a kind of debt to humanity after being saved from near death, a burning desire to make a difference. For his part, Walter emerged from the war with the characteristics that had already been evident in him as a schoolboy more sharply honed, described in his obituary in the *Daily Telegraph* with 'clarity of vision, single-mindedness of purpose, fierce insistence on discipline, fearlessness in the face of both the enemy and his superiors'. The reverse side of the coin was an inability to see others' point of view and an absolute conviction that his way was the correct and only way. He always spoke his mind and put loyalty to his men above all other considerations.

With five older siblings, Ruth was already a resilient and self-possessed character before the war. But surviving near-burial, seeing off a razor-wielding patient and working with the war's burned and battered victims undoubtedly strengthened her already steely stoicism as well as imbuing her with an optimistic, glass-half-full attitude to life.

For Bee, even Gaddis's death did not shatter her natural *joie de vivre*. She remained sociable and gregarious, not broken by her loss. But for Edward the triumph of war was overshadowed by the tribulations of peace.

As for Peter, whose bravery was of a different order from that of his older brothers, the war wrecked his health and his dreams as well as his first marriage. But, with time, he overcame the anger and pain to help others through a compassion born of suffering. His was perhaps the greatest victory of all.

All the Walker children had inherited Dorothea's iron will, the determination to keep going against the odds: '*Nil desperandum*'. But perhaps just as important was Arthur's optimistic 'All will be well': hope is a powerful force indeed.

The war pulled families apart and when they were brought back together, things were inevitably different from how they had been before. Some family members had prospered while others suffered. Hierarchies and alliances shifted. Much as they might try, it was difficult to understand each other's experiences and how they had altered them. From evacuated children, to women who had entered the workplace for the first time, to civilians who became soldiers and people who lost their possessions, health or loved ones, the war years defined the rest of their lives.

After the war, families who lived close to each other had greater opportunity to rebuild their bonds and get to know each other again, to observe and absorb how each other had changed. Not all families weathered the ructions: there was a sharp rise in divorces at the end of the 1940s. But for others the end of the war brought a life-affirming optimism that resulted in the baby boom.

The Walkers, as we have seen, experienced all of these: Edward's marriage broke down but Walter's survived, and Harold, Ruth, Peter and Bee all married within a few years of the war's end. All, bar Edward, contributed to the post-war baby boom.

The Walkers were unusual in that they were as scattered in the post-war period as they had been during the war, with Edward and Walter serving abroad, Peter in India, Ruth in Sarawak and Harold in Nigeria. Perhaps if they had been less far flung, they might have been emotionally closer. But while some bonds between the siblings were strained by their mixed fortunes, others endured, such as that between Ruth and Peter, who had played so happily together in the garden at Tara and remained close all their lives.

Whatever the personal cost of war, not one of them regretted or resented the sacrifices they had made, well aware that others had paid a far higher price. They were proud to have played their part.

Their story is remarkable, spanning Britain, Italy, India, Burma, Malaya and Thailand, the home front and the battlefield, prisoner and victor. And yet in other ways it is typical of the wartime sacrifices, heartbreaks, triumphs and tragedies experienced by families up and down the country and across the world, to whom we owe so much.

Acknowledgements

So many people have generously given me their time and expertise: without their help and encouragement the process of writing this book would have not only been infinitely less enjoyable but impossible.

The most important sources for this book have, of course, been members of the Walker family. By the time I began writing it, Ruth was the only one of the six siblings still alive and her memories, about which I interviewed her and chatted to her over a period of ten years, were the starting point for the book. To her, and to her son Jonathan and his wife Karen, I am grateful beyond words.

Although the other five Walker siblings had died, their children were able to pass on to me the stories that their parents had told them and these became the starting points for my research, along with letters, records of service, photographs and other documents.

One of the most rewarding aspects of writing this book has been getting to know the wider family, many of whom I had met only briefly, many years ago, or in some cases not at all. All, without exception, were kind and generous with their time and memories and patient with my endless questions.

Edward's sons Nick and Hamish, and Tiggy's daughter from her second marriage, Fiona Forsyth, were all incredibly helpful. A special mention must go to Nick's wife Maybe Jehu, who has been a wonderful collaborator, unearthing family photographs and Edward's correspondence during the 1930s and 1940s, his school reports, confidential army reports, record of service, letters and his account of his marriage to Linda, as well as supplying me with family photographs.

Peter's family have also been fantastically supportive. Jennifer, his widow, and his sons Richard and Michael, Adam and Matthew have all shared their memories of their father, and of what he told them, with great generosity.

Baron Godert Van Lawick was kind enough to talk to me about his mother, Isabella, and her marriage to John Fisher.

Harold's widow, Nancy, was sadly not able to talk to me but his daughters Pam and Penny were helpful: Pam was a wonderful contributor, sending me snippets from books and articles about Harold's life. When I told her about the interview Harold had given the Imperial War Museum she was able to play it to her mother, Nancy, who was delighted to hear Harold's voice again.

Bee's daughter Mary, my godmother, sadly died in 2006 but her daughter Iona, Gaddis and Bee's granddaughter, kindly lent me the album of letters that Gaddis wrote to 'Sis', and put me in touch with the Plum family in America. Matt Plum, who was a schoolboy when Bee visited New York with baby Mary, shared his memories via email, for which I am very grateful.

Bee's son from her second marriage, Peter, was endlessly tolerant of my constant questions about his mother, who had told him so little of her wartime years, although she did regale him with tales of her Hong Kong sojourn. Thanks go to him and his wife Estelle for their hospitality and help. It was my uncle Nigel Walker and his wife Janie who told me about their elderly friend who had been one of Bee's Hong Kong admirers – and about decimating Arthur's rose garden. My uncle Anthony Walker also gave me some great stories and set me straight on certain details.

Walter was the easiest subject to research in some ways as he had left a great archive of personal papers, as well as his own privately published memoir, *Fighting On,* and the excellent biography *Fighting General,* written by Tom Pocock. Charles Allen kindly allowed me to quote from the interview he did with Walter for his book *The Savage Wars of Peace: Soldiers' Voices 1945–89* (Michael Joseph 1990). Fortunately for me not one but three of Walter's officers in 4/8th Gurkhas wrote accounts of the Burma campaign. I was unable to trace the families of Scott Gilmore, author of *A Connecticut Yankee in the 8th Gurkha Rifles,* and Denis Sheil-Small, author of *Green Shadows, a Gurkha Story,* but my thanks go to Mary Davis for allowing me to quote from her late husband Patrick's excellent book, *A Child At Arms.*

My mother, Venetia, who started me off on this quest by suggesting that I interview Aunt Ruth about her war years, was a fantastic source of photographs, papers and anecdotes as well as being endlessly supportive of the project, along with my father, Richard. I am grateful to them both for this and for so much else.

My mother-in-law Angela Walters kindly shared Walter's letters to her, in which he wrote about Harold's rescue of Ruth, Harold's own near-death, and about the Battle of Imphal, episodes that he had not written about elsewhere. Thanks go to her and to my father-in-law Martin Walters for their constant support.

Several people have kindly read sections of the book for me and given me advice and corrections for which I an enormously grateful: I consulted Professor Christine Helliwell of the Australian National University and co-curator of *A Matter of Trust: Dayaks & Z Special Unit Operatives in Borneo 1945* on the Semut operations in Borneo; Jonathan Moffatt, author of *Moon Over Malaya* on the campaign in Malaya and Singapore; and Rod Beattie, Terry Manttan and Andrew Snow of the Thai-Burma Railway Centre on the Death Railway material. I am enormously indebted to their generosity and expertise, and to the Thai-Burma Railway Centre for organising an amazing tour of Peter's camps (except for the northern ones that are now under a reservoir) and fielding my many enquiries. Most of the facts and figures I have used come from Rod's excellent book, *The Death Railway: a brief history of the Thailand–Burma Railway,* and anyone who is interested in the subject would be well-advised to pay the TBRC a visit if possible. It is incredibly inform-ative and very moving.

My friend and neighbour the historian James Holland has been particularly kind, reading the book in its entirety: as the author of multiple books on the Second World War and an authority on so many aspects of it, his help, suggestions and encouragement have been of enormous value and I am truly grateful.

I am fortunate in knowing a number of consultants who were able to advise me on their areas of medicine: Graham Branagan talked me through the bowel condition that Peter was born with; gynaecologist Stuart Verdin explained what happens when a placenta is retained; plastic surgeon Mansoor Khan described how pinch grafts work, the difficulties of treating burns and the debt owed by modern plastic surgery to Harold Gillies. I am extremely grateful to them all and to Katie and Martin Cook.

The Gurkha Museum in Winchester opened their archive to me and special thanks go to its director, Gavin Edgerley-Harris, for all his help and contacts. The Tiverton Museum of Mid-Devon Life also allowed me to use their excellent archive. The London Metropolitan Archive supplied me with copies of Ruth's nursing records. The National Army Museum dug out histories and newsletters of the 8th Punjab Regiment and the Surrey History Centre sent me information about Captain Alfie Roy of Camp 226k and the obituary of Colonel Swinton.

Glyn and Ruth Brace, the current owners of Tara, kindly showed me around their home and told me stories that they had heard from Harold and Ruth when they visited Tara.

The chaplain of the Queen's Chapel of the Savoy allowed me to see the marriage register and showed me round this beautiful chapel.

Professor Brian Farrell of the University of Singapore and author Romen Bose were both very helpful on the subject of Japanese war criminals and Pudu jail. Dr Andrew Bamji, Gillies Archivist, British Association of Plastic, Reconstructive and Aesthetic Surgeons (www. gilliesarchives.org.uk) shared with me his amazing knowledge and material on Harold Gillies' work at Rooksdown House. Trevor Stone, author of *Sustaining Air Power: Royal Air Force Logistics Since 1918*, Jan Gore, author of *Send More Shrouds: the V1 Attack on the Guards' Chapel 1944* and Charles Noon, author of *The Book of Tiverton,* were all fonts of knowledge, which they generously shared. Historian and SOE expert Adrian Weale kindly interpreted the acronyms and terminology in John Fisher's SOE file, and Dr Peter Caddick-Adams did the same with Peter Walker's army record, as well as advising on numerous pieces of military lore.

At Blundell's School the archivist Mike Sampson has been fantastically helpful, sending me information about the Walker brothers and arranging for me to visit the school. I have also been helped by the archivists at St George's College, Weybridge, Cheltenham Ladies College and Lancing College, Sussex.

My cousin Lucy Venning was a brilliantly enthusiastic travel companion and collaborator in Myanmar (Burma) and Thailand – and she and her husband Nick were generous hosts in Singapore, while Tina Nixon also gave me excellent pointers for my research there.

Several people gave me advice on visiting Myanmar (Burma). Big thanks to Selina Rivers, Elodie Grant-Goodey, Piers Storie-Pugh and

Alex Shaw, to David Eimer for all his contacts and tremendous help, and to Ian Rigden, who showed me where to access maps from the 1950s that revealed the whereabouts of Taungdaw, without which I would never have found it since it is absent from Google Maps.

Ruth's friend Eve Waring shared her memories of Ruth and of wartime Cairo. Lucie Whitmore and fashion historian Dr Bethan Bide were incredibly informative on the subject of Bee's wedding dress.

Although Ruth told me much about her nursing career, particularly her work with Harold Gillies, she did not remember all the details of her daily routine as a probationer. These details and other background information I was able to glean from records left by nurses who had served at St Thomas's during the war, and had written about their time there for the *Nightingale Fellowship Journal*, or were the subject of short obituaries published in the *Journal*, held at the Royal College of Nursing's archive. The quote from the nurse who recalled a patient's mother breaking down at Rooksdown comes from Eileen Willis, then a student nurse who was interviewed for *Sisters: Memories from the Courageous Nurses of World War Two* by Barbara Mortimer in association with the Royal College of Nursing.

I also read a short account by Anne Radloff (then Reeves), held at the Imperial War Museum, who was buried in the rubble the same night as Ruth. Other important sources on St Thomas's were copies of the *St Thomas's Hospital Gazette*, held at King's College Archive, in which Harold wrote about the night he was bombed. A shortened account of this also appeared in *The War Diary of St Thomas's Hospital 1939–1945*, a slender but informative history published by a former surgeon, Frank Cockett, and his wife, Dorothea Cockett (see bibliography). I am grateful to the IWM for allowing me to quote from their audio recordings and personal papers.

Much of the information about the camps in which Peter was held comes from the war crimes files at the National Archives but I have also consulted several books (see bibliography), among which Julie Summers' outstanding biography of her grandfather, *The Colonel of Tamarkan: Philip Toosey and the Bridge on the River Kwai*, Jack Shuttle's memoir *Destination Kwai* (my thanks to TuCann Books for permitting me to quote from it) and Cary Owtram's diary *1000 Days on the River Kwai* were particularly valuable. For the aftermath of the war, *Captive Memories: Starvation, Disease,*

Survival, Far East POWs & Liverpool School of Tropical Medicine drew my attention to the 'Guard your Tongue' order and provides moving testimony of the lasting effects of their imprisonment on the prisoners of war. Among the sources I used for the Burma retreat in 1942 is Felicity Goodall's oustanding and moving *Exodus Burma*.

Social media has proved to be enormously helpful: the FEPOW Facebook group brought me into contact with the families of Far East Prisoners of War, several of whom have shared documents and other material with great generosity. Particular thanks go to Jonathan Moffat, Cec Lowry and Martyn Fryer. I am indebted to Tim and Alice Holmes for putting me in touch with the TBRC.

Numerous friends have provided support and acted as sounding boards, including Catherine Hill, Kate Minto, Vanessa and Tobyn Andreae, Louisa Hallowes, Julia Weston, Sue Wharmby, Pam Clover, Emma and Henry Flint, Rachel Holland and my sister Belinda Venning. At the *Daily Mail*, Sandra Parsons, Susie Dowdall and Sally Morris have been endlessly supportive.

Enormous thanks to my wonderful agent and friend Patrick Walsh, who has been a believer in this book from the earliest days, and to John Ash, his superstar assistant. I am full of gratitude to the fantastic team at Hodder & Stoughton: Rupert Lancaster, Drummond Moir, Maddy Price and Ian Wong, Becca Mundy and Caitriona Horne, and to Hazel Orme for her brilliant copy-editing.

On the home front, my children Will and Alice have been extremely tolerant and enthusiastic, while my husband Guy Walters has been a tremendous support, reading and commenting on the manuscript, helping with my endless IT issues and generally cheering me on. I could not have done it without him.

But my greatest debt is to the person who is, sadly, no longer here to be thanked: Ruth.

Most of the photographs are from the author's collection.
Additional sources: Getty Images, p. 5 above, National Army Museum/Bridgeman Images, p. 6 below.

Sources & Select Bibliography

＊─◆─＊

I have not detailed here all the interviews with Ruth and other family members as I have discussed these in the Acknowledgments. The sources listed below were the principal ones used. As I have not included footnotes I have referred to many of these sources within the text. On occasion there have been small differences between people's recollections and the documentary records concerning date and time: as a general rule I have deferred to official and contemporary records.

IWM = Imperial War Museum

GENERAL

Assam Planter by A.R. Ramsden, John Gifford, 1945
Inglorious Empire: What the British Did to India by Shashi Tharoor, Hurst & co., 2016
Raj: The Making and Unmaking of British India by Lawrence James, Little, Brown, 1997
The Book of Tiverton by Charles Noon, Halsgrove, 2008
Devon in the 1930s: the way we were by Gerald Wasley, Halsgrove, 1998
Blackshirts in Devon by Todd Gray, Mint Press, 2006
The Thirties: An Intimate History by Juliet Gardiner, Harper Press, 2010
Nine Pints: A Journey Through the Mysterious, Miraculous World of Blood by Rose George, Granta, 2018
Raiders Overhead: A diary of the London Blitz by Barbara Nixon, Scolar/Gulliver, 1980
The Blitz: The British Under Attack by Juliet Gardiner, HarperPress, 2010
Wartime Britain 1939–1945 by Juliet Gardiner, Headline, 2004
The Little Blitz: The Luftwaffe's Last Attack on London by John Conen, Fonthill Media, 2014
Clementine Churchill by Mary Soames, Littlehampton Book Services, 1979
How We Lived Then: A History of Everyday Life in the Second World War by Norman Longmate, Pimlico, 2002
London: Bombed, Blitzed and Blown up: The British Capital Under Attack Since 1867 by Ian Jones MBE, Frontline Books, 2016
The War in the West: A New History, Vol 1, Germany Ascendant by James Holland, Transworld, 2017
The Second World War: The Hinge of Fate by Winston S. Churchill, Folio Society, 2000

For information on births, marriages, deaths, passenger lists and the 1939 register I have used the subscription sites ancestry.co.uk and findmypast.co.uk.

For contemporary newspaper reports, such as those I have used: britishnewspaperarchive. co.uk for UK newspapers such as the *Tiverton Gazette* and other Devon and Surrey newspapers, as well as national papers such as the *Daily Herald* that covered the St Thomas's bombings. The reports on the shooting down of the Catalina flying boat were on the free resource www.trove.nla/gov.au.

Among the many websites I consulted, www.westendatwar.co.uk has been particularly useful along with newhamphotos.com for accounts of Black Saturday, the first day of the Blitz.

RUTH

Unpublished Sources:
Ruth's nursing record: Courtesy of London Metropolitan Archives.
Ann Reeves' account of the first St Thomas's bomb: Mrs A Radloff, private papers, IWM

Published Sources
The Story of St Thomas's: 1106–1947 by Charles Graves, Faber & Faber, 1947
Accounts of the St Thomas's bombs on 13 and 15 Sept: *Hospitals under fire: but the lamp still burns*, ed. George C. Curnock, Allen & Unwin, June 1941
St Thomas's Hospital by E.M. McInnes, George Allen & Unwin, 1963
The Nightingale Training School: 1860–1996 by Roy Wake, Haggerston Press, 1998
No Time for Romance by Lucilla Andrews, Corgi, 1997
A Very Private Diary: A Nurse in Wartime by Mary Morris, ed. Carol Acton, Weidenfeld & Nicolson, 2013
Eileen Willis interview: *Sisters: Memories from the Courageous Nurses of World War Two* by Barbara Mortimer, in association with the Royal College of Nursing, Hutchinson, 2012
Gillies: Surgeon Extraordinary by Reginald Pound, Michael Joseph, 1964
Plastic Surgery and Its Origins: The Life and Works of Sir Harold Gillies 1882–1960 by Richard Petty, 2013
Park Prewett Hospital: The History 1898–1984 by Dilys Smith
Faces from the Front: Harold Gillies, the Queen's Hospital Sidcup, and the Origins of Modern Plastic Surgery by Andrew Bamji, Helion, 2017
Send More Shrouds: The V1 Attack on the Guards' Chapel 1944 by Jan Gore, Pen and Sword, 2017
Cairo in the War: 1939–45 by Artemis Cooper, Hamish Hamilton, 1989
Zamalek: The Changing Life of a Cairo Elite, 1850–1945 by Chafika Sliman Hamamsy, The American University in Cairo Press, 2005
An Englishman at War: The Wartime Diaries of Stanley Christopherson DSO, MC, TD. 1939–1945, ed. James Holland, Transworld, 2014
Nurses' accounts of PTS, training and bombing of St Thomas's: *Nightingale Fellowship Gazette*, held at the Royal College of Nursing archive
gilliesarchives.co.uk - with thanks to Dr Andrew Bamji

www.guysandstthomas.nhs.uk/news-and-events/2015-news/september/20150810-st-thomas-nurse-remembers-London-in-the-war.aspx

A nurse's memories of Rooksdown: www.basingstokegazette.co.uk/memory_lane/4491429.gillies-the-genius-of-rooksdown

JOHN FISHER

Unpublished sources
National Archives:
WO 169/19035 (John's SOE file)
Conversations (via email) with Professor Christine Helliwell

Published sources
White Rajahs by Steven Runciman, Cambridge University Press, 1960

Sylvia, Queen of the Headhunters: an Outrageous Englishwoman and Her Lost Kingdom by Philip Eade, Weidenfeld & Nicolson, 2007

Story of spy with gold incisors: *British Intelligence: Secrets, Spies and Sources* by Stephen Robert Twigge, Graham Macklin, Edward Hampshire, National Archives, 2008

Beaulieu: The Finishing School for Secret Agents, 1941–1945 by Cyril Cunningham, Pen & Sword, 2005

Silent Feet: The History of Z Special Operations, 1942–1945 by GB Courtney MBE, MC, Slouch Hat Publications, 1993

Ring of Fire: Australia's Ferocious Guerrilla War against the Japanese – The Untold Story by Dick Horton, Panther Books, 1984

The Most Offending Soul Alive: Tom Harrisson and his Remarkable Life by Judith M. Heimann, Aurum Press, 2002

World Within: A Borneo Story by Tom Harrisson, Opus Publications, Kota Kinabalu, 2008

Borneo Story by Keith Barrie: https://s3-ap-southeast-2.amazonaws.com/awm-media/collection/AWM2017.7.126/bundled/AWM2017.7.126.pdf

https://www.awm.gov.au/visit/exhibitions/a-matter-of-trust

The Sarawak Gazette, 1930s. Available online.

HAROLD

Unpublished sources
Interview, sound archive, IWM, 1998
National Archives: HO 250/18/758A (George Medal citation for Harold's rescuers)

Published sources
Obituary: British Medical Journal, 2001

Harold's account of bombing: 'Fifty Years on: A Survivor Remembers', *St Thomas's Hospital Gazette*, Summer, 1990

Sam Maling's letters and Pat Barnden's 'A Secretary's Tale' are quoted in *The Bombing of St Thomas's Hospital* by Dr Moira Ockrim.

The War Diary of St Thomas's Hospital: 1939–45, ed. Frank Cockett, Dorothea Cockett, Starling Press, 1991

'pink-faced and prosperous-looking': *Rh: The intimate history of a disease and its conquest* by David R. Zimmerman, Macmillan, 1973

PETER

Unpublished sources

Peter's Indian Army Service Record and prisoner of war record are held at the British
Library; his prisoner of war index card and liberation questionnaire are at the National
Archives.

The medical records of Far East Prisoners of War are held at the National Archives and
Peter appeared in the following:

WO 347/14-59 Index to Hospital Registers: Japan, Hong Kong and South East Asia
WO 347/36 Hospital Book 27 (reference book)
WO 347/38 Hospital Book 29 (Nakom Pathom)
WO 347/39 Hospital Book 30 (Roberts Hospital)

In addition:
WO 344/406/2 Liberated Prisoner of War Interrogation Questionnaires
WO 344/330/2 Liberated Prisoner of War Interrogation Questionnaires

War crimes testimony:
WO 311/381, WO 235/924, WO 235/867, SWO 235/963

Imperial War Museum:
Reverend G.E. Chippington, private papers
Captain R.B.C. Welsh, private papers
Major G.A. Graham, private papers
J.A. Richardson private papers,
Maj G.A. Graham Private papers
Interview with Douglas Finlayson, sound archive

Published sources

8th Punjab Regimental Magazine 1931–1947 (National Army Museum)
Unfaded Glory: The 8th Punjab Regiment 1798–1956 by Major Rifat Nadeem Ahmad and
Major General Rafiuddin Ahmed, Baloch Regimental Centre, 2006
Eastern Epic, Vol 1, September 1939–March 1943 by Compton MacKenzie, Chatto & Windus,
1951
Moon over Malaya: A Tale of Argylls and Marines by Jonathan Moffatt and Audrey Holmes
McCormick, Tempus, 2002
Singapore: The Inexcusable Betrayal by George Chippington, Self Publishing Association,
1992
The Defence and Fall of Singapore: 1940–1942 by Brian P. Farrell, Tempus, 2006
Sinister Twilight: The Fall of Singapore by Noel Barber, Cassell, 2002
Singapore Burning: Heroism and Surrender in World War II by Colin Smith, Penguin, 2005
Malaya and Singapore: The fall of Britain's Empire in the East by Mark Stille, Osprey,
2016
Spotlight on Singapore by Denis Russell-Roberts, Times Press/Anthony Gibbs and Philips
Ltd, 1965
Railroad of Death by John Coast, Hyperion, 1946
The Death Railway by Rod Beattie, OAM MBE OON, TRBC, 2015
*Captive Memories: Starvation, Disease, Survival, Far East POWS & Liverpool School of Tropical
Medicine* by Meg Parks and Geoff Gill, Palatine Books, 2015

The Colonel of Tamarkan: Philip Toosey and the Bridge on the River Kwai by Julie Summers, Simon & Schuster, 2003

The Man Behind the Bridge: Colonel Toosey and the River Kwai by Peter N. Davies, Athlone Press, 1991

Destination Kwai by Jack Shuttle, Tuccan, 1994

The War Diaries of Weary Dunlop by E.E. Dunlop, Penguin, 1986

The Railway Man by Eric Lomax, Vintage Digital, 2009

'Final Disposition of Prisoners' document: *War Ministry to Commanding General of Military Police, Taiwan, 1 August 1944*, Document no 2710/record group 238/Box 2015, National Archives and Records Administration, Washington DC. Cited in *The Final Betrayal: Mountbatten, MacArthur and the Tragedy of Japanese POWs* by Mark Felton, Pen & Sword, 2010

Obituary of Lt Col G.E. Swinton MC: *Journal of The Queen's Royal Surrey Regiment*
fepow-community.org.uk

singaporewarcrimestrials.com

BEE AND GADDIS

War and Children by Anna Freud, Medical War Books, 1943

Sustaining Air Power: Royal Air Force Logistics Since 1918, Trevor Stone, Fonthill Media, 2017

Profile of Elisha Gaddis Plum: *Over the Front: Vol 12, No. 4, Spring 1997*

Yale Men Who Died in the Second World War by Eugene H. Kone, Yale University Press, 1951

Township of Ocean by Marjorie Edelson and Kay Zimmerer, Arcadia, 1997

EDWARD

Unpublished sources

1 Jaipur Infantry War diary: National Archives

Interview with John St John Baxter, sound archive, IWM

In the mountains of the Appenines with the Jaipur Infantry, MWY 69, film archive, IWM

Published sources

The Moon's A Balloon: Reminiscences by David Niven, Hamish Hamilton, 1971

Niv: the Authorised Biography of David Niven by Graham Lord, Creative Books, 2013

Love Lessons by Joan Wyndham, Virago, 2001

Italy's Sorrow: A Year of War 1944–45 by James Holland, Harper Press, 2008

War in Italy 1943–1945 by Field Marshal Lord Carver, Sidgwick & Jackson, 2001

The Tiger Triumphs: The Story of Three Great Divisions in Italy, HMSO India 1946, Pickle Partners Publishing, 2013

The Campaign in Italy, 1943–45 by Bisheshwar Prasad, Pentagon Press, 2001

One More River: The story of the 8th Indian Division in Italy, Anon., War Department, 1947

The Last Maharajah: A Biography of Sawai Man Singh II, Maharajah of Jaipur by Quentin Crew, Michael Joseph, 1985

Lugo memorial: http://www.comune.lugo.ra.it/Citta-e-territorio/Eventi-e-Manifestazioni/Calendario-Eventi/Lugo-celebra-le-Truppe-indiane-nel-74-anniversario-della-Liberazione-dal-nazifascismo

WALTER

Unpublished sources:
Personal letters and service records
4/8th Gurkha Rifles War Diary: National Archives
Tony Brand-Crombie's diary: The Gurkha Museum
Scott Gilmore's letters: The Gurkha Museum
Interview with Charles Allen 1989, sound archive, IWM
Transporting Men and Supplies across Irrawaddy for 7th Division: JFU 32, film archive IWM
7th Division establishing a beach head across the Irrawaddy, JFU 32, film archive IWM

Published sources:
The Battle of Taungdaw: a Commanding Officer Remembers, by General Sir Walter Walker KCB CBE DSO★★ PMN PSNB, Bugle & Kukri, 2001
Fighting General: The Public & Private Campaigns of General Sir Walter Walker by Tom Pocock, Collins, 1973
Fighting On by General Sir Walter Walker KCB CBE DSO★★ PMN PSNB, New Millennium, 1997
Bugles and a Tiger: My Life in the Gurkhas by John Masters, Cassell & Co., 1956
Exodus Burma: The British escape through the Jungles of Death 1942–43 by Felicity Goodall, The History Press, 2011
Retreat into Victory by Field Marshal Sir William Slim GCB GCMG GCVO DSO MC, Cassell & Co., 1965
Burma: The Forgotten War by Jon Latimer, John Murray, 2004
We Gave Our Today: Burma 1941–45 by William Fowler, Weidenfeld & Nicolson, 2009
Fighting with the Fourteenth Army in Burma by James Luto, Pen and Sword, 2013
Burma '44 : The Battle that Turned the War in the Far East by James Holland, Bantam Press, 2016
Imphal: A Flower on Lofty Heights by Lieutenant-General Sir Geoffrey Evans KBE, CB, DSO and Antony Brett-James, Macmillan, 1962
Green Shadows: A Gurkha Story by Denis Sheil-Small MC, William Kimber, 1982
A Child At Arms by Patrick Davis, Hutchinson & Co., 1970
A Connecticut Yankee in the 8th Gurkha Rifles: A Burma Memoir by Scott Gilmore, Brasseys, 1995
The Sparks Fly Upward by Geoffrey Armstrong DSO MC TD, Gooday Publishers, 1991
Tributes to Walter following his death: *Red Flash: Journal of the 8th Gurkha Rifles Regimental Association (UK),* No. 25, March 2002
Newsletter of 4/8th Gurkhas 1938–1946
Story of women found dead on the route out of Burma wearing evening gowns: https://www.independent.co.uk/news/world/asia/dunkirk-of-the-east-how-thousands-of-brits-travelled-the-road-of-death-in-burma-7566790.html
A Savage Dreamland: Journeys into Burma by David Eimer, Bloomsbury, 2001

These cartoons, by an unknown
artist, depict the Walker siblings
at the end of the war.

Champion Lady at Police Military Sports
Cairo.

Ruth

Recovered by Allied Forces
Bangkok.

Peter

"Gentlemen—My Rare Case!"

Harold

"Bee — the Modern Miss.

Bee

G.1. 1/8 Gurkhas
Siam.

Walter

Jaipur Guard.

Edward

Index

An invitation from the publisher

Join us at www.hodder.co.uk, or follow us
on Twitter @hodderbooks to be a part of
our community of people who love the very
best in books and reading.

Whether you want to discover more about a book
or an author, watch trailers and interviews, have the
chance to win early limited editions, or simply browse
our expert readers' selection of the very best books,
we think you'll find what you're looking for.

And if you don't, that's the place to tell us what's missing.

We love what we do, and we'd love you to be a part of it.

www.hodder.co.uk

@hodderbooks

HodderBooks

HodderBooks